Communication Toolkit for Introverts

Find your voice in everyday business situations

Patricia Weber

Impackt Publishing
We Mean Business

Communication Toolkit for Introverts

First published: November 2014

Production reference: 1241114

Published by Impackt Publishing Ltd.
Livery Place
35 Livery Street
Birmingham B3 2PB, UK.

ISBN 978-1-78300-068-5

www.Impacktpub.com

Credits

Author

Patricia Weber

Content Development Editor

Vaibhav Pawar

Reviewer

Arslan Ali

Copy Editors

Roshni Banerjee

Simran Bhogal

Maria Gould

Ameesha Green

Paul Hindle

Karuna Narayanan

Faisal Siddiqui

Acquisition Editor

Richard Gall

Project Coordinator

Venitha Cutinho

Proofreaders

Simran Bhogal

Maria Gould

Ameesha Green

Paul Hindle

Production Coordinator

Melwyn D'sa

Cover Work

Simon Cardew

About the Author

Patricia Weber is one of the first people since 2006 to lead the way in support of introverts, as "America's #1 Coach For Introverts (and extroverts reluctant to sell)", and is an introvert herself.

Working with individuals, groups, and on the speakers' platform, she supports introverts to experience more personal energy, more vitality, and in the end, more success.

Since 1990, Patricia's coaching has transformed the lives of introverts who typically sell reluctantly or lead with less than stellar personal power. She has helped them as her clients to become people who are beacons of success for others in their organizations.

An award winning, top selling salesperson and sales manager, Patricia has assisted her business clients reach higher sales goals and simultaneously improved organizational leadership. She has taught many people to speak with more confidence, deliver effective presentations, and increase sales by more than 100%.

About the Reviewer

Arslan Ali has more than 14 years of experience related to the IT Industry and training institutions with experience of 5 years exclusive in teaching various disciplines and projects in an IT institution. He has worked in various roles in the capacity of software engineer, software tester, trainer, and quality assurance. The major focus of his expertise lies in coordination, implementation, and testing of ERPs and customized applications. He is also a trainer for context-driven testing for various companies and individuals.

Arslan is currently working at Sidat Hyder Morshed Associates as a Sr. Consultant—Information Solutions; but besides that he is also an active founding member of TestersTestified (www.testerstestified.com) (@testtified), Outtabox! (www.outtabox.co) (@OuttaBoxPk), and OISOL—Open Integrated Solutions (www.oisol.com) as a training consultant for software testing and context-driven testing workshops.

You can follow him on Twitter @arslan0644 and on LinkedIn at pk.linkedin.com/in/thegoodchanges/.

I would like to thank Impackt Publishing for this opportunity and my father for his reading habits that he successfully inculcated in me!

Contents

Chapter 4: Your Hardworking Wrench: Tighten or Open up Your Listening   71

Chapter 5: Your Headband Light - Succeeding in the Business Meeting   97

Chapter 6: Tape Measure Your Success for Powerful Presentations   123

Chapter 8: On the Level to Negotiate with Success 181

Chapter 9: Power Tools of Influence, Persuasion, and Selling — 201

Chapter 10: Quiet Communication can Triumph — 229

Preface

Why write a comprehensive business communications skills book for introverts?

"Just how do I position myself, my uniqueness, as a business coach? The field is so competitive," the budding coach asked.

"Well it's right here. You state it in your biography," the life coach observed.

"I do?"

It took a life coach to jolt my awareness of that personal uniqueness in a successful business career that could apply to a then budding new career, years later as a business coach, that something special each of us live with on a daily basis is not necessarily easy to find. After all, how could you notice? It is almost as unremarkable and taken for granted as the air you breathe. Often, it takes an outsider to make such observations for you.

For me, the uniqueness as a highly successful sales person is that I am an introvert.

In my online blogging about almost everything introvert, it's been exciting to see the number of people who are introverts and position themselves to help other introverts as either coach, or speaker, or author is growing since 2007 from just the two of us to dozens of people today. Over the years, introverts have become able to find information to discover a variety of techniques, ideas, and skills that are either innate to their temperament or learned. These skills, once understood and brought together, can help any motivated introvert get to a level of success wanted in business—regardless of the field or profession.

This book is going to be different and, in some ways, more relevant than many those are available to help the introvert in business. It is an all in one place toolkit in which you will find six essential communications skills, which are accepted by many authorities as the most needed to get ahead in a more extroverted world.

With anecdotes, examples, and supportive research, you will recognize your authentic introvert nature is highly valuable in any workplace situation.

Additionally, this is presented by an introvert author and interviews with other introverts and extroverts who have first-hand experience in all the aspects and have achieved best results for them and others involved using these techniques.

What this book covers

Chapter 1, Communication Preferences of Introverts and Extroverts, will fully and clearly define communication differences between introverts and extroverts so that each can work more effectively in an environment that suits their temperament.

Chapter 2, Identify and Count on Your Introvert Strengths, will allow you to appraise the introvert strengths of planning, listening more, self-reflection, thinking things through, and meaningful relationships to have specific actions to leverage them in more communication situations.

Chapter 3, Confident to Communicate, will distinguish between self-confidence and other "selves" to affirm often unrecognized self-appreciation, which helps to compose a personal plan to develop the key to workplace success: communication.

Chapter 4, Your Hardworking Wrench – Tighten or Open Up Your Listening, does a thorough examination of listening, which will increase your understanding of how people listen and what gets in the way. Then, with anecdotes and examples you will have specific ways to go from listening more to listening better and getting your voice heard.

Chapter 5, Your Headband Light – Succeeding in the Business Meeting, will discuss how with a formulation combining introvert strengths and subtle changes, introverts will be in charge of themselves and their contribution in the next and future business meetings.

Chapter 6, Tape Measure Your Success for Powerful Presentations, will discuss the key elements that presenters use in the most successful presentations; using these, an introvert can creatively and comfortably design the elements to make a presentation to any size group with poise and confidence.

Chapter 7, Do You Have an Axe to Grind? Use a Positive Approach for Workplace Conflict, explores how in the next inevitable business conflict situation, you will be more equipped to use your self-reflection and calm demeanor to assert yourself to achieve a positive outcome for all.

Chapter 8, On the Level to Negotiate with Success, will examine the strengths of an introvert in the light of a win-win negotiation process to employ more of what the introvert has going for them than not, for more successful outcomes—from the smallest to the highest-level negotiation.

Chapter 9, Power Tools of Influence, Persuasion, and Selling, will evaluate a variety of comfortable techniques to increase influence in more high-stake business situations, as well as any sales encounters, with a full understanding of the pervasiveness of influence and persuasion.

Chapter 10, Quiet Communication can Triumph, will move you quickly from planning to a prioritized schedule of actions after going through opportunities for self-reflection and thinking things through in the previous chapters.

Who this book is for

If you have this book, you are likely an introvert with a desire to succeed more easily and even more effortlessly in everyday business situations.

One potential problem is that either you aren't aware of the introvert strengths you innately have to help or you think the more extroverted have something you don't in their natural traits.

Or, you could be an extrovert and believe that having a communications toolkit could be useful in mentoring or helping introverts who you work with everyday.

Chapter 1, Communication Preferences of Introverts and Extroverts, starts with a review of the communication preferences and differences of each style, which when understood and used effectively could be your major strength. This chapter will establish how the two temperaments can relate more easily despite some fundamental differences.

Chapter 2, Identify and Count on Your Introvert Strengths, will focus on the strengths of introverts and how these can help in virtually all business settings.

Chapter 3, Confident to Communicate, puts a light on self-confidence, what it is, and how to get it, as is it central to better communications. Then, we will move on to the core communication skills.

Chapter 4, Your Hardworking Wrench – Tighten or Open up Your Listening, is the key to moving forward, because there is one skill the introvert has more than any other in their waking hours: listening. This chapter is the beginning of chapter self-assessments. You may not have considered listening this way, but when you know how to turn up your listening ability, you can get your voice more easily heard.

These first few chapters explore who you are naturally, at your core, when you are feeling relaxed. The intention is to take a break and consider that there may be more in those innate traits than what you give credit to for effective business communications.

Chapter 5, Your Headband Light – Succeeding in the Business Meeting, examines how to bring all those ideas in your head to the typical business meeting so that whether you are the leader or a participant, you can be better in charge of letting the ideas be heard.

If you have given a presentation once, or even more than once, it is highly likely you know that public speaking is a fear that people everywhere have in common. *Chapter 6, Tape Measure Your Success for Powerful Presentations*, discusses ideas and techniques of public speaking and how you put things into action. With these ideas, you can stand up with confidence to the one communication skill even extroverts fear: public speaking.

Once a church pastor remarked to me, "Relationships are messy." Then, there are the things that make them messy, like the next inevitable conflict. *Chapter 7, Do You Have an Axe to Grind? Use a Positive Approach for Workplace Conflict*, will equip you with actions that take advantage of your natural strengths to walk away from handling that next encounter, the person you have it with, and yourself—all in a more positive state.

Negotiation can be formal or informal as needed. Theories generally identify types of negotiation. While illustrative examples might include a discussion of some high profile negotiations, the focus in *Chapter 8, On the Level to Negotiate with Success*, will be to help you identify negotiating skills for those everyday business needs such as a salary increase, or the corner office, or a tough sales prospect.

Sales, often considered as a career that introverts avoid, draws on many skills that stand on their own, including public speaking, negotiating, and conflict management. In *Chapter 9, Power Tools of Influence, Persuasion, and Selling*, the more silent skills of influence and the sales side of persuasion come together for when you have to balance people-savvy with presenting yourself and ideas to get others to act.

Chapter 10, Quiet Communication can Triumph, may be the end of the book but it is the beginning of your action. It will build on your thinking around "Thoughts to Contemplate" and concludes to move you from getting out of your head into a prioritized schedule of actions.

If you are an introvert, you will find that there are some things that you do already and some things you can do more easily and confidently. Once you understand how and what you can do to bring yourself to act in certain ways without ever compromising who you are at the core of you, your energy will soar and that freedom alone will elevate your everyday business successes.

If you are an extrovert, you will discover a greater understanding of what helps and what hinders the introvert to contribute his or her best self in everyday situations. With this broader understanding, you can either change how you behave to create the best environment or know how to encourage your introvert associate.

Finally, here are some suggested tips to navigate the book to your best advantage:

➤ The best place to start in this book, with both reading and putting ideas into action, is at the beginning where you are now.

➤ *Chapter 5, Your Headband Light - Succeeding in the Business Meeting*, and the rest of the content, guides you to put the ideas and actions you read about into practice, and flows from basic to more advanced skills.

➤ Beginning with *Chapter 5, Your Headband Light - Succeeding in the Business Meeting* if you find you would rather skip to a chapter that can help you with an immediate business situation, please do it. The chapters are however designed to flow from core skills to more encompassing ones.

➤ One effective way to get the most out of any one chapter from 4 to 9 is to take the self-assessment at the beginning of each chapter.

➤ I encourage you to keep in the forefront of your thinking that you already have much innate strength to pull into each of these communication skill areas. The goal is to either help you strengthen them or identify what you can act on and begin to start using them.

Conventions

In this book, you will find a number of styles of text that distinguish between different kinds of information. Here are some examples of these styles, and an explanation of their meaning.

New terms and **important words** are shown in bold.

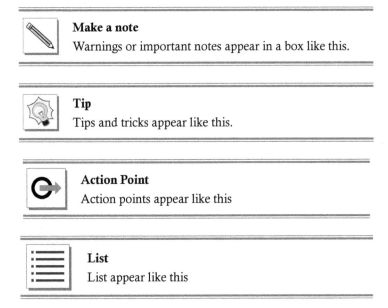

	Make a note
	Warnings or important notes appear in a box like this.

	Tip
	Tips and tricks appear like this.

	Action Point
	Action points appear like this

	List
	List appear like this

Reader feedback

Feedback from our readers is always welcome. Let us know what you think about this book—what you liked or may have disliked. Reader feedback is important for us to develop titles that you really get the most out of.

To send us general feedback, simply send an e-mail to `feedback@impacktpub.com`, and mention the book title via the subject of your message.

If there is a book that you need and would like to see us publish, please send us a note via the **Submit Idea** form on `https://www.impacktpub.com/#!/bookidea`.

Piracy

Piracy of copyright material on the Internet is an ongoing problem across all media. At Packt, we take the protection of our copyright and licenses very seriously. If you come across any illegal copies of our works, in any form, on the Internet, please provide us with the location address or website name immediately so that we can pursue a remedy.

Please contact us at `copyright@impacktpub.com` with a link to the suspected pirated material.

We appreciate your help in protecting our authors, and our ability to bring you valuable content.

>1

Communication Preferences of Introverts and Extroverts

"Life is not about pretending to be someone else, or trying to be like someone else. It's about being who you are regardless if it makes you different."

- *Nishan Panwar, writer*

A husband and wife each took on the role of a C-level position in their newly started small business. He, Bob, was a more contemplative and conscientious style communicator and she, Barbara, was more talkative and lively.

The newly appointed Sales and Marketing Manager, Sandra, would always plan differently for meetings with each of them.

For Bob, Sandra did her homework, often supporting facts or statistics with a chart or graph. She purposely spoke more slowly and sought for agreement at every step. They each would often make notes of something they wanted to revisit for further discussion. In particular, this approach was important when Sandra was asking for a salary increase.

For Barbara, Sandra would plan for twice the amount of time for a meeting than was scheduled. Quite often, by the time the conversation turned to the original purpose of the meeting, Sandra would have to jokingly state the main agenda item when Barbara laughingly said "But we are way off track now!"

Fortunately Sandra used her understanding of personality styles from early in her sales career when she was communicating with almost everyone. After all, as human beings we tend to enjoy more successful communications when communicating with people who are more like us. Sandra intended to master her communication with these influential people at that early stage in her career. After all, these two people would determine at least her salary and her position in the small company of 75 people.

In this story I am Sandra. It's important you know this so you understand the ideas, tips, and strategies I share with you come from my own life learning experiences.

Additionally, when I choose to introduce someone else's stories to you, it's because I know they too have successfully managed everyday business situations you want to know about as an introvert in a business environment.

Knowing about the communication preferences between the introvert and extrovert will help you better navigate your daily communications.

We'll cover the following topics in this chapter:

> ➤ You will understand how the introvert and extrovert may be both different and the same in their communications.
>
> ➤ You may surprise yourself finding out that different styles can work together productively.
>
> ➤ If you currently think you have to change to be more extroverted to succeed, that will no longer be your thinking.
>
> ➤ To give you practical ideas that you or your manager can do to make your environment more conducive to both the introvert and extrovert preferences.

What does introvert, extrovert, and ambivert mean?

Carl Jung, a Swiss psychiatrist and psychotherapy, is noted for his work regarding two major personality traits. Jung theorized and then decades later after studying his work, Katharine Briggs and Isabel Myers created the Myers-Briggs Type Indicator® (MBTI) questionnaire.

After a person answers the questions, their preference of four personality continuums are determined. The assessment gives a person a broad and full awareness of their preferences. The four preferences of the MBTI® are:

> ➤ Introversion and extroversion: A person gets their energy either from themselves or from outside themselves

> ➤ Intuitive and sensing: We process information either based on patterns of information or on sensory details in the present

> ➤ Thinking and feeling: We make decisions either in a logical, detached, objective manner, or our bias is toward an attached manner with values we hold

> ➤ Judging and perceiving: A person takes action either from a planned or a more spontaneous approach

The first preference, the introversion and extroversion continuum, reflects what the answers reveal regarding what energizes the assessment taker.

No one is solely more introverted or extroverted.

Someone more extroverted is more interested in attention toward the outer world, to include talking and interacting with others. Someone more introverted prefers the inner world of quiet reflection and ideas, thoughts, and imagination.

Even though each person moves up and down the continuum all day long and in various situations, we each tend to have a preference, one where we are most energized with the activities of the day.

Most current conversations in the research community suggest that more of us are actually ambiverts. This means our personality has a balance of introvert and extrovert preferences. For example, we can enjoy networking but recognize that how we prepare for it might need to be with some quieter activities before such events. Or, we can enjoy, even thrive, as a public speaker, but need to recharge after giving a presentation.

What are the differences between introvert and extrovert communication?

Using the introvert and extrovert model of styles, while not the only model, is the most often referenced work of Carl Jung, whose work dates back to 1921. He is acknowledged as the first person, a Swiss psychologist and psychiatrist, whose work typed people into the introvert and extrovert styles. Since this finding, the fascination with the introvert and extrovert spectrum of temperament is being referenced in many studies.

Through research, studies, and observation, we can identify some key differences in the communication styles.

Extrovert and introvert communication preferences are as follows:

Extrovert preferences	Introvert preferences
■ Talk out loud to sort through their ideas	■ Think things through before speaking
■ Communicate freely with anyone about themselves	■ Openly talk about themselves with people they know and trust
■ Visibly gregarious	■ Visibly stay in the background
■ Prefer communicating on the telephone or in-person	■ Prefer to communicate in writing including e-mail exchange
■ Usually prefer getting input from as many people as possible	■ Prefer one-to-one conversations over meetings

As you read this table, you may have a question in mind about whether the introvert preferences either indicate someone is shy or that introvert equates to shy.

The way psychologists and introvert authorities explain the difference between the two styles comes down to this.

Extroverts get energy from everything around them, including activities like talking and interacting with others.

Introverts get energy from the playground of their mind, including being alone in and with their own mind in reflecting and thinking.

Someone more introverted is not necessarily less socially engaged because of shyness. It's more a situation that an introvert does not need much outside stimulation to be engaged. But when a shy person is not socially engaged, it is more because of anxiousness over the socializing.

Tip

Bernardo Carducci, psychology professor and director of the Shyness Research Institute at Indiana University Southeast in New Albany, uses a party scenario to illustrate the difference between an introvert and a shy person.

Make a note

The introvert isn't afraid to talk to people but might stand in the corner to take a break from the crowd. The shy person stands in the corner because he feels he has no choice. And the shy person can be an introvert or an extrovert.

In my own management training of different theories about people styles, there is one relevant point, which also applies to effective communication. Your greatest power in communicating lies in your awareness of the how and what of differences. Once we are aware of how an extrovert communicates differently to an introvert, then we can either make a conscious choice to modify our style to be more like theirs or accept those differences.

As you consider this communication preference can you understand how the preferences are energy-based and are at the heart of communication differences?

Is ambivert a real word?

Most people fall somewhere in the middle of a bell curve of introvert and extrovert and this might mean you are an ambivert.

Why would this matter?

As far as communication preferences, it means an ambivert naturally balances talking and listening, and has a more flexible communication style.

In the 1998 *MBTI® Manual* the reference of a USA National Representative Sample identifies the introvert (I) and extrovert (E) population breakdowns: (E) 49.3% and (I) 50.7%.

According to Adam Grant, Ph. D., organizational psychologist of The Wharton School, University of Pennsylvania, ambiverts are the new sales ideal. Ambiverts have it over extroverts and introverts.

If his assumption was correct, it would be in regards to one of the key business communication skills, which we will investigate in *Chapter 9, Power Tools of Influence, Persuasion, and Selling*, where it means ambiverts trump extroverts in this area. Maybe you have heard that extroverts excel in sales? Be prepared to be surprised.

And how is this beneficial for the introvert?

In an interview Grant stated, "My findings suggest that less-extroverted people may be missing out on productive careers," he said, "and hiring managers may be missing out on star performers."

Grant's study confirms that innate introvert skills also found in the ambivert, like listening and being less apt to be overexcited, add more value to a successful sales process.

How can introverts and extroverts misunderstand each other?

What is the real difference between an introvert and an extrovert? It is simply how a person finds their energy. How we get energy is not a reason for communication problems.

Several years ago my husband and I were interviewed by the *Wall Street Journal*. In that editorial *When Innies Love Outies: How Odd Couples Cope*, the author, Elizabeth Bernstein, quotes another author and psychologist Laurie Helgoe, "What looks like communication can actually be a problem." As the quieter introvert seems to be listening, an extrovert can take that as a cue to keep on talking.

This interpretation of listening invites a communication problem of interpreting listening in different ways. Listening for many introverts means "I'm thinking this over, and give me a few moments to reply," but to the other often more extroverted person it may mean "Great. I must fill the silence with more talking."

Often when networking with my husband he will introduce me to someone and then go on his way. Since I am quite comfortable with silence, I listen a lot, and more to understand than to respond. When I do respond I ask questions either for clarification or out of curiosity. Frequently some time after such an event my husband tells me that John, Judy, or whoever he introduced me to complimented me. When I ask about what it is almost always, they said you were a wonderful person to talk with.

This is the other side of the interpretation of effective listening.

Communication myths

Misunderstandings contribute to communication mismatch. A communication mismatch between an introvert and extrovert may mean a lack of understanding of the preferences to think before speaking which many introverts do, versus speaking being thinking out loud, which many extroverts do.

If left unchecked misunderstandings can become a myth. We want to free ourself of any myth that may have an incorrect hold on us. If as an introvert we are going to find our voice in any business situation, then believing a myth will keep us stuck. Be certain to know a myth from the truth. Here are some common myths:

> **Introverts don't like to talk**: Being quieter does not mean as introverts that we are shy or unknowledgeable. It is more usual that we are thinking before we speak. More often than not, we listen to understand and then speak to be understood.

> Some people may be prompted to believe this myth upon first meeting someone more introverted because small talk is not something comfortable for many introverts. It is fast moving but not necessarily fulfilling. Most introverts seek the more meaningful conversation and often feel the bridge to get there; small talk, is not worthwhile.

> **Introverts have difficulty knowing what to say**: This might mean being mistaken for a shy person. While shyness is a social anxiety, introverts do, however, speak their mind.

> To someone who does not understand the introvert preference, what seems like a quiet demeanor, is usually more of taking time to think something through for its usefulness in the conversation.

> **Introverts are anti-social**: Can we agree that both introverts and extroverts can listen, converse, remember someone's name, and give feedback, all of which show they are being attentive? We develop our personal social side by developing interpersonal skills and techniques in many situations in life.

> If your co-worker is declining an invitation to happy hour fun after hours, it is more likely that they need to charge up their personal energy than it is they are anti-social.

> **Introverts can fix their problems by becoming more like an extrovert**: Introvert, extrovert, and ambivert are natural, brain-wired temperaments. Each style has its own strengths. It's more a situation of fixing the communication problems, not the people.

> What works best for most people is not to become more like someone else or something else but instead to be the best version of themselves in any situation.

Let's work together better

Susan Cain, author of the book *Quiet: The Power of Introverts in a World That Can't Stop Talking*, argues "forcing everyone to act like extroverts harms the quality of our work and our lives."

There are strategies we can use in communicating with extroverts, and there are strategies extroverts can consider using when communicating with us. When we put actions in place, there is a stronger foundation as we more effectively use essential business communication skills for success. Here are the foundational beginning points:

> **Step one is to be aware**: We are all aware of differences between men and women, or being left-handed or right-handed. With this awareness we might behave or set up the environment differently. Be aware of the introvert and extrovert differences as were described in the extrovert and introvert communication preferences table just before this section.

➤ **Move awareness to clarity**: Myths, misunderstandings, or wrong assumptions can lead to job dissatisfaction and take a toll on employee retention. Observable differences are easiest to recognize in the two prevalent personal types. Moving beyond that to understand the how and why of the differences leads to correct information.

➤ **Respect our differences**: In a step forward to accept ourselves as who we are, we can begin by respecting our differences. Whenever we compare ourselves to others, someone either comes up short or rates better. Comparing in this sense does little to resolve a divide. Even in our differences, we can put ourselves in a position to be able to more easily recognize our own excellence.

➤ **Understand there is no all or one**: We all move along the continuum of introvert and extrovert behaviours and preferences all day long. Regardless of what our work is, we may find ourselves immersed in research, which we love, or giving a presentation to a board of directors, which some of us love. We each will find we are more energized more often on one side or another of the introvert and extrovert continuum. And some of us are more in the middle, and those people are ambiverts.

Reasons why an introvert may not want to act like an extrovert

Let's say you aspire to a leadership position in your company. You have the time in your current position, and the background of practical experience in your role. Right now there is a supervisory or management position open. Your boss is looking for someone who speaks up in meetings and shares lots of ideas.

Immediately, your thoughts begin to focus on questions of how to be more vocal and speak your ideas out loud.

Is behaving more extroverted your best strategy now?

Each of us needs to decide how much energy we are willing to put into any changes that we believe will help us if we are interested in moving up in a work position. Depending on our comfort for change, then it may be useful to be more extroverted more often, when it is appropriate.

For example, maybe we would like the freedom to basically write our own paycheck and go into sales. Then could we tolerate adding more interacting with customers and other staffers with the quiet kind of product research that also goes into the role?

In the situation of a supervisory role opening up, would we want to be interacting more with people on a daily basis to get the perks of having the perks that go along with the responsibility of management?

The sales route worked well for me as a business track to that often-aspired management role. Even if I knew then what I know now, I would likely take the same route. Knew what? If I knew the prevalent thinking was, and still is; as an introvert I would not be suited for sales.

But you may or may not want to be in sales.

The biggest advantage of being in a sales-related position is to have the ability to write the amount of your own paycheck as this is directly related to your efforts. You help more people buy your products or services and you earn more. However, if money is not a big motivator for you, then rule out a career in sales.

Now back to your desire to have that vice-president-like title and role.

You do not have to act like an extrovert to succeed in business. This is not to say to ignore what might be your weaknesses. It is to suggest you direct your attention to leverage your strengths, which we will examine in *Chapter 2, Identify and Count on Your Introvert Strengths.*

The honing of our strengths approach outweighs trying to be something or someone we are not, nor care to be. Here is an example of what can happen when we start thinking the best approach is to use our strengths.

When I was in sales I wanted to be a sales manager. It so happened that a new location was being built and my managers were interviewing internally for the position. One of them told me flat out that I was too much of a loner and not enough of a team player to likely have management work successfully. But undeterred, and planning for this objection, I am confident my answer won over the last of the three people making the decision.

"If I may ask you John, what would be the main area in which you would want me responsible as your sales manager?" was my lead in question to further the discussion instead of being turned down.

"Look Patricia, we know you are the number one sales person, your numbers show that. But we would want you to turn many other sales people into star performers. How would you be able to do that?" John asked with a confidence that hinted he thought I might back off.

But I had planned for his objection, just as I was trained to plan for a customer objection during the buying and selling process.

I am convinced what I replied is what won him over to the other two yes votes for me as the new sales manager. What was my answer? It was a follow up to my original question to him.

I took a few seconds to gather my thoughts and looked at him to reply, "If you want more star sales performers, I'm confident I can both model and create a training program for other salespeople in my approach. Then in the training, they could adopt the key parts to their own style."

What I shared with him next were certain behaviors that my customers told me on the exit interview of a sale I knew I was engaging in that helped them decide to buy from me. I continued saying to him, "Based on what many of my customers tell me, they like that I focus on helping them to buy just the right product for their needs. They feel like when we talk I am listening to them, instead of just trying to sell them. So if what you want are more star sales performers, you'll get them with my training ideas and leadership."

We are talking about a more extroverted strategy of asserting ourselves confidently. Indeed we are the only ones who know as much as we do about our strengths. It is not a situation to be hesitant or shy, instead when a promotion is within your reach, shine the light on your strengths.

That was on a Friday and on the following Monday I got the telephone call of congratulations.

Think about how the conversation may have differed if I decided to, even with planning, focus on what he saw as my weakness.

It might have been more of a defensive strategy. I might have asked about training. We might have focused on how the company could support me in learning to be a team player as they viewed it. Over time, anyone can become better at what they are weak in. John and I likely would have agreed on these points. The thing I knew in this situation is that the three managers wanted a new manager on their team to build more superstars, and the sooner the better.

When we focus on using our strengths and innate abilities, we have to produce a broader or bigger benefit. Why? Because this raises our motivation to plan the best course of action so results are better in some way. That is what is called playing to your strengths.

With the promotion, training did help me develop leadership skills. I learned to manage meetings, make presentations that got results, manage conflicts, and build a better team. Indeed my awareness was raised about how taking advantage of my strengths helped me improve my weaknesses.

As you sort out your strengths, you will find you can count on them to get you through almost any business situation.

Should you pay attention to studies that show extroverts are generally happier?

What if you knew being happier would help you be or at least appear more gregarious and lively and so then likely to increase performance?

Which approach would you take: play to your strengths or reinforce your weaknesses?

Wake Forest University published findings in a 2012 article in the *Journal of Personality*, which show that when introverts act extroverted, they too feel happier. It is a compelling finding that may invite introverts to move over to the extrovert way of being.

One theory put forth is extroverts are happier because they have a greater sensitivity to dopamine; they need more of it to make them happy. It wires the extrovert brain to act more motivated to get a reward, like giving a presentation and then either hearing applause or being recognized for good work.

But there is no conclusive evidence of why this happens. It's actually more scientific evidence that all is not always what it appears to be.

Furthermore, no one has broadened the study to explore whether this dedicated concentration to go against what nature wired us for is going to use up energy.

When we act in ways that are not natural to us, there can be a battle between what is comfortable and what is not comfortable. When our nature is to be prepared and suddenly we are called on in a meeting to make an impromptu presentation, guess what happens to our energy? We struggle to make it a winning performance and in the end, all the air is out of us like a popped balloon.

Here is one possibility of why acting like we are something we are not normally may work in the short term, but not necessarily in the long term.

If we have too much dopamine in the introvert brain then we can feel over stimulated, and have "stimulus fatigue". Our brains have a longer pathway of blood flow, and more blood traveling to it, making us even more sensitive. More dopamine just exhausts us and depletes our energy. That same longer pathway is activated by acetylcholine, which gives us a happy feeling that extroverts don't get from just thinking and feeling.

While studies may conclude introverts are happier when they act more outgoing, if it is at the expense of daily exertion which could lead to energy exhaustion, then it may work in smaller doses, not all day long.

Alice Domar, Ph.D., a psychologist and author of *Be Happy Without Being Perfect*, says, "If you think you should feel happy nearly all the time, it's going to make you miserable."

If being more extroverted means striving for constant contentment, then Domar's advice for the introvert might be to strengthen the introvert within.

If focusing, researching, and planning make you happy, then would it be more accurate to conclude, "do what makes you happy, not what someone else says makes them happy."

How managers can create a work environment for both introverts and extroverts to thrive in

Extensive research about effective working environments finds that lighting, noise, color, and even air quality affects employee productivity. These factors stimulate the introvert and extrovert differently.

Because our environment is all about energy like the energy from the people in the room, the energy from the way things are arranged, or the energy from either clutter or organization, by far this is one area that affects us from the moment we get to work until the end of the workday.

Leaders and staff would benefit immensely in creating an environment that serves both the more introverted and more extroverted if they know how to set things up to play to each preference.

Lighting

While extroverts can better tolerate bright light, partially because of not being so affected by sensory stimulation, introverts do better with more subdued and indirect lighting.

Lighting companies know the type of lighting can affect both our mental state and therefore our performance.

By our very nature as introverts, we prefer calmer places. In the lighting world, this can mean more indirect lighting.

Extroverts are not as affected by such sensory factors. Bright lights might even energize them.

Lighting will affect alertness and activity in people differently. The best way to know how you are affected is by trying different kinds and checking their effect on your work.

Music

In a workspace occupied by introverts, music is more of a distraction than a factor that might help concentration and focus.

Numerous studies have examined the effects of music on performance. A current study by Adrian Furnham and Anna Bradley, Department of Psychology, University College London, UK, found that depending on both the task and the temperament of the employee, music while you work can mean either better or worse performance.

If you asked yourself was it introverts or extroverts who performed better with music, even pop music, and you answered extroverts, you are right.

Even background music may cause introverts to lose focus and have worse performance.

Choice

In the design of an office the optimal situation is to have both quiet and open spaces that give people the type of space needed for the task at hand.

A recent study by the design firm Gensler found both open-plan layouts and the lower cubicle setup do more to compromise some workers' ability to concentrate and be productive. The findings from surveying 2,035 employees found that it is when employees are given their choice between quiet spaces and collaborative spaces that productivity is optimal.

This actually applies to introverts and extroverts alike in cases where the task is more knowledge-based.

Collaborative office space can be an open-plan office design. Credit is often given to German designers, post-war, for the open plan office design still in many offices today. Replacing traditional factory style line up of desks for what was once thought to a better arrangement, with workers facing the boss like in schools where students were facing the teacher, now there was not necessarily a hierarchy of seating.

Cubicles, possibly the last chance for an introvert to have privacy, are on the way out.

Faux privacy

Faux privacy is where privacy by personal office is not possible or impractical in the company space, earplugs or even headphones can serve to dampen the surrounding noise.

Founded in 1994, when in 2012 Yahoo CEO Marissa Mayer took the position she quickly got the media's attention: she ended telecommuting for all of their 11,500 employees working in that way.

It turns out research finds that telecommuting is almost an ideal work environment for an extrovert. Suppositions are it is because of their quicker decision-making style in a more volatile environment. They can better manage inevitable interruptions that might happen because of looser rules at home. And regardless of where they work from, they stay connected with people.

Introverts just may thrive in the structure of the office environment and schedule.

Mayer and the human resource people believed in-person interaction is still best for communicating even for these knowledge workers. E-mail would not serve the purpose as well in particular as the company was going to be forging new territory.

Part of the changes also included redoing the office space to create a more collaborative atmosphere.

What kind of work might many of the employees be involved in that requires concentration, focus, even research?

Apparently the jury is still out on the changes Mayer made. As relates to our personality style, there are proponents for both the more introverted and more extroverted being affected the most.

Mayer seems to bring in to this decision to end telecommuting what she learned at Google in terms of where innovation comes from: discovery, collaboration, and fun.

The more you research Mayer's move you find firms like Apple, Facebook, Zappos and more, with data supporting evidence of how more interaction, in part from collaboration, fosters faster decision-making and more innovation.

If extroverts do thrive with people connections, they could benefit from being lassoed back to an office where people and interactions abound.

If introverts excel with a quiet and alone space, and offices have nothing but this stated collaborative environment, there is doubt their productivity could also thrive.

However, privacy can both quickly and inexpensively be created if the environment is an open office plan. Headphones are one option for those who want to block out the buzz around them. One step up from this would be creating a sectioned-off quiet work place when someone needs more focus, concentration, and privacy for the work at hand.

There is not a win-lose in the situation for any personality group as a whole. We have to know our preference for our privacy at work, considering there are various other personal traits and preferences that affect our productivity in any environment. The key is to know there are options if you are an introvert whose clear preference includes more privacy.

Summary

The communication preferences between the introvert and extrovert are real but certainly manageable. With the completion of this chapter you either are reminded of, or have found new learning in this chapter about the introvert and extrovert communication divide. You are at the point where you:

> Understand the key introvert and extrovert differences in communications

> Have deduced that the differences in communication styles identified are all about you or the extrovert satisfying a need to be energized

> Understand you might be an ambivert who on balance has energizing needs from either end of the introvert and extrovert bell curve

> Have a greater understanding of some prevalent introvert myths and now know the truth of each

> Recognize some foundational beliefs you have to adapt to go forward in being able to better communicate with extroverts

> Have a real-life understanding of both sides of either taking on your weakness or playing to your strengths so you can decide the best strategy for you

> Have practical ideas you or your manager can use to make your environment more conducive to both the introvert and extrovert preferences

Thoughts to contemplate

As you reflect back on this chapter, about the communication preferences of introverts and extroverts, ask yourself these three key things:

> ➤ How has your belief or disbelief of commonly stated introvert myths helped you or hurt you in your everyday business communication?

> ➤ Once you decide on the effects the myths have on you, what will you either continue to do, or do differently, going forward in order to increase your business communication successes?

> ➤ Whether you work at home or in an office, can you prioritize the four office environment factors that work to your benefit?

Bibliography

> ➤ Carducci's report on shy versus introverted: http://www.shyness.com/documents/1999/SHYENC599.pdf

> ➤ Adam Grant's abstract report on ambiverts: http://www.philly.com/philly/business/20130412_Study__Extraverts_not_always_best_for_sales_positions.html

> ➤ Online assessments for ambiverts, introverts, and extroverts:

>> ➤ http://lonerwolf.com/introvert-or-extrovert-test/ - most comprehensive description of results

>> ➤ http://www.danpink.com/assessment

>> ➤ http://www.thepowerofintroverts.com/quiet-quiz-are-you-an-introvert/

> ➤ *Coping Strategies for Introverts Married to Extraverts* is an article from the June 28, 2011 edition of the *Wall Street Journal*

> ➤ Image for the *Thoughts to contemplate* section, courtesy of Stuart Miles can be found at http://www.freedigitalphotos.net

> 2

Identify and Count on Your Introvert Strengths

"If summer resisted fall, it wouldn't really be summer or fall. Better to celebrate the season you're in...Especially those of your wonderful life. "

-Mike Dooley, author of Notes from the Universe, http://www.tut.com

In some ways we are like a sailboat. A sailboat can have problems. These problems are like our weaknesses. There could be holes in the sails or, worse yet, holes in the boat. If any kind of hole in a sailboat is not patched up there will be trouble! Sailboats also have sails to manage their travels. Consider sails like our strengths. Sails get hoisted, trimmed, and deserve attention to be paid to how they are working and the condition they are in. If we don't pay attention to maximizing what the sails do, we can find ourselves not going anywhere, going slower than we want, or not at all.

In coming across this metaphor in my research online, it seems to be appropriate to the importance of counting on our introvert strengths.

Keeping this sailboat metaphor in mind, how do you use your strengths, your sails? Do you use them to help manage your weaknesses to a greater advantage? Or do you take too much time focusing on patching up holes, possibly creating a headwind that slows your progress down?

It tends to be a human trait that we most often focus on the negative, our weaknesses relative to how as an introvert we might show up in an extrovert world.

Do you know of anyone who does not have one or two weaknesses? If you are human then weaknesses are part of you.

One secret in any business communication success is if and how you use your strengths in communicating. This chapter considers how the top strengths we have as introverts can help our everyday business success by putting those strengths into our communications. By the end of this chapter, you will understand:

> ➤ The effectiveness our predisposition with self-reflection can bring to communicating

> ➤ How planning affects almost every key communication skill, and how we can use this strength to help organize our thinking and actions to reach an intended outcome

> ➤ How much more time everyone spends on listening over any other communication skill, and why it is that introverts listen more than extroverts

> ➤ To harness at least three key introvert beliefs to put more passion in communication, your way

> ➤ To take what we know that positively charges our one-to-one relationships and put this into our general business communications

"There are three principle means of acquiring knowledge...Observation of nature, reflection, and experimentation. Observation collects facts; reflection combines them; experimentation verifies the result of that combination."

-Denis Diderot, French philosopher

Understanding self-reflection and how it helps

Self-reflection is conscious introspection. In our thoughts and through our talking, we examine our beliefs, feelings, and observations to improve our self-awareness.

One of our introvert preferences is to seek depth over breadth in issues and ideas. This often comes out as thinking before we speak, needing to let thoughts percolate over night or acting on specific practices, like meditation and journaling. It's likely this extra time we need to make some of our decisions that may drive some extroverts crazy.

A 1999 study's findings by Gustafson and Bennett seems to blend the best of introversion and extroversion to deduce what kind of environment might be the best for fostering self-reflection. There is no general acceptance of a definition for self-reflection, not even among researchers. There are however some simple (and some more complex) definitions.

Gustafson and Bennett define self-reflection simply as thinking over a longer period about experiences and in that practice seeking out what is common, what is different, and anything interrelated. Self-reflection is purposeful thinking activity over time.

This particular 1999 study examined the variables in the reflective behavior of military cadets over a period of three years, using diaries as a means of deep reflection. The conclusion supported other research in the finding that self-reflection is difficult to accomplish, at least in a diary format.

One interesting finding is that the most promising kind of environment for encouraging self-reflection is an interpersonal environment. It is here we find the blending of extroversion and introversion at its best. On the surface it seems contrary to what we believe may help any introvert thrive, until you take it through its premise. "Social interaction may enhance motivation and prolong engagement with the task. Social interaction would almost certainly bring forth more information and ideas that could be shared and perhaps result in deeper thinking about the subject."

In the end it doesn't matter if this interaction is formal or informal, or during or after some kind of learning activity. The act of interacting is that little extroverting charge that an introvert can benefit from in their own self-reflection.

Self-reflection is the sister of self-awareness. It is one thing to think while in a situation and quite another to think on the situation to produce an effective result, in large part because of our awareness.

Early in my sales career, a highly extroverted manager, as most in sales are, shocked me by almost forcing me to make a decision right on the spot about additional responsibility. To not have the time to think things through for an introvert is about as comfortable as an army of ants at a picnic. We feel better about our decisions with self-reflection time.

This turned out to be one of the times we have to either play a role or recognize the situation for what it is and flow with it.

He did allow me to ask a couple of questions, which served to fill in some knowledge I wanted, as well as acting as small decision points along the way.

Then he went further in his explanation helping me understand what it would mean if I succeeded and if I failed. He pressed for the decision again, this time saying if I did not want the opportunity he would take it to someone who would.

Time was out, and instead of feeling the pressure to make a decision right then I decided to trust myself to take on a challenge that might push my current abilities as I saw them.

My answer was "Yes, okay, I will do it".

Fortunately it worked out positively and recognition of my work prevailed. In light of his apparent greater confidence in me, and the positive outcome, there was only that immediate feeling of stress with a decision that was on the spot and that time was gone.

Our personal power from self-reflection cannot be underrated, although in situations when time is not flexible, we can make it work for us. The power we get at times when we are reflecting on an experience is to have a stronger self-awareness of our own and other's emotions and what effect they might have on the situation. With that awareness, we can often then better self-manage and adapt to changes that can happen at work.

If self-reflection helps us become more self-aware with even just one situation, we can take that learning forward with us into an upcoming setting. We can find commonalities and differences in the settings but also discover new ideas.

Make a note

Self-reflection can also often be an inner clearing mechanism. Being comfortable listening to our inner thoughts and even feelings we can generally make better decisions.

A short time before I was about to be promoted to sales manager I encountered a challenging situation. A gentleman came into the computer store I worked in reeking of alcohol. It was only once we were both seated to start his shopping experience that I could smell this as it took a few minutes for the smell to filter through the air to me. When it hit me, anxiousness flooded me. I felt uncomfortable knowing from personal experience the unpredictable behavior of someone under this influence, and did not know how to deal with such an unfamiliar scenario in business.

I held in my mind that I would do something about the situation as soon as an opening became apparent.

Then it happened. He wanted to talk about another computer model than what he originally came in to ask about. This is the only time in my sales career I recall being delighted to have a chance to possibly turn a prospective client over to another salesperson.

As I excused myself from our meeting claiming this model was not my expertise, questions started to flood in my mind. I purposefully slowed down my walk.

Why did I attract this drunk man? How can I get out of working with him? Who else can take this on? The questions streaming in triggered a plan forming in my mind.

At first it occurred to me to ask for help from the first available salesperson I could find and then, leave the demonstration. However, as I turned off the showroom floor to the sales bullpen to do just that, it occurred to me a better plan might be to inform the manager of the true situation and ask for her help.

Fortunately, even in the short time to think and plan I was able to analyze this new situation and decide on the most effective alternative to get the best outcome. In the end I was able to calmly introduce the man to the more knowledgeable salesperson for that product.

With greater self-awareness, we better understand our feelings or emotions, which can direct our actions. Our actions, to include how we communicate, affect all people around us. The more effective our self-reflection the more successful our communication can be.

As an employee you want to be able to manage your personal relationships with co-workers. As a leader or manager you must often be able to help move the situation from being stuck when you are called to intervene in a situation.

While a book can teach you techniques of self-reflection, it is a distinct advantage most introverts have at hand, who by their nature find it natural and empowering. Let's count on it in our everyday communications.

How to use our love of planning to work to our advantage

Planning is a process with a range of actions: assess the current situation, set a clear goal, identify priorities and action steps, inspect what you expect, and clarify, possibly communicate a plan before implementing. There are many decisions that get made along the way of planning. Depending on what we are planning we could end up with a written plan. And of course with the plan complete, we may either want feedback or need to communicate feedback ourselves.

What is it exactly that gives introverts somewhat of an edge in this process?

There is one explanation that Dr. Debra Johnson and John Wiebe are credited with in their study of cerebral blood flow and personality. If you are interested in the study you will find it referenced at the end of this chapter. The men and women selected were close in their temperament scores. Using a positron emission tomography with 18 people they showed images of events and people to detect what areas of the brain in both extroverts and introverts are active when thinking about personal memories and plans for the future. Their research supported what previous but less sophisticated research found: there are blood flow differences between temperaments.

The differences are to where and how much blood flows in the brain. There is more blood flow in the introvert brain in the frontal lobes, which controls more cerebral activities like thinking, planning, and remembering, as well as the anterior thalamus, which has a role in learning and memory.

The extrovert brains showed more blood flow to three different parts of the brain:1, the anterior cingulate gyrus, where emotions and thinking are governed; 2, the temporal lobes, which relays information from the ears and is involved in visual recognition,; as well as 3, the posterior thalamus, which regulates body heat.

The advantage is hard-wired. This of course does not mean that extroverts cannot plan or plan well. It simply means as introverts we are naturals at the process because of our physiology.

But what does the extrovert, not always so keen on planning, do differently?

The sister to planning is risk-taking and it is more characteristic of extroverts. In her book *Quiet* ,Susan Cain references the research of Dr. Janice Dorn. Dorn is a Ph.D. in Neuroscience, a psychiatrist, and a day trader who counsels other traders. It is the extrovert's brain that seems to crave more reward seeking actions, driven by the limbic system, often called the pleasure center. This dopamine chemical reward is what fires up an extrovert to take more chances and risks as well as blind-siding them to consider signals of danger that might come from some planning.

It turns out that Dorn believes introverts are more likely to stick with their investment plans than be carried away with their emotions of excitement. Better to be smart with investing to retire comfortably, than to be fired up with excitement and risk too much to possibly be uncomfortable in retirement.

Planning things through usually helps to minimize risk taking since by its nature planning identifies potential problems.

When communicating with others, we do not always get the opportunity to plan. Consider a conflict with someone in the middle of a heated discussion. It is not likely we can say, "Let us pause, and get a plan of action to work this out." I suppose we could, but is it likely?

While we might want to have time to think things through during the moment of a disagreement, it just may not happen.

With many parts of planning being mostly in the head, and being what lights up our introvert brain, we have a decided advantage.

How can we learn to love and use this advantage in different communication skills?

The following sections are intended to put our love of executing a plan in almost any situation in a positive light, as helpful to all essential communication skills. Rather than possibly considering it as a hindrance in the workplace, planning is a powerful component for success.

Powerful presentations require planning

Organizing and rehearsing are the best preparation to more clearly communicate a message or to get people to act or be inspired via words. You cannot know what the final delivery of a presentation on the platform will look and sound like, but rehearsing key components will help you sound and feel more confident, appear and feel more knowledgeable, and prepare you to handle the unexpected.

Effective meetings depend on planning

How often have we attended a meeting that goes nowhere? People will often ask "Why did we have that meeting?" Or they comment, "I could have accomplished more at my desk."

A relevant TED Talk by Jason Fried communicates some of his 10 years of research, titled 'Why work doesn't happen at work?' He opens the 18-minute video with a question to people, "Where do you go when you really get something done?" He gives many answers but none include, "I was in this meeting and wow, being in that meeting is when the work happened."

TED Talks is a global conference non-profit organization with "talks" that are no longer than twenty-minutes, designed to inspire, and all videotaped around the world. With access to the Internet they are readily accessible.

This kind of thinking is highly likely because of the global agreement that meetings can be a waste of time. Often not all the right people are there, sometimes there is no agenda, and if there is an agenda often it is not prioritized. When a meeting starts with planning it ends up being productive and even appreciated. In well run meetings, people who attend are those affected with the topics, someone manages the process with an agenda, people who can take action are either assigned or reporting on a task, and there is a follow-up from the organizer, usually in written format.

Conflict management benefits from planning

Often in conflict management, it is not possible to resolve differences immediately. This is when a plan can emerge.

Managing any conflict is dependent on planning—planning what we intend to say and planning what action steps need to happen to go forward to a better solution or relationship.

A plan to help resolve a conflict may be an ongoing process to simply have more communication to discuss differences as they come up.

The best negotiations happen with planning

Without planning we go into a negotiation with less confidence and a less effective plan of action. With preliminary planning we can anticipate the other party's issues, needs, and even actions.

Knowing these types of issues ahead of time allow us to consider different outcomes. Prioritizing the most to the least significant issues can help us decide what we would be more willing to concede.

Thinking through potential questions, objections, and concessions is better than being blind-sided without planning.

Helping someone to buy results from thoughtful sales planning

Whether it is goals to meet or targets to hit, planning takes much of the guess work out of how many calls to make, who to make them to, measuring our results, and changing our approach if necessary.

If we are selling on a team then of course this involves sales meetings. In addition, sales team meetings benefit only if the sales team members can leave a meeting motivated to sell.

Regardless of the communication skill, particularly the key communication skills we are reviewing how to use our strengths in, planning helps to organize thinking and actions to more successfully reach an intended outcome. This strength works for us all the time.

Being aware of the value of natural listening capability

You are in a conversation with a co-worker. It is a conversation to help each of you complete a particular project you are tasked with as a team. You find yourself being interrupted, regularly. Your co-worker often looks away from you to acknowledge something going on or someone walking by; you find they have more interest in something other than your current conversation. Then something you say sparks your co-worker to say, "You know that reminds me…" and the conversation goes off target.

Does any of this sound familiar?

Have you found yourself more like the victim than the perpetrator with lack of luster in listening?

It is not realistic to believe that when we start to talk others start to listen. It is more likely accurate that the person we are speaking with may not be ready to listen for various reasons.

Hearing is different than listening. Unless you are hearing impaired, we hear passively, and this is usually little effort. If the environment is noisy or otherwise distracting, for healthy people to hear usually requires no effort. The hearing impaired may actually be forced to listen with more effort because of their impairment.

Listening, however, requires you to make a conscious choice to pay attention, understand, and engage.

Studies over the years have found the primary daily communication skills are reading, writing, speaking, and listening. Many studies are compiled by the International Listening Association, and conclude every time that listening is our most frequently used communication skill. Listening is also the least learned or studied communication skill.

Put in perspective how much more time is taken to teach these main skills compared to the percentage of time we use each skill in everyday life.

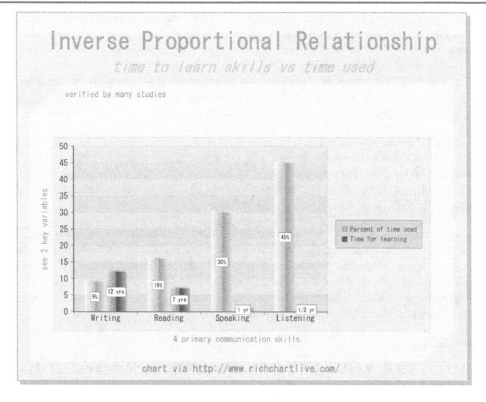

Most of us have schooling, with most of that time teaching us to write, quite often for 12 years, and yet in life we spend the least time, just 9 percent of our time, using our writing skills.

We are learning to read, on average, for 7 years in school, although we use this skill just 7 percent of our time.

If we are lucky, we might get about one year of presentation skills or public speaking training, and we speak about 30 percent of the time.

We spend more time listening, about 45 percent of our time, but spend the least time learning to listen, with only about 6 months if we are fortunate enough to get some training at our work.

All aspects of our daily communication are important to our success in everyday business. The perspective of the inverse proportion to each skill area to the amount of time to use it is meant to bring to attention: Being able to acknowledge that our introvert natural inclination to want to listen is to be valued. With a little effort, we can learn what to do to improve listening and find both quick and valuable results from doing so.

There is a theory that introverts listen better. The only truth in this commonly held belief is introverts do more listening than talking by nature.

As introverts, we spend more time processing thoughts than verbalizing them. Talking takes much less time than thinking those same thoughts through. Most extroverts think while they talk. When we talk, unless we are thoroughly prepared, as introverts we are not always at our best. That means we do not get as much of a gratifying response from others. The lack of positive response can tend to affect our confidence and we may want to speak less. However, extroverts thrive on the external response so they show up in their best light while talking, and that moves them to talk more.

There is little evidence that because by our nature to listen more that we listen well or that we listen better. Even the significant and often referenced study in 1988 of Neil Rackham with 35,000 sales calls supports just one thing: Introverts have a natural gift for listening that contributes to their sales effectiveness. Both major account and successful relationship selling include effective listening and good questioning.

It can make a difference to understand our advantage to better focus in on what we already do more easily and quickly improve on this. We can also learn to hear our inner dialog in a deeper way to help us manage listening better. Listening elicits ideas, and helps clarify thinking, both of which are rewarded in the workplace. In *Chapter 4, Your Hard Working Wrench: Tighten or Open up Your Listening*, we will look at some specific ways to further hone and tweak the skill of listening.

Allowing your true passion to show up in your communications

Could you have ever imagined you would "tweet" about relevant news stories or research findings that interest you? Or did you ever think you would share ideas for people to "like" on Facebook with simply writing about them? Maybe posting a discussion question or an idea in a LinkedIn group is your preference if you are online?

Many people claim that the Internet and online social media give an advantage to introverts.

Others say this communication venue gives people, including introverts, the excuse to show up differently from who they really are.

Our communications, whether online or in-person, come from both our head and our heart. As introverts, our passion to communicate comes in part from being able to be authentic, and connect with people at a genuine and often deep level.

In allowing connected communication online or person to person to develop, there are some things that might get in our way. Whether we call these things misconceptions or myths, if we hold on to beliefs in one certain way we might hold back the passion we want in our communications from showing up. It is in letting go of beliefs that do not serve us or in beliefs that are simply not true that we can help our communications deliver the passion we want them to, without jumping up and down as we speak.

Several beliefs contribute more than others to unlocking our communication success; we'll cover these beliefs in the following sections.

Energy source

If we get our energy more from being alone than with other people, where or how will we be able to tap the passion we have about something to communicate?

Once I had the opportunity to be in a training program at the Zig Ziglar Corporation. Zig was a legendary successful salesman turned international motivational speaker. In attending the facilitator training course in his town, the attendees heard some memorable stories. Once Zig was standing in a dinner serving line with people who would be attending his program. He overhead a woman say to someone she was with about him, "He doesn't look very motivational." Zig commented, "Ma'am, how does motivation look? I am standing in a line."

Passion or motivation look different for each of us. When I am passionate about a topic it comes through in what I say with energy. When something is close to our heart, it is likely we will speak and, when doing so, speak with conviction and courage. Any negative feelings like worry or anxiety melt away. I do not believe it is possible for passion and something like anxiety to occupy the same space.

Whether more of an extrovert or introvert, each type has the energy, enthusiasm, and excitement we often associate with passion.

The key as an introvert is not to waste that energy. These days, almost all of us use e-mail. This is advantageous for us because it gives us the ability to communicate in a way we prefer. We can take our time and think things through when we interact. We have the writing option to give us more control to communicate instead of the often spontaneous face to face or telephone options.

While more of our communication will still likely be face-to-face or in-person, we can use writing via e-mail to our advantage. While we remain true to ourselves—taking time to think, choosing when we interact and how—we will fuel our energy. And that fuels our passion.

Smaller groups

Early 1990s research by McCroskey and Richmond of West Virginia University and Sallinen-Kuparinen of University of Jyvaskyla examined the comparison of communication between Americans, the Finnish, Australians, and Puerto Ricans. The results found similarities in all four cultures in the study of communication fears and self-perception of communicating. It also found the differences are mostly in the willingness to communicate and introversion, with Finns being more introverted and less willing to communicate in groups. Meetings are highly regarded for decision-making in Finland and many formal procedures guide a meeting. But interestingly Finns saw themselves as more competent at communication.

If the research findings prove anything beyond cultural differences it is that there is truth to the idea that introverts do not like group work. Maybe it is more of a question of what size of a group we enjoy working in.

Because we generally thrive on genuine connections, smaller groups are also where our passion can shine. In business, passion allows ideas to spring up that businesses are always trying to tap from employees.

Depending on the work task we quite often work in groups. If we are in leadership we have an advantage of being able to decide if a group is deemed the better direction, how big that group can be, and other factors.

If we are in more of a support role or frontline position at work then we may not have a say in either of these options. Then we must be able to bring some of our natural skill set into play.

If, as a leader, we designate a group assignment, then remember that a larger group can always have its smaller group assignments within it. Having been a corporate trainer and facilitator, this type of format often leads to the most productive moments.

As staff, if we are assigned to work in a large group, can we step out of our way and step into a path of acting to make the group work for our benefit? Can we do this in a beneficial way so that our best ideas are on tap?

We do have options.

First, find out which people are going to be in the group. Meet with all or any of these people ahead of the scheduled large group meeting. Since we enjoy connecting with one person at a time this will create more of a relationship and at the same time allow us to do some preparation. By the time the large group meeting begins we will feel safer, more comfortable, and become more willing to express our ideas as a result of meeting beforehand.

Once the large group meetings begin and we find ourselves with the typical exercises as an icebreaker, or large group discussion, we have also created a base comfort level. Then, little surprises that come up and force us out of our comfort zone do not have that much negative affect upon us. Our energy is better preserved and again, that allows our passion to come through in our communications.

Small groups can work in helping us to both turn our passion up and let it show more.

Thinking things through

We can turn ideas over and over in our mind, never voice or act on them, and then fool ourselves to believe we have achieved something. But can we have an over active mind? Can our mind be too flooded with ideas? Can we use our preference to think things through only to end up procrastinating on taking action?

One of the times thinking things through is ineffective is if we use it to fool ourselves into thinking it can replace action. Thinking is comfortable for us, acting is not always so. What we must be confident in is that our planning, part of that thinking, will take much of the risk from moving into action.

How does possible over thinking affect workplace communications?

Communication, while difficult to define, is not difficult to engage in. Think about when you are in the flow of a conversation with someone who you know well, someone who you enjoy the company of and someone you feel have the same interest in a topic:

➤ Is the communication complicated?

➤ Is it stilted?

➤ Does the conversation move deeper or wider?

➤ Are you interested in the topic?

The communication likely was easy, flowed naturally, and may have even gone deeper or wider. It did not take a formal plan of action to make this happen. Effective communication in business can be the same way.

Since better communication is one of the easier ways to improve working performance while we want to focus on it to improve it, we can still keep things simple, rather than over complicate it.

What if you tried to explain how to put a coat on? You and your body know how to do it. But if you have to think about the easy process, could the mental attention you give it make the communication worse?

A 2013 University of California Berkley study in the Journal of Neuroscience by Robert S. Blumenfeld of the Helen Wills Neuroscience Institute and Mark D'Esposito of the Department of Psychology have some of the answer of why such over thinking might over complicate things.

A transcranial magnetic stimulation (TMS) was used to briefly interrupt the function of two different parts of the prefrontal cortex, the dorsolateral and ventrolateral. It was used in a specific visual processing task where participants were shown kaleidoscopic images and asked to distinguish between them by providing details. It was found that there is indirect harm to the implicit memory processes controlled in this brain area.

"The results of disrupting the function of the dorsolateral prefrontal cortex shed light on why paying attention can be a distraction and affect performance outcomes. If we ramped down activity in the dorsolateral prefrontal cortex, people remembered the images better," said Lee.

When the researchers disrupted the ventral area of the prefrontal cortex, the participants' memory was just slightly worse. "They would shift from saying that they could remember a lot of rich details about the image to being vaguely familiar with the images," Lee said. "It didn't actually make them better at the task."

Over thinking something before we engage in communication about it may not be the best approach.

How do we get the same satisfying and easy results as in one-to-one communications with people we know well into our everyday business communication?

If we can stop and listen to our thinking, we can consciously stop ourselves. We can even decide to anchor a word or physical action like either, "Enough," or a soft slap on the head to get us to stop the over thinking.

Then we might want to distract ourselves from the head conversation. Any physical distraction would likely be your best action at this point. Do not go back into your head. Stand up and stretch, a lot. Take a walk. Do something physical away from where you caught yourself ruminating.

Edward M. Hallowell, a psychiatrist in Concord, Massachusetts, and an instructor of Psychiatry at Harvard Medical School may have the final step to disengage our over thinking in what he calls the human moment.

Once you have caught yourself (the anchored word or slap on the head) and then broken your preoccupation with being in your head, move into action with a face-to-face conversation. You will have your energy back with your physical presence putting you in the present moment and you can put that energy into the conversation that brought up all the over thinking.

Make a note

These three main introvert habits, when used appropriately: how we get our energy, putting the best of us into small group work, and thinking things through, can fuel our passion to shine through in our work.

Using your close connection communication habits in your work

"What I hear, I forget; what I see, I remember; what I do, I understand."

-Old Chinese proverb, sometimes attributed to Confucius

We can hear about how to do something new, but we forget it. We remember a little more or a bit better when we read about or see some new idea in action. The best learning comes from understanding and doing the thing you wish to learn.

Yes, we see or read about an introvert's strength and we do understand. We already act in these ways with our customers, close business associates, and friends. The learning is ingrained.

In the brief discussion earlier in this chapter we found how we can use our authenticity in three specific areas to pull our passion into our communication. Now let's also bridge our natural tendencies in close friendships to the wider workplace to keep grounded and maintain energy.

When we talk with someone we have a close relationship with, we are more comfortable and less inhibited. If we examine more closely what happens as we interact at these times, we can find certain natural personal resources, habits, and characteristics we bring to these more comfortable relationships.

When we identify these natural tendencies we can choose what might work better for us in a less comfortable conversation. We can also keep any or all of these characteristics in mind to bring to bear, as we need them in communication situations we are not as fond of. This can broaden our success in communications with almost anyone. If we discover things that do not work so well for us, with just that awareness we can decide to let them go or change them to be better.

To bring this chapter to a close, we will consider those natural tendencies and characteristics we already understand and do in one context, in communicating and building close connections, and broaden it to workplace connections.

Meetings, presentations, managing conflicts, negotiating and influencing—the sound of all these extroverting activities can exhaust us.

Yet if we think about our most fond relationships, unless you are at the extreme end of the introvert and extrovert continuum, it is likely all this is going on in them as well.

Seek out a quiet place

It is likely that the most comfortable conversations with people who you know well are between just the two or few of you. And when you want to be heard you are. A quiet place will energize you. Even if it is a large meeting or presentation, using a quiet place ahead of time will give you both energy and confidence.

Time your communications if at all possible

There will not always be this luxury, however, many events in business are scheduled. If you are involved in the scheduling, plan things for when you know your energy will be at its best. If I have to meet with a client or prospective client, morning is my preferred time. Several studies claim that their findings show that morning types tend to be more introverted and evening types are more extroverted. Think about when you know you are at your best in those one to one relationships and make that kind of scheduling work for you.

Keep on track

Many meetings in the work place last longer than either planned or even scheduled. Even when we are with close friends our batteries need recharging. Be the one who volunteers to keep track of time and make it work for you. Just like you make time your ally with your close friends.

Use your natural curiosity to your advantage

When we are with a person we know, we explore, discover, and are sincerely interested in their experiences. This helps us use our listening more and when the situation is right, and the offer is welcome, we give our perspective. Whether it is knowledge for its own sake or because we are in a valued relationship, bring curiosity with you.

Make a note

A few example phrases to get you started to show your curiosity:

- "Tell me more about ..."
- "Help me understand what you mean by ..."
- "What an interesting point. Tell me ..."

Keep on listening

I have heard many introverts say what I often have happen. Sometimes I can meet someone for the first time and do very little talking. I will listen. I often ask questions. I hold back on being self-revealing. If we do meet again, or if the person meets someone who I know well then word gets back to me that this new acquaintance thinks I am so interesting. Listening helps us to both maintain positive relationships and sync up new relationships positively.

Bring your trustworthiness with you

A 1997 study by Ramsey and Sohi in the Journal of Academy of Marketing Science established that a customer's perception of how well a salesperson listens has a positive association with trust. Trustworthiness goes far in both building relationships and helping us in our career.

Be prepared

Trainique partnered with Nightingale Conant and surveyed 2,663 sales organizations. Most were in the USA but 20 percent were in the UK. The results showed that 82 percent of the organizations had a poorly defined sales process, which helps us to understand why customers often think we do not understand their business. Planning covers preparedness.

Deepen a higher relationship

Where is it written that we have to wait for a formal review from a manager before we flush out what we might need to do more of, or do better to reach our work's goals? Likely there is nothing written to prevent you from building a one-to-one relationship with a supervisor or manager.

We do not have to sabotage our business success by hiding our strengths. What would be more beneficial, for us and the people and the company we work with, is to bring our strengths with us into everything we do.

Are we perfect?

No.

Are we better than extroverts at communicating?

In some ways we are more natural, in some ways they are more natural.

Are we competent?

Yes.

Developing meaningful communications goes beyond having a lot of connections, being upbeat and friendly. We have to understand the position of the other person, and listen to their conversation to find meaning and understanding.

We can pull in our authenticity that shows up in our best or closest relationships into our everyday communications. If we do that, we can bring our introvert personality into any workplace situation for the greater good.

The biggest obstacle we might have is self-confidence. But the good news is that is not an inherent trait. We will explore this in the next chapter.

Summary

Our introvert strengths, like the sails on a sailboat, can help us better navigate daily communications and their challenges. With this chapter completed, you may find yourself feeling better about being just as you are. At this time you know or are reminded:

> ➤ Self-reflection can guide our communication behavior to the advantage of all concerned

> ➤ Self-reflection leads to self-awareness, which is particularly helpful in negotiations and conflict management

> ➤ Self-awareness puts us in touch with our emotions, other people's emotions, and our actions

> ➤ Planning is integral for success to every one of the key essential business skills that most of the content of this book is about

> ➤ While our brain is wired to be a brilliant planner, we often need to be flexible to take what we have and go into a situation with confidence in our preparedness

> ➤ Our introvert tendency is to listen more, which gives us actual practice to hone this central skill

➤ Crucial to our success in business, or life, is to fuel our natural energy source

➤ Mastering our boundaries to over think things can move us into action with courage

➤ The same habits that we are comfortable with in one-to-one close relationships and small groups can work positively for us in all relationships

Thoughts to contemplate

Just like paying attention to the holes in the sails of a sailboat, when we focus on our strengths to build our weaknesses we can usually expect better results.

It is actually in our strengths that we build upon any weakness and if need to pull that strength along side to do it.

As you reflect back on this chapter about the introvert strengths that can help you achieve better results in your everyday business communications, ask yourself these three key things:

➤ How has your belief or disbelief of commonly stated introvert myths helped you or hurt you in your everyday business communication?

➤ Out of the many strengths cited in this chapter, or even different ones you might think of, what are the top three you feel you can count on even under stress?

➤ When you think about your closest and most treasured relationships, what are the communication habits that you bring to them that boost them to that level of success? How do you see yourself pulling in those same habits to future relationships?

Bibliography

> 1999 *Self-Reflection Studies* by Gustafson and Bennett: `http://www.nwlink.com/~donclark/hrd/development/reflection.html#Interpersonal`

> Dr. Debra Johnson and John Wiebe, *Cerebral Blood Flow and Personality*: `http://psychiatryonline.org/data/Journals/AJP/3697/252.pdf`

> TED Talk by Jason Fried: `http://www.ted.com/talks/jason_fried_why_work_doesn_t_happen_at_work.html`

> *Willingness to Communicate, Communication Apprehension, Introversion and Self-reported Communication Competence*. `http://www.as.wvu.edu/~richmond/articles/kuparinen-will.pdf`

> International Listening Association: `http://www.listen.org/`

> UCSB Study Reveals That Overthinking Can Be Detrimental to Human Performance: `http://www.ia.ucsb.edu/pa/display.aspx?pkey=3080`

> 3

Confident to Communicate

"Confidence contributes more to conversation than wit."

-Francois de La Rochefoucauld, 17th century French author

Who will listen to us in a business meeting if we sound less than confident? What will audience members walk away with from a presentation if our body language says we are not quite sure what we are saying? If we are in a conflict situation and lack confidence, what might be the kind of potential outcome? Why would the party across from us in a negotiation believe in either our knowledge or our conviction in the absence of confidence? How do we persuade someone to buy or act on our recommendations if we are second-guessing something we said?

In these essential skills of business place communication, each of them has at least two common denominators: listening and confidence. Any communication situation like the examples above can move along although they succeed with best results when the speaker is listened to.

But without confidence, communication results can be as disillusioning as finding out that your favorite restaurant serves its tuna from a can. We just cannot be effective without confidence in communications.

Both listening and self-confidence are skills that are impossible to hold in a hand, just like the essential communication skills cannot be held either. Yet, it is undeniable what confidence can do for a person. Each of us likely has days when we are feeling less than stellar, but suffering from a serious and enduring lack of self-confidence can hold us back.

In times of self-doubt, confidence can come through for us in dealing with the most difficult situations and people. And the more confident we are the more often it happens. Self-confidence is quite like a body muscle in that, the more we experience it, the more we feel its positive effects.

Karen M. Caito is a Confidence Coach for Introverts. She is a Certified Professional Coach (CPC) through the Institute for Professional Excellence in Coaching. She is a master practitioner authorized to give the ELI, Energy Leadership Index assessment. The tool helps you discover your level of energy based on your attitude and perspective of your world, helping people move from being overwhelmed to feeling energized.

She did not plan this direction but it happened as person after person said to her: "I need more confidence." What Caito found in her training to be a coach is our energy level can affect our confidence level. She says if you have ever heard the encouragement from people around you, different variations of "Be more confident," then one of the best actions you can take is to first understand what the meaning of confidence is. We will start at the place of clarifying some of the "self-words".

Self-confidence distinguished from other selves

Understanding the differences between self-confidence, self-efficacy, self-esteem, and self-image may be something to give you just the boost you need. Because they are so intertwined one can make the other stronger like in a braided cord. At the very least, as we go forward with this chapter, we have the same understanding of at least each of these four words.

Maybe more importantly, as we assess the degree we each think we need to boost our confidence, it may or may not be what is keeping us stuck in certain situations. Then we can decide to let it go or do something about it.

With varying dictionary and psychological differences in the definition of each of these self-terms it may make sense to consider either the Greek or the Latin root words of each. After all with more than half of English words coming from Latin, and a smaller percentage from Greek, it is in the root words we find the original meaning.

For example, "ego" is a Latin root word and means "self". In Greek, the root auto also means "self". It seems our "self" is on auto—autopilot, automatic. Unless we take the time like right now to stop and reflect, our ego will run our self-confidence level for us without even recognizing that it may be increasing or decreasing.

I was not always as confident in myself as I am today. Even when I was in college there were times that I wondered, "How did I even get so lucky to be here?" The courses were difficult. The environment was devoid of any long-lasting high school friendships I had. It was difficult to make friends. That was a further continuance of my faithless feelings and thoughts mostly acquired in high school.

Fast forward to getting jobs, which eventually steered me onto the entrepreneurial path. The one thing I was confident about when I took this step; I knew I had demonstrated for years that, for other people who were my managers and supervisors, selling is something I could do successfully.

Self-confidence

Self-confidence is from the Latin word confidentia or confide, which means to have full or firm trust, reliance or faith. Going to the Greek word of "fid", we find the meaning of trust. We have confidence because we have faith in our abilities and ourselves.

An interesting thing about self-confidence, this faith we have in ourselves, is what can inspire others: our boss, our peers, our customers and whoever our audience is. When other people see we have confidence, they trust and respect us.

Building more self-confidence is somewhat dependent on building on the confidence you already have. If you have ever been labeled or called timid then you could be looking in a mirror in front of you confirming lower self-confidence.

It may be worth the time to look back to identify what success you have already had in various communication situations. Identify some and you will begin to feel the lower self-confidence transforming into higher self-confidence.

Because our everyday work is about getting tasks done, often with and through other people, this could be just the boost you need.

Self-efficacy

Efficacy has a Latin root word *effectivus*, which means creative, productive, and effective.

Albert Bandura, a psychologist who studies self-efficacy and is most often quoted about how there is a distinction of confidence through examining self-efficacy: "Confidence is a nonspecific term that refers to strength of belief but does not necessarily specify what the certainty is about." For example, we might be confident our presentation will be a disaster or be confident a conflict with someone else will continue.

In other words, the word confidence on its own does not always point to a positive outcome.

To distinguish what is at the heart of the aspect of positive confidence when we use the term self-confidence, Bandura illuminates, "Perceived self-efficacy refers to belief in one's agentive capabilities; that one can produce given levels of attainment."

We have to believe we are able to do what tasks we are assigned or what role we have to fill. Self-efficacy affects our positive belief in our capability to do things, and this affects our faith in ourselves, our self-confidence.

If we have a strong sense of self-efficacy, we will view challenging situations as something we both can do well and recover from quickly if we fail. If we are someone with a weak level of self-efficacy, we will likely focus more on the impossibilities of a task or situation and likely suffer from the effect of losing or lowering self-confidence in our abilities.

What is the learning point in this relationship between self-confidence and self-efficacy?

When we face a difficult situation, if we can minimize our stress and improve our mood we will find the creativeness and productiveness (one's agentive capabilities) to move forward with full faith and trust to be effective or successful.

Self-esteem

Self-esteem is originally from the Latin word *aestimare*, which means to assess the merit of, appraise, or estimate. Another derivative of it is from mid-15th century showing up in old French as estime, meaning high regard.

If self-confidence is having the faith and assuredness about what we can do, then self-esteem is our overall appraisal of our worth. Other related words would be self-worth or self-respect.

Low self-esteem could limit our self-confidence. If we believe any of the introvert myths–introverts don't like to talk, we have difficulty knowing what to say, we are anti-social (go back to *Chapter 1, Communication Preferences of Introverts and Extroverts*, for a quick refresher of examples of the main myths)—then of course we question our own value as a person.

Self-image

In the word "self-image", the root word of image means something symbolic in both Latin and Greek. It is our own idea or concept of a collective representation of oneself that mostly comes from learning from images of who we are that are reflected back to us from others.

Carl Rogers, a 20th century psychologist, believes our self-image is one part of our self-concept. Our self-concept is all the beliefs we have about ourselves that both others projected to attitudes, as well as what we tell ourselves about our own experiences. Our self-image is one of the more difficult things to change but not impossible.

Make a note

To summarize, self-confidence relates to our faith and assuredness in who we are, self-efficacy is more of a positive belief that we have in our capabilities to get results, self-esteem is our evaluation of our worth, and self-image is who we think we are.

Have you assessed your self-confidence?

Assessments are helpful to identify where we currently are, to give us some direction of what to focus on in order to get where we want to get to. Have you already assessed your self-confidence? Is it the same, better, or lower since that assessment? What have you done to boost your confidence since the assessment? Are there some things you know you need to give more attention to?

Consider the degree to which self-confidence is either as strong as it can be or needs some strengthening to be helpful in particular, in your everyday communications.

Stop and take time to answer the following statements with just one of the words in the scale of words. Do not try to force your thinking of what the assessment will mean and then answer accordingly. The truer your answers are the greater understanding you will have of your self-confidence when you read the interpretation.

Self-confidence assessment

Scale of words	Never	Rarely	Sometimes	Often	Almost always
I'm proud of my accomplishments.					
I believe my past success can create future success.					
I feel energized by results of daily business communications.					
I add value to conversations with listening.					
When in a business meeting I make sure I am heard.					
I welcome the invitation to speak in public.					
If a personal conflict arises, I act to clear the air.					
If I want something, I ask for it.					
If asked for something, I can say no.					
I can do what others do as well or better.					
I am able to solve difficult situations.					
I am resourceful in new situations.					
I listen to but am not convinced by critics.					
I admit mistakes and learn from them.					
I don't have to hear, "Good job," to feel good.					
I accept compliments.					
I have more positive than negative self-talk.					
I can easily name my top three to five qualities.					
I have a positive view of the future.					
I set and reach goals.					

Interpeting your score

Give yourself the following score for the words you identified with each statement:

> ➤ Never: 2 points

> ➤ Rarely: 4 points

> ➤ Sometimes: 6 points

> ➤ Often: 8 points

> ➤ Always: 10 points

The highest score would be 200. The higher your score, the more self-confidence you have. You have full faith in who you are and your abilities. The actions, thoughts, and beliefs you have on a daily basis are helping to raise your self-confidence.

The lowest score would be 40. The lower your score, the more you should identify what you are willing and can easily do to improve your confidence. You may need to find reassurance, or put a new plan into action. A key is to know that you can likely improve your confidence. It is within your ability.

Action Point

Focus first on acknowledging and continuing to use your strengths first, which is are those statements you answered with Sometimes, Often, or Always. Too often we want to slide right into the mindset, "What am I doing wrong?" So wait. Acknowledge that you have confidence working for you in various ways.

Next identify what statements have an answer of Rarely or Never. As you pull in what you already know about self-confidence as well as make new discoveries in this chapter, decide what actions you can and will take to improve these areas.

Can you use your strengths to boost your confidence?

Most people cannot change their personality but can choose different behavior to get results they want, according to Karen Caito. When it comes to confidence you should always look to "capitalize on your talents, strengths, or unique gifts, so you can be who you really are and be confident in that." Discovering how you can change is more effective than going down a path to try to act like someone you are not.

Do you often have a difficult time making decisions because you think you will make the wrong decision? It could stem from over-analyzing. Then since we don't have the confidence to make a decision, we do not act.

It is quite likely your research went beyond the norm in gathering data and evidence.

A male chef, who Caito coached to actually secure the position, was soon up for a promotion. But because he was so quiet, management was concerned. In a twelve-week program with Caito, he realized being quiet showed up as being aloof to others. It was not being quiet that caused the concern but the perception of what was the outward manifestation.

Does being labeled something like aloof sound familiar?

Caito helped the chef get to the core of understanding how his passion could help if he could communicate it. That is when he moved towards being more confident. He transferred his passion into his communication.

A high-ranking US Army officer approached Caito because he lacked confidence. Caito helped him build his confidence by looking back at all the accolades he received through his career. But while the degrees and recognition made him feel good, they were merely to ward off a lack of any recognition with his family. Many of us have those gremlins from our younger life. It is the "not good enough" syndrome. When he realized these recognitions pointed more to his intelligence, his compassion and the like, his confidence began to bloom. He even named himself, "warrior," to help visualize his confidence.

Just think about the physical posture that comes to mind with the word "warrior." Or if you are able as you are reading about this now, stand up and get in the warrior pose. Just like the positive effect you get if you are forced to smile when you are feeling down in the dumps, you will find this pose in one that the warrior pose brings on a feeling of confidence.

Eventually the officer stepped out of the shadows and became more confident about initiating conversations with new staff, which he could never do before his transformation.

Each person is different with unique talents, often things we do not easily acknowledge.

So we have to start with being able to feel better about who we are by taking inventory of our strengths. You can work with any personal strengths you have as a person, or for now we will use generally accepted introvert strengths.

Move your strengths forward

Caito claims an exercise of writing down 10 to 20 success stories in your life helps in focusing our attention on our strengths. Ask yourself at any period of time in life from childhood to where you are now, what did you feel great at doing? Then ask why?

This is the start to connecting the dots.

Looking at the essential skills you will discover you can improve your success with, let us tie some of our introvert strengths to each skill. Then for what we want improved results in, let us connect some dots.

Listening

Listening is foundational in all other communications essentials we are discussing. Our role in listening is core to the outcome in each situation of a business meeting, a presentation even when we are the presenter (more about that in *Chapter 6, Tape Measure Your Success for Powerful Presentations*), in conflict management, for negotiations, and in any kind of influence. As introverts, we tend to listen more so we are in the most advantageous position to master this skill.

Business meetings

In *Chapter 2, Identify and Count on Your Introvert Strengths*, I mentioned how Jason Fried in his TED Talk states there is a global agreement that most meetings do not accomplish much. In almost all meeting management training that I have either facilitated or been a participant in, the most mentioned "must do" that most often gets overlooked is to plan a meeting from start to end.

Planning a meeting implies that at least an agenda to come around to reaching the meeting goal needs to happen ahead of time. This is a time when thinking before we act or speak allows us to bring our strength of thinking things through to the event.

If we are not in charge of a meeting, we may have to speak up and either offer to help the meeting leader with this, or at the meeting, ask for an agenda. The leader will likely take the hint and either give it or build it then.

Presentations

For some people, the only business situation that is worse than sitting through a poorly run meeting is being bored to either tears or near death by a presentation. Regardless of what the point of the presentation is, most people try to cram too much information into time in an appealing way; this is often labeled death by presentation.

We are naturals when it comes to preparing. This is a time when we can pull in our creativity around ideas. Rehearsing is the best step to a well-received presentation. You will find you can research, plan, and revise your story until you have it as concise and clear as it can be.

Being more high touch than high tech with public speaking and presentations is more effective.

Conflict management

When we think of conflict, we might think of emotions being tangled up. I do. Usually we are adept at being calm and taking a broad perspective. This gives us time to more clearly identify the problem and propose something mutually agreed upon in the end.

Being calm in uncertain situations, such as when there is conflict, can allow us to bring cohesiveness to a noncohesive situation.

Negotiation

Successful negotiations usually do not happen quickly; there is preparation, there is making our case, and uncovering what works to our advantage on the opposing side.

To discover, there has to be a search. We have to be willing to explore and find common ground.

Negotiating successfully also means to give as little information as possible. It is like being able to have that "poker face" in the card game of poker. It is about listening more than talking.

Go deep and go wide. We have to find out what is important to the other person, what we are willing to give up, and be willing to stay the course. We love exploring most things in depth.

Chapter 8, On the Level to Negotiate with Success, reviews negotiating with success.

Make a note

Relevant research: If you are now up for a salary increase, or a corner office, or an up-front parking space, and want to skip ahead to negotiations, consider this:

- Researchers speculated that women are more anxious than men about negotiating
- An online survey results showed 2.5 times more women than men feel apprehension about negotiating: 55% of women to 39% of men
- Men negotiate about four times more than women
- Men and women who do negotiate salary can earn about $1 million more in their career

As introverts, with business structures changing and economically often less than ideal situations, we owe it to ourselves to know we have a strong natural foundational to better negotiate for what we might want.

Influence, persuasion, and selling

We know that customers often do not feel listened to, particularly in selling. The customer knows we hear them, but being listened to is what they want. Many sales people feel obligated to give their pitch and rush into it. This usually turns off customers. We are happy as introverts to let people talk while we listen. When we listen, we are able to pull in more information that someone else might share into our own experiences. What happens in the process is rich ideas get even richer by going wider or deeper. Put aside for a moment that you may feel you do listen, but it could always be better. The fact is we listen more than the people who are more extroverted. So take it all in, and listen to carefully when you are in a situation of influence, persuasion, or selling.

Make a note

Basic strengths of essential communication skills:

- Think things through
- Prepare
- Be calm
- Go deep
- Listen more

Do you agree that typical everyday business skills go from business meetings to selling, influencing, and persuading?

Do you agree that the basic tendencies necessary to succeed are ones you naturally possess?

Hopefully you agree we have the beginning of a small inventory to acknowledge who we are at the core. Then we connect the dots to see that the tendencies we might take for granted are actually vital to the success in almost all everyday business communications. So let's not be distracted.

Are you distracted by pesky introvert myths?

Earlier, we learned about the meaning of self-confidence, and interpreted it as the faith we have in ourselves. We continued with further confidence from three other selves:

➤ **Self-efficacy**: A positive belief we have in our capabilities

➤ **Self-esteem**: The image we have of our worth

➤ **Self-image**: How we see ourselves

Unless we are aware of the truth about who we are, including what our strengths and weaknesses are, myths can keep us stuck regardless of which self-word we may identify distorting our thoughts. Low self-confidence can prevent us from taking action, action necessary for our essential communication skills to be effective. If you can identify with low self-confidence, it may be time to examine a possible central problem.

Because so much credence is given to what others project to us about how they see us, often based on some unproven collective belief, we can often confuse the projection with the truth.

When I was midway through my sales management position my confidence soared. My career grew from my sales being at the top of a sales leader board, to a team on the top of the world, being in the top ten percent of 700 locations around the world. My request for a raise was honored. My suggestions for some restructuring were underway.

My actions were reaping positive results.

On a cool fall weather Saturday I headed to a luggage shop. Someone there who looked out of context to me offered to help. It took less than a minute for me to recognize a former salesperson on my team.

She helped me find a piece of luggage for my next trip. Then we were standing at the register completing the sale.

I decided to ask how she liked her new work. "Oh, I love it here," smiling as she commented. "And you know I learned a lot from you even though you always were so intense."

In sales we recognize the phrase "even though", or the word "but," as negating or canceling out the words that came before it. Actually all of us have found the word "but" in a conversation with someone else only to feel the sting of it. "That meeting was terrific but ..." or "We loved your presentation but ..."; yikes. Everything just before the "but" just went down the drain.

Wanting both to answer my curiosity, and salvage what was likely meant to be complimentary, I asked what she meant by intense.

"You were relentless with ideas about what we could be doing to sell more to reach our goals. I never knew anyone so determined. So focused."

Had I not asked for further explanation of what came after the energy drain word "but", I may have walked out of the store wondering, "How bad was I as a manager?" "Intense" generally indicates something of an extreme. Walking away from the brief conversation at that point would have meant possibly leaving me in a low-confidence place with self-reflection.

But regardless of the former salesperson's take on intensity I was comfortable learning from my probing that I was successfully doing what my role needed.

There are so many lists about myths of introversion. Whether it is just five items or thirty-one, the highest number on a list I discovered, we can be distracted from truth when, out in our daily encounters, one of them grabs our attention.

Sadly these are myths we accept without question because they are pervasive and can lower our self-confidence. It is important that you recognize which myths you believe, and then turn them around. This is why it made sense in *Chapter 1, Communication Preferences of the Introvert and Extrovert*, to bring up four of the most common myths as they relate to how introverts and extroverts can miscommunicate.

Not all introverts are the same

Many of us discover our introvert preference through the Myers Briggs Type Indicator®, MBTI. There are of course other assessments but this one stands out. It measures four different traits, not just the introversion/extroversion energy preference.

The MBTI® also factors in how we take in information, either from a reality-based interpretation of things from the past and present or from a pattern of information considering everything including the future.

A third is the decision-making trait where one way of drawing conclusions is preferred over another. We primarily either use the thinking side of the brain or the feeling side.

The fourth trait is what guides us into action with a preference toward either judging or perceiving. If we are more of a judger, we tend to approach the world with a plan. If we are more of a perceiver, we go along in a more flexible way taking things as they come along.

An ISFP and INTJ, two introvert MBTI® types who might be in the same situation will react quite differently. There is more to us as individuals than our introversion.

Make a note

The MBTI® four-preference scale includes the following:

- **Introversion/extroversion**: How we get our energy with introverts thriving from the inner world of thoughts and ideas, and those more extroverted finding more life from everything outside them in the way of activities, people, and things.
- **Sensing/intuitive**: In how we perceive information, the more sensing is perceptive about present sensory details, which the intuitive speculates about the future from many past experiences.
- **Thinking/feeling**: How we make decisions may lean more toward thinking by relying on facts, deduction, and an objective manner or it may lean more toward a more feeling and subjective manner considering what is important to ourselves and others.
- **Judging/perceiving**: This is related to how we take actions. The more judging approach is to have an organized plan in a structured way. The more perceiving approach would be a spontaneous way of making decisions as you go along.

Any style assessment analysis will include more than one dimension of our style or personality.

Susan Steele, Digital Confidence Builder at Quietly Fabulous says, "Don't think because you're an introvert that everything you read about introverts holds true for you. You are unique and special. Find your own kind of introversion and revel in it."

Even when we factor in the other traits with the energy trait of introversion that we might share, we might forget that it is not who we are in whole. That is when we want to be ready or at least be aware that we can take actionable steps to break down those myths to invite self-confidence in.

Break down myths and boost self-confidence

One of the most recommended ways of boosting self-confidence is through the use of affirmations. Have you used them? Do they work for you? Over time people find these empowering statements replace limiting old beliefs with more positive new ones.

They often get you results in any area of life you have used them. Self-confidence affirmations top the list. We also use them for improved health, being successful, better relationships, and advancing our career. We can also craft several to turn around a myth. Otherwise, myths have a possibility of keeping us stuck with a belief that we might intuitively question.

For example, maybe you have been under the spell of believing introverts are soft-spoken. A suggestion for a positive affirmation to move you away from what might not be true for what you want is "I am excited to meet and talk with new people."

For years there were times I would write down positive, personal, present tense statements, with a positive verb. Then I would read and say them aloud throughout the day and night. I always read statements like "I enjoy attracting more than enough success in my business" and "I gratefully learn from my mistakes and increase my experience from them" with enthusiasm.

Updating affirmations

Affirmations do not work for me. I have found other practices to be more effective for me. I recently found myself attracted to afformations created by Noah St. John. Years ago he claims he asked himself a question brilliantly propelling him to author *The Book of Afformations*. The insight came to him while showering; St. John asked himself, "If human thought is the process of asking and searching for answers to questions, why are we going around making statements that we don't believe?" He then started with his simple, but not easy, afformations.

An afformation is an affirmation in a question format. It is still positive, personal and in the present tense acts like an affirmation.

In examining some of the lists of myths we could take anyone of the many of them and create a perfect afformation to help dissolve them. After all, by our nature we ask lots of questions to be able to understand things better. Here are five myth buster suggestions, by way of afformations, one for each of the essential communication skills thatwill reinforce acknowledgement of a personal strength.

If we know that we are people who already listen more, maybe even better than most, an afformation reinforces what we already know to be true. What an inspiring way to lead this kind of self-talk.

 Action Point

Myth: Introverts do not get involved in talking a lot.

Afformation: Why does my listening more get better results in virtually all business communication situations?

This afformation around our natural tendency to think before we speak stands up to any misconception when you might be asked "Why don't you speak up in meetings?" This example will both allow you to recognize your strength and begin to see how it helps your effectiveness in a business meeting.

 Action Point

Myth: Introverts seem to be slow to contribute in conversations.

Afformation: Why do I like to think before I speak or respond?

You might start to feel anxious when you are asked to give a presentation. This feeling by the way, affects not just introverts, but many ambiverts and extroverts. But what if you could acknowledge personal preferences, which actually increase the delivery of a confident presentation?

Action Point

Myth: Introverts do not give the best presentation.

Afformation: Why does my planning and preparation give me self-confidence in front of my audience?

Conflict in the workplace usually happens because of differences in style and personality clashes around handling a task or issue. Often our first reaction can be to avoid the situation. By recognizing what we already know to be true and positioning against a myth we might be familiar with, we both build our confidence and help the myth dissipate.

Action Point

Myth: Introverts don't like people and often seem unfriendly.

Afformation: Why do I work well with others, especially one-to-one relationships?

Negotiating can be uncomfortable. Research as stated above finds both men and women avoid it. Many conflicts during negotiations happen because of different interpretations. As introverts we have a trait to help during this time challenging negotiations.

Action Point

Myth: Introverts can come across as intense.

Afformation: Why does my ability to focus and concentrate help me more easily negotiate to an agreement without giving in?

Persuasion is influence, and it requires communication. Verbal communication is not always needed to influence. Sales or selling incorporates each of these. The skill of persuasion requires the skill to bring what both sides want into the decision-making.

Action Point

Myth: Introverts are soft-spoken.

Afformation: Why do I prefer a thoughtful and creative approach when helping others to make an important decision?

As you use these examples or other afformations you come up with to counter a popular introvert myth, it is highly likely to find your negative feelings about yourself or low confidence in your capabilities start to dissipate.

While creating afformations is a simple technique, it is not easy to have the discipline to use them daily. If you can get to that point, you begin to see your confidence grow and open up your strengths up to your advantage.

Go inside your head with visualization

Affirmations and even afformations are not everyone's answer to a boost in confidence. Since as introverts we spend time in our heads, why not take some of the time while we are there to make the best of it in boosting our self-confidence?

Research in sports and health has found that guided imagery, used interchangeably with the word visualization, can help improve certain situations. A popular study we might hear about is an athlete using guided imagery to see himself achieving a certain outcome, and as a result he gets his best score in golf.

There are studies like one conducted at the University of Chicago that report a group of basketball players who, with daily practice of nothing but guided imagery, compared to a group that might be physically practicing basketball free throws, collectively improved their free throw shots by as much as 25 percent.

Another study at the Cleveland Clinic Foundation in Ohio, reveals that by only using guided imagery a person can increase muscle strength.

Other studies and findings point to visualization enhancing not just the body but personal motivation.

The more studies you read with such positive results leads to a conclusion that imagery affects ability, consistency, and confidence. More specifically, this mental toughness gained with visualization includes self-confidence, intrinsic motivation, focus, and composure.

The next time you feel you are getting insecure or doubtful about yourself, take what we know to be the best of visualization to imagine yourself stepping into a circle of confidence. As a Neuro Linguistic Programming certified practitioner, here is a visualization I have used to guide many clients through, before a team meeting or a presentation or a difficult customer situation, to ground themselves with confidence. It is called the Circle of Confidence Visualization.

In general, visualization starts with taking two or three deep breaths to let go of anxiousness and relax. Closing your eyes is recommended if it will play out totally in your head, in particular if you find that even in a quiet spot by yourself you will be distracted. Then you begin to get into your head. In the version here, the suggestion is to get your body involved. Your physiology is as important to the success of this particular technique as is the imagery. Remember what we learned earlier–we can force a smile and that results in us feeling happier. But if you prefer, you can do this entire visualization process in your head.

Use a situation like wanting to be confident to share a unique idea you want to share at an upcoming business meeting. Use any upcoming communication situation that might have you doubting yourself.

Lists

- Remember a time when you were at your best and felt most confident. It does not matter from where in life you felt confidence. It could be a business meeting or a family picnic. The idea is to remember the feelings at the time when you felt this self-confidence; hear the sounds at the event that may help you remember; see how you and others around you looked in this most positive situation; feel how you may have been standing or sitting. Take a minute or two to bring the whole situation into your mind.

- Stay with the picture, sounds, and feelings about this confident time for another minute or two.

- Next, imagine a circle in front of you. Yes, the Circle of Confidence. Note the appearance of it including color, shape, and even texture. You also might want to bring in any sounds or tones it may have.

- When you get your visual recollection of your confidence experience to so that it moves your feelings to as confident as you want to be at this upcoming meeting, maybe a minute or two, and it is fully satisfying to you, step into the circle.

- Now you are in the circle. Visualize yourself in this future upcoming event; picture it in the environment if you know where it will be. Feel the self-confidence you now know you have, which you can take to any future situation. Hear the sounds and tones that communicate confidence to you. Be in the moment of that positive feeling and picture. Stay here in your head with this complete multi-sensory image for a few minutes.

- Step back out of the circle. Shake the entire event and feelings with it off of you. Go ahead. Actually shake your hands, your arms, or whatever you would do to shake something off of you. Maybe take just a minute to do this.

- As you are out of the circle, again recall yourself feeling the confidence you know you have in that original successful situation or even another; see, hear, and feel yourself as confident as you want to be for another minute.

- Now step back in the Circle of Confidence and again access those feelings, sights, and sounds that made you feel your best and most confident. Stay in your head for a few minutes.

- As you stay in the circle, decide on a physical touch point—it could be holding your hands together, it could be tapping your hand on the side of your thigh, or it could be putting your finger on your chin as if in a thoughtful pose. You are creating a physical anchor to feeling this positive, self-confident state that you can access whenever you want to bring it forth to you in a situation. Take no more than a minute.

Lists

- Step back out of the circle. Shake this event and feelings with it off of you. Do this for no more than a minute.
- Now, either step into the circle or don't, but use that anchor as you think about the upcoming meeting where you are going to confidently be sharing an idea you have come up with. If the visualization process worked for you, in particular with the anchor, in these 12 to 15 minutes, you are now feeling confident.

Understand that you are able to step into this circle in any future situation that calls for you to have high self-confidence, and you can just access this physical anchor. If you find the good confident feeling subsides as you use the anchor, take yourself through the complete process again. This is assuming you have time just before the upcoming meeting, presentation, or communication event that might be causing you to feel anything but confidence.

Whether you use afformations, visualization, or something else, there are introvert friendly actions to use any time you find yourself stuck with one of those introvert myths reducing that reduce your belief in yourself. The ideas I am sharing here are researched, get positive results, often quickly.

Free yourself from myths comfortably with social media

As fast as information spreads throughout the Internet, each of us has control over our speed of the use of it. We can decide to what degree we want to use it. We can choose what online websites we want to show up on. Ultimately, we get to set both the time and location of when we want to respond to another individual.

Using social media makes it easy to connect, move conversations forward, and showcase our expertise. How does all this affect our self-confidence?

Let's remember that self-confidence relates to the faith and assuredness we have in our abilities and self-esteem is our confidence in our worth and abilities.

There are some interesting findings about both personalities and effects on self-esteem. From these we can relate our actions to boosting our self-confidence in a way to take into all communications. Studies continue to reveal findings that can guide our actions in a more natural way.

While what researchers call, OSA, Objective Self-Awareness supports a more negative theory; the Facebook profile format supports what researchers more recently call the HM, Hyperpersonal Model. OSA implies that focusing our attention on ourselves can lower self-esteem because we become more aware of our limitations. But the more recent HM has results that support the premise when we select what information to share it can have positive effects. If in our Facebook profile we shine a positive light on ourselves then it would follow that even having a Facebook profile would increase our self-esteem as we are the ones in charge of creating what we say about ourselves.

A 2011 Cornell University study found that because we want to make the best impression we can when communicating, Facebook can provide a quick confidence boost. Some people will often voice that "People are fake or phony online." The study does not support this; it is not a deceptive image but a positive, supportive one we are communicating. It better supports the HM theory.

Three studies around Facebook in 2011 at the University of Waterloo, Ontario, Canada, found although there is an attraction for people with low self-esteem to use Facebook, as it often causes them to be more comfortable with communications, although stating more negativity in their comments. The result is even friends may not give positive feedback. But when sharing more positivity, introverts' interpersonal outcomes were better.

One hundred and thirty-nine subjects participated in a 2008 study, of which sixty-nine were active Wikipedia members. This is more like an online encyclopedia than social media. What makes it relevant to our discussion of self-confidence is people who are contributors, members, do have to collaborate to a degree. Digging into the true interpretation is important because of a possible typo in the report to a possible reversal of the charted results.

This study found the members who contribute to the content feel more comfortable expressing themselves on the Internet than they do in real life. Personality differences were assessed in Wikipedia members and non-Wikipedia members in agreeableness (helping or selflessness), openness, and conscientiousness. Members score higher on agreeableness and openness. More women than men members score higher with conscientiousness.

While a small study, it demonstrates with an open collaborative process of this collective encyclopedia that people who are the members contribute just as much for the overall improvement of information as they do for their ego. Apparently debate is a common occurrence on Wikipedia and the results point to that it may be because of the member's passion to share information.

One last recent study shifts more positive findings of most studies to at least the use of Facebook possibly being more harmful. This one concluded it may have negative effects for our self-esteem. In 2013, researchers from the University of Michigan tracked moods from one minute to the next over two weeks' time of eighty two college age people, men and women, from various countries. The lead researcher, Ethan Kross, said the more a people used Facebook, the more their mood dropped. There was no correlation to likes, or shares, or commenting so of course further research would be warranted.

With varying degrees of supporting evidence from research how can the more social media venues such as Facebook, Twitter, or LinkedIn help build our confidence?

One takeaway from the survey results is social media content sharing, whether it be Wikipedia contribution or blogging, can be good for self-esteem. And since behavior reflects self-esteem it would follow that confidence is helped when those kinds of online actions are successful.

Studies are studies but with experience we can decide how we need to act and what would be our best bet behaviors to get a positive boost from social media. Moving forward with our use of social media in a way that boosts our self-confidence means to take what we are like innately and apply those preferences to the moment.

The following is how we can use social media to our advantage:

> ➤ **There is no pressure for a quick or specific reply**: When we are face-to-face communicating, the conversation flows. A statement might be made, a question gets asked, and talking and questioning go back and forth. Talking usually moves fluidly along and we grab, maybe even relish, those brief interludes of silence to collect our thoughts to keep going.
>
> But online you can take your time to reply whether it's 10 minutes or 10 days. I have an online presence with LinkedIn, Twitter, Facebook, and my blog. On none of them do I reply to anything quickly. I often take time to think and take advantage of the conversation being just one-sided up to that point.
>
> Treat online communications as you would a personal one to one conversation. Sometimes you will have something of value to add. Other times you will have a question. On other occasions, the topic will not be of interest to you. You get to decide how to reply in real life and online.

> ➤ **Shine a light on your expertise**: By taking time to think through on an online profile, the very act can often build our confidence. And if we do respond to e-mail communication, blog our ideas, or just comment on a blog of interest, the best of us will come through because we allowed our innate nature to infuse the communication.
>
> Again, the process that allows us to take our time, is also a process that, along the way, helps with a confidence boost.

> ➤ **Take your in-depth preference and go wide:** People are online seeking value whether it is in content or being social. But, there is no one right way to make social media work for you if you are using it for a business presence. Certainly there are better and worse, good and not so good approaches. But there is not a one-way only approach.

> ➤ **Engage when you have energy**: Based on the research, it will serve your confidence best if you engage online when you have high and positive energy. If you have had an otherwise extroverting kind of day, that is, a presentation, some conflict at work, or a failed negotiation, skip a day. It will still be there tomorrow.

> ➤ **Select the best community for yourself:** My family and some friends are on Facebook but I am rarely there. I would rather telephone these people or have a cup of tea with them. For me, Facebook is a drag on my business. I find myself often feeling down because there is so much negativity about world events.

➤ **Put your analytical hat on:** We tend to prefer thinking things through and often getting as much detail as we can. Online there are various tools like Klout and Trustcloud that give a big picture assessment of how your online presence is affecting others. You need to have strategies to measure your online social media presence if it is for business.

➤ **Be more positive than negative:** Rather than risking revealing, Revealing flaws which is a natural tendency regardless of introversion or extroversion. when we are feeling down about ourselves, sharing online best serves us when we focus on positive events, situations and comments.

The structure of social media suits most of our preferences for communicating. While we do have to engage to claim we use social media, our confidence in being ourselves will happen when putting all of who w-e are into how we use it.

It's not how many times you fall down, but instead how you bounce back

"The law is simple. Every experience is repeated or suffered till you experience it properly and fully the first time."

-Ben Okri, author of Astonishing The Gods

If self-confidence relates to the faith and assuredness in who we are, what happens if actions you take or things around you are not going so well? As human beings we tend to focus on, "what did I do," and that can be when our resilience suffers.

There are big setbacks and small setbacks in life. Sometimes there can be a terrible event and other times we have to know how to cope. When the economy is uncertain and global bad news catches our attention we can find ourselves caught in the negativity of the situation. That can spill over into everyday business situations.

We might become frustrated to a point of withdrawing if we are not able to have our voice heard in a meeting or even in a negotiation. Not being able to manage conflict over time with the same person we have to work with daily can wear us down. Some of us are even knocked down if we get stuck in a traffic jam.

How we react to setbacks can depend on the level of being derailed. Sometimes we recover and sometimes it seems whatever we do we cannot solve things. It is not just that we should do something, but instead more of finding the how to do something differently to change a situation.

History shows many individuals and people who have shown resilience that helped them through obstacles. We read about Helen Keller, Thomas Edison, and Abraham Lincoln as well as various countries where their people have overcome nature's disasters of tsunamis, tornadoes, and hurricanes.

Who comes to your mind either in the public eye or in your social and family circles?

Every day, regular people show resilience. Relying on research, there is not one doubt that everyone has the innate ability to bounce back. It is not a trait but instead a process.

In researching the resilience process as defined by many researchers and psychologists, we discover resilience pulls in some actions, attitudes, and beliefs of what from both introverting and extroverting styles.

When we overcome a setback at work or in life our own evaluation of our worth, which is our self-esteem, goes up. Self-esteem nurtures our self-confidence. So if, or more likely when, a similar event happens, we know that we can face the challenge successfully.

As a business coach I have often heard other coaches use a tree as a metaphor for resilience. A tree naturally lives and flourishes through weather and seasonal changes. In some of the worst storms I have watched in my own backyard, high winds might cause a tree to bend, and some smaller or older branches to break, but the tree stands secure. It has roots that go deep to keep it grounded. It is the trees with shallow roots that get uprooted in a storm.

This is what we are like in the face of problems. When we get knocked down in some way, we find we can pull in our ideas, experiences and strengths to deal with the event.

There are several online assessments that can determine your personal resilience strengths. Most of them are short in time, 10 minutes on average. There are just two of them noted in the appendix but any Internet search for "personal resilience assessments" will find more. Most of these have some common themes to consider as we examine our own process.

After taking several of these assessments it became apparent that distinct commonalties could be useful for anyone to make improvements to their resilience process to ensure that their self-confidence is either preserved or strengthened. One by Metcalf Associates has a more inclusive and whole person approach. While three of the following four categories come from this assessment, the ideas are extrapolated from my perspective of the difference between an introvert being able to easily take certain actions and what would be different for someone more extroverted.

Emotional

If we get quiet in our head we will quickly be able to see all the details of a situation. Being in our head as much as we are as introverts, turns out to be an asset when faced with a challenge that might for the moment be keeping us stuck.

We, more than extroverts, can easily examine our thoughts, our feelings, our behavior, and our personal understanding of a situation that we label a setback. This can give us the knowledge of what we need, what would be most helpful for us, what to prioritize to move forward, and even when it is time to draw on social support.

Since our emotions factor into any decisions we make, it is important to take time to recognize what those are for us. That way so we can draw on them to make the right moves to get back on track in any negative event.

Social

People who are the most resilient reach out to others for social support. Now I hope you have not just been sucked into the warp of one of the introvert myths and thought "But, I am not that social." If so, refer to this definition of social: "support accessible to an individual through social ties to other individuals, groups, and the larger community."

The more introverted we are we will have a close friend or two that we can discuss a situation, get out our feelings and bounce around ideas.

Every new friendship uses our energy so because of this we prefer deeper relationships with a few people.

While extroverts might have more of a social circle, the process will be the same. The key in getting out of our own head and seeking some counsel, whether with friends or professionals, is to broaden our perspective, bring in more ideas, and just express our emotions while feeling safe about it.

Mental

We each realize we do not, and we cannot, have all the answers. We also know answers will come forth. But it is also going to be our attitudes and beliefs that will help us stand strong like a tree and bend rather than break in a negative situation.

This can mean stepping back to look at the big picture to get creative with a solution, or even several solutions. As we gather knowledge from our own experiences, our thoughts, and the feedback from others, we will move toward a plan that will get us positive results.

And we certainly know about planning! We can gather all the information we need to, think things through and somewhere along our bounce back, and reach out to our closest connections to pull a plan together that we are motivated to follow.

Physical

Very few assessments focused on anything physical adding to the resilience process, which is interesting to me as a person who exercises regularly. We are all here in the physical after all.

When we encounter a setback of any sort, our body can be affected. We can feel tired, our posture might slump, or we might lose our appetite. As introverts are sensitive to preserving our energy, physiological and physical aspects to the resilient process need consideration. Our bodies respond to the way we feel, and think. We often hear about the "mind/body connection" referring to this.

If you have an event or a situation that is affecting you negatively it can show up in any kind of physical manifestation. Recently, being somewhat of a caretaker in the last year for my sixteen-year-old poodle, my husband and I realized we were more keeping her here for us rather than doing the right thing for her. A day before we made the gut-wrenching decision to put her to sleep I had a dental appointment.

My dental assistant always takes blood pressure before even the most routine cleaning visit of a cleaning. My blood pressure was in the 170 range, which is not normal for me at all, as I'm usually around 120. I could only logically attribute it to the stress of the situation.

Depending on what the setback is the level of stress could be low to high. Doing a quick body check of aches and pains that you might not normally suffer from – back pain, no appetite, tiredness, lightheadedness, upset stomach and more – can help you decide what you might have to do to take care of your health.

Consider each of the four key aspects for resilience—emotional, interpersonal, mental, and physical—for our discussion of the relationship between self-confidence and being resilient. If resilience is not an innate skill then anyone can create their preferred process to cover each of these aspects to bounce back from negative events.

Looking back through the explanations of the four aspects we will find ideas that we feel more comfortable with doing than not. The key question is, by doing just what you are comfortable with and only those actions, how resilient are you?

If the answer is along the lines of "I bounce back easily" then you are taking care of yourself, and your self-confidence. Every day business situations are likely not negatively affected.

If your answer to how resilient are you is more like "What is resilience,?", then step up your process. Keep doing what is easy for you, but also step up to learning new actions and new ideas. Let go of what is not working for you and create a plan that will work.

How acting on two-minute ideas can boost your confidence

When I was speaking with Caito about confidence-building, she talked about coming across the TED Talk that I want to share with you. It is about how our body language both affects how others see us, and more importantly for our self-development, how it also can change the way we see ourselves.

Let me introduce you to Amy Cuddy.

Are you ready to easily super charge your confidence?

Amy Cuddy is a social psychologist and Associate Professor at Harvard Business School. Cuddy asks everyone to freely share her scientific findings and the ideas to put into action. She wants to significantly change people's lives. Her TED Talk has over seventeen million views. Her research shows that regardless of our personality we can control those feelings of anxiousness or nervousness in those situations when we need more sense of power or well-being.

Cuddy and coauthors Dana R. Carney and Andy J. Yap of Columbia University have an article in Psychological Science reviewing the results of an experiment. Forty-two male and female participants were randomly assigned to a high- or low-power pose group. None were told what the study was about.

We will get define the exact description of the poses.

Saliva samples were taken before and after the posing measuring testosterone, the hormone linked to power and dominance, and cortisol levels, the stress hormone.

The people in the high-power group were given two open poses for two minutes each: first, hands behind the head with feet propped up on a desktop.

The second pose was standing and leaning at a desk with hands on the desktop.

A third power pose revealed by Cuddy is what is commonly called the Wonder Woman pose: feet shoulder width apart and hands on the hips.

There are actually five of these power poses, which take up space whether you are standing or sitting.

The people in the low-power group were posed for the two-minute time with more restrictive space poses: sitting in a chair with arms and hands folded close to the body. The second stance was standing with both arms and legs both crossed.

Either the low-power pose, or more that are similar, make you smaller and feel powerless. We make ourselves small.

The experiment included rolling dice to win $2 or $4 to introduce risk tolerance. The risk tolerance factor attributed to more seemingly high power people is high.

What do power poses actually do?

The poses are not about what they communicate to other people. They are about what the poses are communicating to you; how changing your behavior is changing your mind, which is changing your results.

The high-power poses reduced the cortisol around 25 percent and increased testosterone around 19 percent for both men and women. And as you might suspect now, the low-power poses increased cortisol about 17 percent and reduced testosterone about 10 percent.

The real evidence is in the reported feelings of the people: high-power poses of both sexes claimed to feel both more powerful and able to take charge.

So when you want to feel in charge, or you are in charge and want to communicate that, you want your body to be in an expansive mode, taking up more space regardless of whether you are standing or sitting.

Assertiveness, confidence, optimism, more creative thinking, and more risk taking are typically associated with more powerful people. But you want to maintain the calmer demeanor of our typical introvert nature while inwardly and outwardly appearing powerful.

Cuddy says "Our bodies change our minds, and our minds change our behavior and our behavior changes our outcomes." But she also knows about feeling like an impostor; she struggled with it herself. Her story is one actually what she says "Don't fake it till you make it. Fake it till you become it."

In the end, your effectiveness in everyday business situations is about how we you connect with each other. The poses are just two-minute tools to do in an elevator, in your office with a closed door or yes, even in a restroom.

You can achieve these results by doing any of the high-power poses before a meeting, or when getting ready for a presentation or negotiation.

These power poses are actions you can take and likely feel good for a short period of time, along with a quicker positive result. They are handy to have while waiting for longer-term foundational self-confidence to take effect. Since confidence gets eroded over time, boosting it more permanently takes time as well.

Who knows? It just might speed up your entire confidence makeover and help with more success in your the next communication event.

Summary

We were not born with low self-confidence; we learned it, and we can unlearn it or learn to have greater self-confidence. Doing something consistently to increase it will do this. The more tools you have in your toolbox, the more repair work you can do. So it is with a low self-confidence level.

Undoubtedly, there are a vast number of action steps to help with self-confidence. Some that you could do on a daily basis and some that you could do as needed. Self-confidence grows like money in the bank. You can make a deposit, or you can make a withdrawal to the bank of self-confidence everyday.

Starting with this chapter summary, think about what you already do if that makes you better in your communications, and then add in some additional confidence boosters.

When we have healthy self-confidence, supported by high self-esteem and self-worth, we have a high comfort level in our communications. All of these self-words are related to one another. With the completion of this chapter some ideas likely were review for you, or if you found some new learning about your personal level of self-confidence. We can say that you:

> ➤ Understand self-confidence, self-efficacy, self-esteem, and self-image more clearly.

> ➤ Can perceive how some of your top tendencies of thinking things through, preparing, being of a calm demeanor, analyzing important issues, and listening more have a positive effect on any essential business communication.

➤ Have tools to dissolve introvert myths that might be holding your self-confidence level in a lower state: affirmations and afformations.

➤ Understand how using social media at a comfort level for "who you are" will improve your self-confidence and more positively affect any face-to-face communication.

➤ Will be able to plan a more complete process to include the emotional, mental, social and physical domains in order to become more resilient and overcome most of life's inevitable setbacks with greater speed.

➤ Know how to overcome most inevitable life setbacks for a speedier resilience.

➤ Know how to visualize the Circle of Confidence or get into two two-minute power poses for a charge of confidence anytime you need it.

Thoughts to contemplate

Thinking back on the ideas presented in this chapter about self-confidence and its effect on our communications:

➤ Considering your renewed understanding around some of the main self-words, self-confidence, self-efficacy, self-esteem and self-image, in what area are you at a high level? In what level area are you at a low level? What are you willing to do to raise the low level self?

➤ Prioritize how you see your ability of the six essential communication skills. Identify specifically how you can boost your self-confidence even further in your top three:

  ➢ Listening

  ➢ Business meetings

  ➢ Presentations

  ➢ Conflict management

  ➢ Negotiations

  ➢ Influence, persuasion, and selling

➤ Determine what upcoming planned communication events you might have such as a presentation, a sales meeting, or a negotiation meeting.

➤ Consider setting up an action plan for the next 30 days.

➤ Use any of the suggested actions to reinforce your self-confidence for the first upcoming event. Assess your confidence and the actions you took. Go through this process until you find the action steps that work best for you.

Bibliography

➤ Karen M. Caito, Confidence Coach for Introverts: `http://www.caitocoaching.com`

➤ McLeod, S. A. (2008), *Self Concept - Simply Psychology*, retrieved from `http://www.simplypsychology.org/self-concept.html`

➤ Albert Bandura on confidence versus self-efficacy: `http://en.wikipedia.org/wiki/Self-efficacy` and his study `http://www.ou.edu/cls/online/LSPS5133/pdfs/bandura.pdf`

➤ Leary, Mark R., et al, *Self-esteem as an interpersonal monitor: The sociometer hypothesis. Journal of personality and social psychology* 68.3 (1995): 518.

➤ Noah St. John, author *The Book of Afformations*: `http://noahstjohn.com/`

➤ Our Facebook walls boost self-esteem, study finds: `http://www.news.cornell.edu/stories/2011/03/facebook-walls-boost-self-esteem-finds-study`

➤ Kross E, Verduyn P, Demiralp E, Park J, Lee DS, et al. (2013) *Facebook Use Predicts Declines in Subjective Well-Being in Young Adults*, PLoS ONE 8(8): e69841, `http://www.plosone.org/article/info%3Adoi%2F10.1371%2Fjournal.pone.0069841`

➤ *When Social Networking Is Not Working: Individuals With Low Self-Esteem Recognize but Do Not Reap the Benefits of Self-Disclosure on Facebook* by Amanda L. Forest and Joanne V. Wood, University of Waterloo, Department of Psychology, 200 University Ave. West, Waterloo, Ontario N2L 3G1, Canada

➤ *Personality Characteristics of Wikipedia Members* by YairAmichai–Hamburger, NaamaLamdan, RinatMadiel, and Tsahi Hayat.CyberPsychology & Behavior, December 2008, 11(6): 679-681, doi:10.1089/cpb.2007.0225.

➤ *The Misunderstood Personality Profile of Wikipedia Members* by Scott A. McGreal, MSc., `http://www.psychologytoday.com/blog/unique-everybody-else/201303/the-misunderstood-personality-profile-wikipedia-members`

➤ *Women Don't Ask: Negotiation and the Gender Divide*, `http://www.womendontask.com/stats.html`

➤ Resilience Self Test: `http://stress.about.com/library/resilience/bl_resilience_quiz.htm`

➤ Resilience Assessment Tool, `http://www.metcalf-associates.com/resilience-assessment-tool.html`

➤ Amy Cuddy: Your body language shapes who you are at `http://on.ted.com/Cuddy`

4

Your Hardworking Wrench: Tighten or Open up Your Listening

"Listening is a rare happening among human beings.

You cannot listen to the word another is speaking if you are preoccupied with your appearance, or with impressing the other, or are trying to decide what you are going to say when the other stops talking, or are debating about whether what is being said is true or relevant or agreeable.

Such matters have their place, but only after listening to the word as the word is being uttered."

– *William Stringfellow, Writer, Friends Journal*

Writers want us to listen.

Speakers hope we listen.

Teachers complain of students not listening.

Our peers, our customers, our coworkers, our staff, and even our managers all hope we listen to what they say regardless of how they communicate with us.

Often when I meet someone new, my tendency is to listen more than speak. As someone more introverted are you like that too? Occasionally, word gets back to me from the person who introduced me to this potential client or new friend that the new person commented that they believed I was incredibly interesting. This always has me giggling because those are usually the conversations where I spent more time listening than speaking.

As Rene Henry, author of *Communicating in a Crisis: A Guide for Management* says, "Remember the less you say, the more someone else will remember what you say," which might give rise to this kind of feedback. Or it just might be we get that effect of someone thinking we were interesting because we are good listeners. Such an evaluation is not so uncommon in effective communication.

You may recall from *Chapter 1, Communication Preferences of Introverts and Extroverts,* listening is the communication skill we learn the least about through any kind of training but it is the skill we use more than any other including reading, writing, and speaking. In my business career, I have attended just one course but from there I have facilitated dozens of workshops about listening. We learn as much when we teach.

Listening is seldom given the time to be explained or practiced in any environment. Yet, we listen about 45 percent of the time throughout our days.

It is also estimated that most of us filter out approximately 70 percent of what we hear in all communication. This means that what we filter out through a variety of personal things amounts to only 30 percent of what someone says being heard in the way they meant it. Filters include our culture, values, beliefs, interests, attitudes, biases, mood, distractions, vocabulary level, body language, and even the way the speaker looks. In the end, this can amount to listening for what we want to hear instead of the intended message.

Somewhere between our rapid thinking speed and our attention to what we want to say next, miscommunication can result. The fact that as introverts we listen more puts us in a strong position to become better at something that we already do a lot of. Just as the wrench as a tool allows the user to open or close its end to better tighten, fasten, or loosen an object, listening can be our tool to tighten (strengthen) or loosen (open up) any weakened communications.

Make a note

In this chapter, we will consider our introvert predisposition to listen more and learn how to meet communication challenges in and out of work by using breakthrough and time tested skills. By the end of this chapter you will:

- Know more about how we listen
- Assess your listening skills with one of the most widely recognized listening assessments
- Clearly understand the general benefits of listening
- Understand what gets in the way of better listening and what to do about it
- Be able to use at least five different ways to power up your listening
- Identify specific benefits of listening in relationships
- Clarify how listening can get your voice heard

Assess your current listening habits

Listening is one of the top ten skills that consistently gets ranked by employers who are asked what qualities and skills they want to know their employees have, whether hiring them for the first time or considering someone for a promotion.

Understanding how we listen can help us improve communication, the results we get, and our relationships. We can hear and be attentive to someone's message but still not get the entire meaning of the message if we do not listen properly.

A typical dialogue involves a rotation of the roles of listener and speaker. Generally, a conversation will move along without any acknowledgement of how the parts and pieces interact together. Face-to-face, telephone, and even e-mail communication includes a message delivered by a sender who encodes what he says through his own perceptions.

Left unattended without effective listening habits, we may or may not get "the message'." Both the sender and the receiver have to engage their hearing to listen for the meaning of the message.

Years ago in the corporate training I received, one particular listening assessment would show up in workshop after workshop by different presenters, none crediting the original work. I decided to find the developer and found it is credited to Dr. Ralph Nichols, Professor Emeritus, University of Minnesota, author of *Are You Listening?*, and pioneer in the study of listening. The assessment below is credited to him. Before you jump into the Listening Habits Assessment, be aware the scoring is different from the Self-Confidence Assessment in *Chapter 3, Confident to Communicate*, in these ways:

> ➤ The word "always" is tweaked to "almost always."

> ➤ Instead of low to high, ratings of the Scale of Words go from high to low. Selecting Never versus almost always gives you a higher score, not falling victim to an ineffective habit.

The results will still help you understand your listening ability with a similar specificity.

Remember the best answers are not what you perceive to be the "right" answers. Instead, be accurate and honest about how you know yourself to listen, which will give you the best opportunity to tweak your listening going forward.

Listening habits assessment

	Never	Rarely	Sometimes	Often	Almost Always
I tune out uninteresting subjects					
I criticize the speaker's delivery or mannerisms					
I can react emotionally					
I listen primarily for facts					
I try to take notes on everything					
I fake my attention					
I allow myself to get distracted					
I avoid difficult material					
I ignore emotional words that are often triggers for me					
I waste the advantage of listening speed.					

Make a note

Number 10 in my workshops often has hands going up to ask, "What does number ten mean?"

Let me offer a statistic to clarify this statement for you. On average, we listen three to four times faster than someone speaks. The average speaking rate is 125 to 175 words per minute. In that one minute, we have at least 400 to 500 words of thinking time.

So the more you find your mind wandering when listening to someone speak, the more time you are ultimately wasting.

Score interpretation

Give yourself the following scores for the words you identified with each statement:

➤ Never: 10 points

➤ Rarely: 8 points

➤ Sometimes: 6 points

➤ Often: 4 points

➤ Almost always: 2 points

The highest score would be 100. The higher your score, the better your listening habits. When you practice developing listening habit strengths before building up weaknesses, you should focus on improving the habits you rated Sometimes or Often.

The lower your score, the more you have to work on improving how you listen. The good news is that listening is something we can all learn to do better. Now is your opportunity. Before we get to those how-to pointers, it is worth taking a small amount of time to more clearly understand the listening process and the relevance of models of listening models.

How and why do we listen?

Hearing is a physiological process. It is something that happens through our ears. As long as someone is not hearing impaired, hearing is a natural event that occurs both during wake and sleep.

Listening, moreover, is slightly different—it takes place, or we could even say is done through a series of mental processes. This is the conscious act requiring us to get meaning from sounds including words and sentences. It might be considered a full package of observing, feeling, and stimuli from other senses. Listening occurs when we are in conversation with others, reading books, notes, and e-mails.

These are the two most fundamental processes but we can find between six and a couple of dozen types of listening.

Instead of reviewing a particular model any model of how we listen, I thought it would be more effective to share a widely used definition of listening. It turns out definitions are as countless as types so it's not a simple task. According to Michael Purdy, professor and Coordinator of the Communications Program at Governors State University in University Park, Illinois, there is a valid reason for this variety of definitions. I agree, so see whether you do.

To summarize, Purdy thinks that because we approach listening differently for different intentions and in different contexts, it follows there would naturally be different definitions rather than a widely accepted standard dictionary explanation. He gives many examples, one related to defining listening as researchers listening for predictions to validate or not, to consultants and trainers who want to bring the best practices of learning listening skills into the workplace. Just these two groups of people each have differing end results.

The nature of our work or role is not the only thing that plays a part in the nature of our listening; the venue or context in which we expect listening to happen is also very important. Our listening might include face-to-face listening in a variety of work situations. It can also mean we listen to what is said in a telephone conversation, in an e-mail, or what is being communicated in a written proposal.

I have long followed the International Listening Association, and their definition is one of the broadest yet most comprehensive. It is fitting for our purposes here because it is one of the most encompassing to both process and context I could find:

Make a note

Listening is the process of receiving, constructing **meaning** from and responding to spoken and/or nonverbal messages.(**ILA**, 1996).

It may be obvious, but we engage in listening as an integral part of our daily lives. Think about the different contexts where listening is the central part of our work in our professional lives—whether we are in meetings, presentations, around a negotiation table, or interacting with customers, good listening is absolutely essential. By keeping this in mind and focusing on the importance of quality listening, only then can we get better at it.

How effective is your listening right now?

A quick check-in: as you think about how you are listening right now, do you find yourself victim to any of the ten listening habits that you assessed yourself on earlier in this chapter?

This next topic should give you an insight on how you listen.

Common listening types

One goal in listening is similar to a goal with sending a text message or e-mailing. We want the message that is sent (spoken) to be the same message that is received (heard). For example, have you ever e-mailed someone with one word in all capital letters without explanation that it is for emphasis? If you did, it is likely they replied with something like, "Please stop yelling at me." Generally held knowledge is usually (that is the operative word) all capitals in an e-mail or text means a yelling statement. In this case, the message that was meant only to emphasize a word or a point lost its integrity with how the recipient heard the message.

Listening is generally described as active as opposed to pass9ive because there are many pieces of the process between the speaker and the listener. These pieces, however, do not necessarily go together in a straightforward fashion.

Quite a bit of corporate training focuses on active listening. I say this because as a corporate trainer, it is what usually shows up in my workshops unless we are facilitating some kind of conflict management. Within active listening, there are several types of listening to move in and out of as dictated by what a specific situation calls for. It is helpful in any daily workplace situation and in sales.

There is another common type that is often used in relationship building. It is called **reflective listening**, reflecting back to someone what you heard. It can become almost parroting someone when over used or used incorrectly. We often find this model used in the counseling and therapy fields.

But what is the benefit of any kind of listening? Or any one of the dozens of other labeled kinds of listening?

Julian Treasure, a sound expert, says, "We are losing our listening. "He claims that with such a huge variety of ways to listen, not least because of the way the Internet now dominates daily life for many of us, we are overwhelmed by messages that demand our attention. In this new environment, we might find other senses becoming more sensitive. A text that sounds on a mobile device grabs our attention and we focus on that instead of the person we are walking with. Or we take an incoming call on a mobile phone while waiting for friends at a restaurant and find we raise our voice more than necessary because our "listening" attention is now redirected.

As the world becomes more global and the use of technology grows, all this informational noise makes it very hard to listen as the situation calls for. Treasure advocates listening being taught in schools because although it is used more than any other communication skill we are taught, it can scarcely be found on the curriculum, at least in the U.S.

We might ask, but what types of listening works best for introverts? Or who has more of an advantage in listening well, the more introverted or the more extroverted?

It is more about how do we bring the best of our introvert style into a particular situation where a particular model of listening might be more effective than another.

Listening models

There are numerous models that explain how to listen. It is not the purpose of this chapter to review them—that would require an entire book. Instead, by looking at the listening process and a recent model, we can get a broad picture that will help us achieve a better understanding overall.

It also might be helpful to understand the commonalities of the models. This can help us to see how in our tendency to listen more, there are pieces we will be more comfortable with and confident about. It will also help us to easily decide which of the components might be more deserving of our attention.

Regardless of whose model is referred to, common elements are involved. The following diagram may be helpful in seeing listening in action:

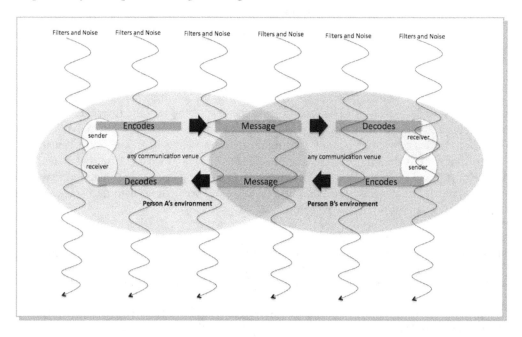

Every listening model includes the interaction between the speaker and the listener, also referred to as the sender and receiver as noted in the diagram. All models attempt to make sense of an apparently simple and passive process, drawing out the way that certain subtle observations, interpretations, non-verbal signals, and emotional cues are built up around the basic physiological instance of hearing.

While these elements are in motion and can take just seconds, there is the tendency for barriers to block or hinder understanding. Then what could be considered to be "complete" understanding is distilled, as meanings are lost or misread. This can, in turn, lead to confusion or waste time that could be used more constructively.

Nichols' research, as well as others research done by others from Florida State University and Michigan State University, moves beyond listening to understand messages in the moment to our recollection of listening further on in time.

Consider the scenario when you might be listening to a manager's presentation. Directly after hearing the presentation is when you remember the most: just eight hours later we forget one-third to one-half of what we heard, and this is only if we engage in talking about what we heard. If we do not talk about what we heard, then our recollection drops. It gets worse. Just two months after, most of us will remember about one-quarter. Improving our listening skills has a direct correlation on remembering more so we do not have to be part of this equation.

The barriers or noises that get in the way of our ability to listen more effectively can be found in our habits. Using the pieces of any listening model should help us to deal with these.

With so many listening models, it can be difficult to remember their most valuable insights. Treasure uses the acronym **RASA** to neatly encapsulate the most important lessons that listening models teach us.

R is to receive and pay attention to what someone is saying.

A is to appreciate the person who you are listening to with those little gestures like a nod of the head or a verbal, "Uh-huh," or "Oooo." Those short cut phrases and grunts that at least say we heard.

S is to summarize what you think you heard whether in your head or spoken in the case of a one-to-one communication. This could include paraphrasing.

A is to ask questions. As with other listening models, it takes place in seconds and seems almost natural in the way it happens.

All listening models have varying elements in their respective processes. Most can be categorized in at least three parts: receiving the message, understanding the message, and then responding to the message.

The issue for most of us is to be more engaged in the process of listening, whether you call it active or empathetic or any of a dozen of names. The practical benefits outweigh the status quo.

What gets in your way and what to do about it

If you look back at your self-assessment, any one of these habits can lead to problems and interfere with the success of your listening. Let's take each habit and both translate more precisely what it is and then identify some specific actions you can take away to improve your listening.

Solution for habit 1– find at least one thing of interest

You might notice signs of people being not interested more when you are the speaker. People doze, they doodle, they even text when in a presentation, business meeting and even during one-to-one communication. We often just shut down our listening when we are not interested.

Yes, the speaker can do some things in this situation. But as a listener, you should try to work with the speaker.

Ask yourself, "Is there anything at all I can use?". Can you listen for a new word? Is it possible that you can discover a new interest or take-away if you listen? The key is to tune in until you find something you can go with. Even if I have heard a topic a dozen times, I listen to leave with just one idea or reaffirmation.

Solution for habit 2 – focus on the content

Early on as a corporate trainer, I would be quite excited reading to read the evaluations. As I looked through them, I soon I began to see how judgmental we can be as listeners. I am grateful that evaluations have evolved over time to paint a broader picture of the speaking or training event.

Usually, the last two questions in a participant evaluation might be, "What did you like best about the speaker?" and "What didn't you like about the speaker?". Of course, being human I was struck more by the criticism than the compliments received. One I remember to this day is, "didn't like the way the speaker touched her hair on occasion." Clearly, this kind of attention can distract us from getting any meaning from what is said. However, if you focus only on the delivery of the message—or worse still, the petty details of your speaker's mannerisms, you will clearly miss the really important part—the message itself.

How much can you miss in a message if you judge the delivery over the content? Quite often, ten years after giving a workshop or speaking engagement, I will meet someone who attended one of my workshops somewhere. They will say, "When I heard you say…". Their memory will be better than mine, and it's likely the case that they focused more on content than mannerisms, which influenced their longer-term memory.

Solution for habit 3 – listen until it's over

Have you ever been listening to someone else for just a few minutes to find that the coworker, manager, or even a customer says something that seems to hit a trigger within you? You may find yourself either wanting to interrupt or even stop listening to this person completely. This is one habit I constantly watch for in myself.

One of the problems in this is that if we stop listening, we might start to draw the wrong conclusion and then embarrass ourselves with an inappropriate interrupting statement.

This is one habit that can pull in every piece of the listening process so we avoid the embarrassment of replying in a way that clearly shows we were not listening.

Solution for habit 4 – listen broadly, then deeply

Most of the people I interviewed when writing this book are introverts. Many introverts prefer communicating in writing, so we e-mail. Almost all of them want an understanding of the broader scope of the book so when they contribute what they can about business meetings or selling, they can be on target with the broader intention.

Too often, when we listen for details we fail to grasp the broader ideas that are being communicated. Remembering facts can be useful but can be distracting. When we listen for and understand the central idea, the facts have context, more purpose, and even a placeholder to go to.

Solution for habit 5 – listen to and question everything

When facilitating a training program, I want people to take away some kind of overarching idea; I want people to see the "bigger picture." Quite often I use statistics, facts, and examples to support what I say, but these are always in service of a wider point.

Consider the "mixing up the forest for the trees" analogy created by Michael Webb, which categorizes some speakers as either "trees" people: those who give concrete and detailed explanations, or as "forest" people: those who talk with a broad overview.

The best speakers of course use both types of examples.

But as the listener, you do not want to either get bogged down in details or go off into the forest with broad generalities.

As the listener, when we listen to grasp the ideas, just as many speakers present them, the facts will help us to remember. As a listener, ask the "forest" speaker to identify the "trees," that is, give specific examples. And ask the "trees" speaker how that fits into the overall picture.

Yes; if you picked up on it, I am a "forest" speaker who readily has "trees" ready to prune. What Nichols found in his listening research is many of us listen to memorize facts, "trees". Does this sound like a similar way to which we are taught in school? Yet, this way of listening can often cause many of us to miss the point, or the "forest."

Solution for habit 6 – be present

When we listen, we use more than just our ears. Linda Eve Diamond, author of *Rule #1: Stop Talking: A Guide to Listening*, and more of an introvert, says "Listening is paying attention, creating a space for the speaker's ideas, and being present."

Diamond says we can create a physical space and a mind space. In everyday communication, if someone wants to talk with you, do not just fit it in between e-mails and voice mails. Make time for the conversation so you will be able to listen. Then, when you have a physical space, create a space in your mind to be focused on listening.

Just like meditation has health benefits, Diamond claims that listening attentively can similarly reduce our heart rate, lower our oxygen consumption, and decrease blood pressure.

Indeed, meditative practices can actually help improve listening and in the next section we will review the highlights of how that can work for you regardless of whether you currently meditate or not.

Solution for habit 7 – focus, don't stray

In the earlier diagram of the process of listening, you can see squiggly lines representing lots of noise. As an introvert, we may be more sensitive to noise than extroverts. Noise comes in all varieties from trains passing by to cell phones ringing to passing thoughts. Anyone can be distracted at any time.

One year, while serving as a sales manager, my department was having a particularly high revenue year. The general manager called to have lunch with me to discuss how to keep improving how sales worked with other departments. We agreed on to meet at a restaurant named The Express. Traveling from the respective cities where each of us worked required at least one of us to get from our respective cities and cross a river through a tunnel.

After waiting for about 30 minutes, the manager had not yet arrived. I called her.

"Did some other priority come up?"

"No, where are you? I've been waiting for you here for 30 minutes."

"Where?" I asked.

"At The Express," I then heard her laugh like I missed that detail.

Then it suddenly dawned on me, "The Express in what city?"

We both laughed. It turns out we met at the named restaurant, in two different locations. Both of us were so distracted by our own department success, we did not question, "Which city?"

Questions in conversations always show we are listening and focused. How many times has your lack of focus, for whatever distraction may have caused it, caused you a misunderstanding? If it is not a regular occurrence, we can get by and tune up our listening next time. In the following section, we will have a tune-up exercise that should help to make your listening a little sharper and effective.

Solution for habit 8 – work out your listening muscle

Do you find yourself shutting down when more difficult information is presented to you? It happens to all of us. Either information is full of acronyms, specialized words, academic words, poorly communicated, or simply an unfamiliar subject.

The person you are listening to is the best source to clarify what might be difficult so do not wait until they are gone to ask a clarifying question. This will help your brain to think creatively. Consider writing down your questions as you go along.

Avoid getting caught in the trap of thinking things over in your head. This can be like listening to two conversations at once. Simply listen to the speaker or read the e-mail or memo before you engage with your own ideas, prejudices, and biases and bring them to the discussion.

You have likely previously or now discovered that listening is a complex enough process. When the speaker makes it more complicated, we have to have practice in any way we can, engaging more of the pieces of the process and less of our distracting habits. This will likely prevent total shutdown.

Solution for habit 9 – open your mind

Anything less than being open minded in listening might be a problem, in particular for those of us who are more introverted. Unfortunately, speakers use words, which for each us of may serve as some sort of emotional trigger.

According to Rebecca Z. Shafir in her book, *The Zen of Listening*, "Judging and attacking ideas that are contrary to our frame of reference is a form of suffering. It is energy depleting, both internally (makes your frustrated and tense) and externally (creates tension between you and the speaker)."

Identify your trigger words; you know them when you hear them. For example, if you are married you might be triggered by the word, "in-laws." Acknowledge you have emotional reactions to certain words or phrases. This can help you to become less sensitive to them and prevent you from shutting down. In the end, it means we will have more energy available for the act of listening.

Solution for habit 10 – get in the listening zone

In clarifying number ten in the initial listening assessment above, I stated a statistical finding that on average, we speak at 125 to 175 words per minute. In that one minute, we think at 400 to 500 words per minute.

Even if we could, why slow our mind down to the same speed of speaking?

Instead, think about how to make the time more effective for listening to understand. We could, for example, mentally summarize what the speaker was saying. We could also ask ourselves to pay attention to the words and non-verbal elements like gestures, facial expressions, and body position. We could even ask ourselves, do I understand the big picture? What facts did I hear that support that? Since we have some spare thinking time, we can use it to put the best of our habits to work to our advantage. All ten habits have this other positive side of them. By clarifying the specific listening habits and generalization of the better side of each, you are ready to move on to some actions to take to power up or fine-tune your listening in introvert style!

Six introvert-comfortable ways to power up listening

We have moved forward in understanding our own listening habits. This should help us clear the way to take on board some of the most effective listening practices. When we factor in our introvert tendencies for introspection and contemplation, we can fine-tune a selection of many ways to practice our listening throughout a day. This sustained practice will power up our listening according to the style with which we are comfortable. Start by choosing just one action in those that follow, and keep adding a tool every so often.

Action 1 – delight in not being a talker

Kicking off these power-up techniques is a simple acknowledgment to act and be comfortable with who we are. A recurring theme in communication circles is that speaking is not all it is cracked up to be. Dr. Arthur K. Robertson, author of *Listen for Success: A Guide to Effective Listening*, has some wisdom for someone more introverted, who might on occasion be criticized for not talking much. "And some of us even worry that if we are not talking we are not in control. … The trouble is that too much talk is a turnoff. Excessive talkers should not assume that they are being heard."

Enter introverts who listen more often than they speak. Pause, smile, and know this can help make your communication effective. We may not have previously considered it from this perspective, that just because someone talks a lot does not mean people are being heard, as in, listened to.

Acknowledge yourself. This is an easy action you can take right now.

Extroverts take heart: you can ratchet down the talk.

Action 2 – listen to yourself first

Given that we greatly enjoy the sandbox of our own mind, let us power up that listening.

Diamond reminds us, "We all have intuition. Put energy into listening to yourself and strengthening that intuition, learning when to listen and when not to." She suggests listening "outside the brain box," if we find that even in listening to ourselves, our thinking, or our gut is not helping us to move forward.

It is about listening to our patterns and understanding how they might affect our choices. "Step back to become an observer of your mind," is what Diamond suggests to get a fresh image of what we want.

Listening to our thoughts, our feelings, how we speak to and about ourselves as an observer, as if we are eavesdropping, can often help us to hear things differently. This approach can help us in improving any one of the ten listening habits.

For example, consider observing yourself if you get distracted, habit number 7. Then when you find yourself distracted, ask yourself "How can I be more attentive?". You have already recognized your distraction. The key is to listen to what you as the observer might see.

Action 3 – meditative learning

Most days I meditate. I find that meditation quiets my mind. With all the outside noise tending to get louder each day with more information, more technology to access it, and more responsibility, it helps to be more present with whatever is happening. Listening is about being present.

I use Headspace, an online-guided meditation that also comes in a smart phone and device app. You can either use it or find some process like it to help you get your mind in a space of better listening.

Each ten or twenty minute session starts out almost the same way.

Some initial deep breaths quiet the mind and body into relaxation. This is to be able to get in touch with the immediate environment of sounds, touch, and smell. Thoughts will come to mind and then you just let them go. Notice them, let them go and direct your focus back to your environment. The idea is to focus on what is going on in the present, not thoughts about the past or future.

Before going into focused breathing, there are a few questions to reflect on: how will I benefit from this quiet today? How will others benefit?

Research from the University of Rochester Medical Center shows that doctors who use mindfulness meditation are more self-aware, listen, and are less judgmental with patients.

If you thought that meditation means silencing the mind, to be clear, it is more about quieting the mind. It is a time to slow the thoughts down and get focused.

This is another approach to help improve any one of the ten listening habits. Consider habit number 3 around reacting emotionally or even habit number 9 and being triggered by something you hear. With your awareness of either your reaction or the trigger, take a few breaths, get mindful of the present, and then ask yourself, "How will I benefit from what I am hearing? How will others benefit?". You might just find your answer.

Action 4 – pull your triggers back

Shafir has several exercises in her book *The Zen of Listening*, which we could consider doing daily given all the listening opportunities we have in the workplace. Here is one to boost the habit that we generally listen more anyway. Just once a day we might select one face-to-face conversation with a co-worker, employee, or manager.

> ➤ Focus on one conversation only.

> ➤ Notice when your triggers are pulled. It might be a trigger word or expression. It could be a particular body language or facial expression trigger.

> ➤ When you do notice it, take your mind off the trigger. Put your mind in neutral to just hear.

Just hear.

Stop evaluating someone's ideas.

This may help to whittle away habit number 2, criticizing the speaker's delivery, which is often from triggers from non-verbals, or even tone of voice. It could also help with listening habit number 9, tuning out emotional words as triggers.

Action 5 – practice

I asked Marc Wong, author of *Thank You for Listening: Gain Influence and Improve Relationships, Better Listening in eight Steps*, for his definition of listening. He says, "Listening is the art and practice of putting someone else's speaking, thinking, feeling needs ahead of your own."

Just how would a person practice that exactly? Putting someone else's communication and feelings ahead of our own?

Wong gave a couple of examples.

We can ask good or better questions than we might normally ask, which give both constructive feedback and specific praise. Specifically questions like, "What is the best, worst, or most likely case?" and "What is the right thing to do?" and "Can everyone win?" Even, "How can everyone win?".

His premise is that there are actions we can take and things we can do to appreciate someone else's viewpoint even if we do not have the same experience or same level of excitement.

As introverts, we already are quite natural with questions. Consider this action a tuning-up of questions to help us take the other person's viewpoint. This can power up our general listening and help us with other listening habits.

Action 6 – go broader

One more practical way to tune up our listening from one of Shafir's several exercises also struck me as being grounded in more introvert tendencies.

The idea is to broaden your perspective on any topic or issue.

Choose a widely read magazine such as *Time*, or *Newsweek*, or even a newspaper, online will work.

Find either the feature article or the longest article you can find. The key is to pick an article that will have readers' comments.

Just from the title, think about what your opinion of the topic is. Then as you read it shift into thinking about the writer's viewpoint, their tone, the accuracy, and even the sources they drew from to write.

Next, find viewpoints that are differing from yours.

Now, go back and re-read the article with these other viewpoints in mind.

The goal is to see whether you either missed key points or maybe interpreted things differently.

Make a note

Insider tip: Practicing a variety of actions all at once can often yield poor results. It will be easier to improve if you practice only one of the above six action steps at a time:

- Select just one action of the six to start with for improving your listening.
- Commit to practicing just that one action for 30 days.
- Take notice of the improvement either by assessing a particular habit or your overall communication.
- We are aiming for improvement, not perfection. Perfection is not likely anyway considering that we are human.
- Then select another action and commit to practicing it for 30 days. Again, how has it helped to improve a particular habit or your overall communication?
- If you take this approach, then in just six months it is likely there will be noticeably marked listening improvement.

How listening benefits business relationships

Think about this "other" perspective that you have found. How might it translate to improved business relationships?

When we are able to cut through the noise, focus on the conversation, and listen to get better meaning, both employee and manager will find benefits for any relationship, in their personal life as well as business.

Increased knowledge

How many times have you possibly sat in a workshop in which you already knew a good deal about the topic? Maybe even to the degree you thought, "Geez, I could be talking to these folks about this." These are times when we want to use our best listening skills. When we listen we increase our knowledge and understanding.

Regardless of how much we know, when we listen to others, we almost always learn something. There has never been a workshop or seminar I have not walked away from with either new piece of information or a new angle on information I already had. Even when it does not feel like we are learning anything, we may well be learning how to put the information we already have to better use.

Increased understanding

Sharon Drew Morgen, thought leader, and NY Times bestselling author gives this metaphor (with permission) of how accuracy is often impaired in how we listen:

> *Think about this for a moment: when we incorrectly hear what is said, each misunderstanding gets compounded until we end up understanding something very different from the initial message. It's just like the game of Telephone we played as kids. For those who never played, kids stand in a circle and one person whispers a secret to the next, who whispers what she thinks she heard to the next, and so on down the line, and the last person says what he heard aloud. The surprise is at the end: the final message is never what the first person said at the start. The words, intent, message, and meaning are totally changed, even with merely six people playing.*

With better listening, we have less miscommunication regardless of how many people the message has to reach, and fewer misunderstandings.

A self-confidence boost

Consider you might have to lead a business meeting or give a presentation and your manager gave you the intention or outcome. By clearly communicating that intended message in how we present our self, we can project a more positive self-image of the moment, which of course, boosts self-confidence.

In the act of giving and receiving, we find the benefit of boosting our confidence. People want to be listened to; it makes us feel valued. So when you listen, you give the speaker personal value and in that giving, at the same time you boost your own feelings of personal value.

Problems get resolved early and quickly

Consider a communication that moved from online video conversation to e-mail. Donald and his partner Mary invited a woman, Jill, to consider collaborating with them for the start of an online teleseminar. The invitation to talk was set in motion and the communication moved to e-mail to schedule mutually agreeable times to go deeper into mutual objectives.

Stuck in the muck of getting three people's schedule to come together took the conversation off track. In this derailment, frustrations grew without being able to find a mutually agreeable date.

In his listening, Donald learned Jill was putting in a number of hours to prepare for what he and Mary called an "exploratory meeting." He wanted to shift the e-mail thread to a (live / online) conversation to clear up any misunderstanding of the meeting purpose because in his filters, hours for preparation were not necessary. He stated, "Might I suggest that the meeting is primarily to connect...".

With a series of e-mail communication, and sentences and paragraphs growing longer, resentment grew and Jill was no longer interested in any discussion. Planning stopped.

Listening in any communication venue can intervene in solving problems at an early stage.

Some clarifying questions early on, or paraphrasing to confirm that both parties are on the same wavelength, or even an e-mail confirmation of the original discussion or going to the online video conversation again might have prevented a big misunderstanding. Certainly face-to-face would be the most effective method, allowing on the spot flow of the listening process.

Motivation

Motivation comes from the inside. But leaders who listen create an environment for employees to be motivated. Early on as a manager of a retail store, I wanted to find out how we could maintain a clean front store to the customer. In a weekly meeting, one of the employees said, "You could buy us lunch." I asked exactly what they meant by that.

What I discovered was that a greater number of staff would work toward achieving certain "clean" criteria if I brought in pizza once a week. They did not want to leave work, they did not want me to eat with them, they just wanted me to order pizza for delivery for them. It was less costly than what I initially thought I heard, until we allowed the discussion and cut through the filters.

Listening in our relationships is like a strong foundation when building a home or other structure. Virtually any collapse can be avoided. If you do not have a solid foundation, then you might as well at times be standing in quicksand.

Besides listening being something that makes communication complete, there are further benefits. It can help with relationship building, improving productivity, and lowering stress.

New ideas

While some of our finest light-bulb moments might come to us in solitude such as when we are in the shower, they sometimes also come when we adopt an open and collaborative mindset in talking with others.

Sandy had been working in sales for about a year, and she was at the store cash register ringing through a sale for a new customer. "This paperwork is such a waste a time," she commented while waiting for the printer to print the order. Since I was standing at the counter writing up a new sale as well, I asked her what she meant, "What are all these copies for?".

The short story is, this paperwork included a copy of the order for the salesperson, a copy for the technician, a copy for the customer, and a copy for—well we did not know who received that fourth copy. It seemed no one questioned it. After all, the accounting staff always received an evening computer transfer of our sales and orders, so it was not for them. It turned out to be a money saving idea because we reduced the number of copies of the hardcopy trail, and at the same time it was one less action for the salesperson to be involved with at the time of ordering.

We have to be listening to get to breakthroughs. If we concentrate on what *we* want to say then we may prevent learning anything new from someone else's speaking.

Fewer conflicts

One year, I did some training in Mauritius. It is one of the most diverse countries in the world with at least half a dozen main languages and at least that many different religions. The country continues to develop, with all its cultures and languages living closely together, partly due to how people listen.

When I was there, meeting with my client, I learned how their listening process works and is likely quite different from the way many people listen.

Tip

When there is disagreement, each party listens to find agreement first, difference second.

How often might we listen to respond because we have found something we disagree with? After all, it is likely that no matter where we are in the world, most of us can hear our differences easier, more and louder. But with real listening, we can discover common ground and reduce conflicts.

Better use of time

It is true that active listening in any model takes time. With this upfront time investment, the other person feels they are heard. We can take time to check our understanding, so if we are wrong, we have the chance right then for clarification.

Have you ever had an experience to walk away from a meeting, move on action you believed you heard was being communicated, only to have someone say, "That is not what I meant"?

When we take time to use listening behaviors at the time, it is the best use of our time to avoid negative consequences of rework.

Time savings equate to dollars, energy, and productivity in the workplace.

Clearer understanding

Each of us knows when we are not being listened to. We can feel not important, or worst, unheard. Can you feel the stress of a situation like this?

But when the person we speak with is asking questions, able to either correctly summarize what we said, and contributing to the general topic, it communicates they do understand.

Rene Henry has close personal experience with how leaders in particular can use listening for clearer understanding. He talks about being on a cruise ship getting ready to leave one port to get to Rome, Italy. The news broadcast was of an anticipated taxi strike close to their arrival port and time. Gregg L. Michel, then president of Crystal Cruises, had a value to "listen and anticipate." This was most evident when Henry arrived in port. Crystal Cruises in their anticipation arranged for vans to take their passengers on any of their land tours and destinations, making a pleasant experience of what was likely nerve-wracking for many visitors of other cruise lines.

What if Michel, in hearing of the possible strike, filtered it through something like, "They have said that before." Would he have understood how plan to circumvent the problems?

Increased productivity

Anyone in a leadership position would appreciate getting the greater productivity from being a better listener. Yes, leaders make decisions. Consider Gregg L. Michel and how he "listens and anticipates."

When you listen fully, you can get all the information you need to make a good decision. It was other cruise line passengers that were inconvenienced, not the Crystal Cruises customers. Imagine the last minute scrambling and likely higher costs to get a solution in place at the last minute.

Trust

So often company leaders say they want feedback. Unfortunately, a recent survey from the Ketchum Communication Monitor found that only 24 percent of employees say leaders are effective, while open communication skills have been ranked number one, for two years in a row, in a leader's communication performance. Many times, solutions are asked for by leaders but are never implemented, leaving a possible impression that they did not listen. Other times, each person's intentions are clearly unmatched from the beginning. People need to hear credible and trustworthy information from their leaders.

Trust is like a bank account. You either build it or take it deduct from it with every interaction. When someone feels listened to, the trust account goes increases. When someone feels unheard, the trust account diminishes. This happens with co-workers, employees, and customers.

There are several studies, one in 1997 by Rosemary Ramsey and Ravipreet Sohi and a more recent in 2005, by Praveen Aggarwal, Stephen B. Castleberry, Rick Ridnour, and C. David Shepherd in the *Journal of Marketing Theory and Practice* that support the notion that listening and trust are closely related.

The earlier study linked salesperson listening and empathy to trust, satisfaction, and future interactions. Empathy is an outcome from effective listening. Listening is positively related to the buyer's trust and the satisfaction they have with a salesperson. But the more recent study concluded that trust and satisfaction from listening can positively affect *future* interactions.

Co-workers, employees, managers, and customers can all find any of these benefits with better listening. Given that as introverts we know we tend to listen more, we should be comfortable taking more time in our listening; we will see its impact in the quality of the results that follow.

How listening gets your voice heard

"I like the fact that "LISTEN" is an anagram of "SILENT".

Alfred Brendel, classical pianist

It might seem counter-intuitive but when we listen more than talk, our voice will be better heard. We all want to be listened to more and better.

If we are a writer, we want the reader to "listen' better to what we are trying to communicate.

As a speaker, we want the audience to listen better.

As a teacher, we hope our students will listen better.

We want our peers, our customers, our coworkers, our staff, and even our managers to listen better.

Why? Because we want to be heard.

Wong says, "Introverts may spend more time not speaking, but they may or may not do more things that actively encourage others to think and feel and to express those thoughts and feelings." We have been revealing just what those things are to make listening an active process with these very results.

Just how is it that listening though can help us to get our voice heard?

People like people who listen

In sales and customer service, there are two radio stations often referenced as etched in the customer's mind. One is **WII-FM**: What's In it For Me. The more important one as it relates to listening is the **MMFI-AM** station: Make Me Feel Important About Myself.

Whether we are an employee listened to by a manager or a team member listened to by others on a team, people are more productive when their ideas are listened to, and better yet, acted on. When we feel listened to, it encourages us to be more creative in the future.

Everyone wants to feel important. So if we are made to feel that way, we will be heard.

Be better understood

Engaging in questions as we listen to others gets close to ensuring the message is more fully understood between people.It also shows that our focus is fueling a desire to understand.

Shafir believes most people want to be able to listen better, but our impulse to want to speak often overrides this. When we get heard fully, it is likely this impulse can be minimized because the speaker feels appreciated. As a more mindful listener, we allow the listening process to flow and give time for clarification, which will ultimately lead to greater understanding. If we are the one who caused this positive kind of listening effect, then when it is time for us to speak, the personal connection helps allow our expressed thoughts to be better appreciated. It is part of the success of being a better listener.

People listen to people with confidence

Confident people know what they know. They tend to listen more because they want to know what others know. Why? Because they want to know more so they can fully understand.

In sales, the way it works is you move your confidence into probing or questioning. When you do this, you can respond more on target than just taking what you want to say down a trail of no interest to the customer.

In negotiating, it works because you have to have an understanding of what the person across the table from you needs. If you do not listen fully, your ability to persuade is compromised. As introverts, we could use our preference to over-prepare to be clear enough in our own mind about our needs first. Then this ensures our intention is on listening to get a win/win.

Build your trust

"If you consistently put people's needs first and can provide value to people, they will respect you and come to you for your wisdom. You'll have influence, and yes, you'll be heard." Wong says this because as you listen fully to someone, they too gain confidence and this results in you being able to directly or indirectly provide insight.

By allowing people to be listened to, they will like you, they will feel more understood, your confidence will increase, and the trust bank account in that connection will be at a high level.

The communicator who listens better has the power to be able to have what they know they want to say to be heard.

Summary

Whether you are a manager, want to be a manager, or are looking to have more success in your everyday business communication, decide to take your listening to a next level. Having listened to this chapter you now:

> Know the difference between listening and hearing

> Have an understanding of at least ten habits of listening and your degree of using them for the betterment of listening effectiveness

> Identified with specific benefits of listening that are most important for you

> Have actionable steps for any of the ten habits that might get in your way of better listening

> Can select from five introvert specific type ways to take your listening to a higher level of effectiveness

> Know how listening gives specific benefits to different kinds of situations in relationships

> Understand that being a better listener can get your voice heard more easily

Make a note

Tom Peters references a Harvard Medical School doctor, Jerome Groupman, who says doctors interrupt a patient explaining their problem within eighteen seconds of the patient speaking. Peters concludes strategic listening is the number one strategic plan to everyday success and everyone who is a manager needs to learn to listen.

Brevity for many things are worthwhile like a storm passing through, or a speaker who stops when they say they would like to conclude their talk. If listening can be effective in eighteen seconds, is the patient going to know or not? And if the patient feels listened to, is it acceptable that the doctor saved a little time? It is the results of the person being listened to that ultimately determine whether the listener was indeed listening?

Thoughts to contemplate

As you reflect back on this chapter about the introvert naturally listening more, but not necessarily on our own more effectively, ask yourself these three key things:

> How has my listening helped me or hurt me in my everyday business communication?

> What am I already doing well in listening that I can improve on? What do I need to learn to do better?

> If you have not done so already, can you come up with a 30-day plan (refer back to the insider tips) to incorporate the listening habits you identified to improve? How would such a plan benefit you in any upcoming communication events you know you will be part of in the next few months?

Bibliography

> Rene Henry, *Communicating in a Crisis: A Guide for Management*, Gollywobbler Productions, 2008

> Ralph Nichols, Professor Emeritus, University of Minnesota, pioneer in the study of listening, author of *Are You Listening?* (Enterprise Publications, 1957)

> International Listening Association, http://www.listen.org/, *Listening Facts* compiled by Laura Janusik, Ph.D., Rockhurst University with assistance from Lynn Fullenkamp and Lauren Partese

➤ Collection of Types of Listening `http://changingminds.org/techniques/listening/all_types_listening.htm`

➤ Michael Purdy, *What is Listening?*, `http://www.academia.edu/603612/What_is_listening`

➤ Julian Treasure, `http://www.ted.com/talks/julian_treasure_5_ways_to_listen_better.html`, TED Talk, *5 ways to listen better*

➤ Michael Webb, `http://www.sklatch.net/thoughtlets/listen.html`, *Eight barriers to effective listening*

➤ Linda Eve Diamond, `http://LindaEveDiamond.com`, *Rule #1: Stop Talking!: A Guide to Listening* (Listeners Press, 2007)

➤ Arthur K. Robertson, *Listen for Success: A Guide to Effective Listening* (Richard D. Irwin Inc, 1994)

➤ Rebecca Z. Shafir, `http://www.mindfulcommunication.com/`, *The Zen of Listening*, (Quest Books, 2000)

➤ Sharon Drew Morgen, thought leader, innovator, NY Times Bestselling author, speaker, consultant, blogger in sales, listening choices. Developed new sales paradigm Buying Facilitation™

➤ Marc Wong, *Thank You for Listening: Gain Influence and Improve Relationships, Better Listening in 8 Steps*, Published by Createspace, 2012

5

Your Headband Light - Succeeding in the Business Meeting

"Our meetings are held to discuss many problems which would never arise if we held fewer meetings."

—Ashleigh Brilliant, author and cartoonist

In general, meetings conducted today are one of the greatest costs to businesses because of their unproductiveness. If you calculate the hourly rate of each individual sitting in a meeting, on average, with maybe six people in a one-hour meeting, with people attending from the front line to top management, it might cost about $6,000, or $100 per minute.

One of my earliest experiences as a corporate trainer was to consider a request for a proposal to facilitate a training workshop about running and being in effective meetings. One reason I can still remember these details is because it turned out that the client brought in a local newspaper reporter who subsequently reported on how to run effective meetings in the work place. The client expressed their need as urgent and urged the reporter to make the message hard hitting.

I opened the training hour by asking the highest-level person attending the first training session to write me out a check for $12,000 in the event that nothing would be changed when I left.

"What!?"

I then explained my reasoning to him. I wanted to give him the benefit of being free to either accept or reject my calculations. So, giving him a tool like a headband light to see what is in front of him more clearly without having to feel his way through any obstacles, I explained the math.

This client had 12 people in our opening training session. Hence, I asked for $12,000.

Business meetings are still often viewed by many as being about as effective as expecting a racehorse to win without a good jockey.

We often find ourselves thinking or feeling that a meeting is an ineffective business occasion when:

➤ People arrive late, with all kinds of excuses

➤ People are distracted by many different things

➤ People don't turn off their cell phones

➤ Someone forgot to send the agenda…

➤ …Actually, there is no agenda

➤ People talk all over each other

➤ The loudest voices get heard

➤ No decisions get made

➤ Not everyone at the meeting needs to be present

➤ There is no follow-up

These actions are probably recognizable to you. They certainly suggest that complaints about meetings being a waste of time have maybe more than a little truth to them. Indeed, some of them can even be counterproductive for introverts.

Still, we cannot do without meetings at work. The question is: how do we make them work for us?

There are leaders who understand some of what it takes to make meetings more productive where a range of different personalities is present. Actually, isn't it more the situation than not that there will be a diversity of personalities in meetings?

Adam Grant, a Wharton School of Management professor, writes in a research study with two co-authors, Francesca Gino, Harvard Business School, and David Hofmann, University of North Carolina Business School, about why extroverts are not always the most successful leaders. Discussing the findings of his research, he mentions his experience of working with a Fortune 500 company leader. The CEO started the meetings with 15 minutes of silence. Since the CEO was more extroverted, he recognized getting excited about ideas would often leave the extrovert talking exclusively, while leaving others in little position to contribute. Starting a meeting with silence might not be every leader's choice, but it can quickly set a different tone for everyone to follow, including the leader themselves.

Of course, leading a business meeting is very different from participating in one. As a meeting participant, we can still be responsible for our actions in a way to help the meeting be more productive, and hopefully, more successful. Whatever our role is, there are actions to take before in preparation, during to ensure the meeting effectiveness, and after to help move the meeting forward and to communicate results.

Make a note

Plan and apply some better and maybe lesser-known tactics when either leading or participating in your next meeting. By the end of this chapter, you will:

- Appraise your own meeting skills.
- Recognize the tools available to strengthen your research and planning to improve your contribution to future meetings.
- Recognize how you can express yourself in an extroverted way if needed in a meeting while still being authentic.
- Feel comfortable with contributing to different parts of a meeting.
- Recognize that your contribution to a meeting is just a small part of your organizational contribution.
- Find how your style best fits into the varying meeting parts, and select what you can most comfortably contribute.
- Distinguish various body language communicators to use in upcoming meetings for your own evaluation.
- Have actionable ideas to use in your next meeting to be better prepared and to make use of the benefits of being an introvert.

Assessing your meeting skills

The first step in developing your skills is to take some time to reflect on your general effectiveness in meetings.

Stop and answer the following statements with just one of the words in the Scale of Words. Remember, the more honest your answers are, the better understanding you will have of your meeting approach. That will allow you to make the best choices of actions to take for improvement.

Personal meeting assessment

	Never	Rarely	Sometimes	Often	Always
I have note-taking and scheduling materials with me					
My report or task is ready to present or report on					
When presenting, I request my equipment in advance					
If leading the meeting, everyone receives an agenda in advance					
If leading the meeting, I open with "housekeeping"					
If not leading the meeting, I ask for an agenda					
During the meeting, I avoid needless side conversations					
I add value in a meeting in what I say					
When I have enough information, I ask questions					
I avoid interrupting others					
My comments are on and to the point					
I help keep discussions on track					
I sit in a powerful place					
I have some fun					
There is a follow-up: minutes, communications, and actions					
I apply lessons learned in the next meeting					

Score interpretation

Give yourself the following score for the words you identified with each statement:

- ➤ Never: 2 points
- ➤ Rarely: 4 points
- ➤ Sometimes: 6 points
- ➤ Often: 8 points
- ➤ Always: 10 points

The higher your score, the more effective you are at leading meetings and participation. The lower your score, the more you need to examine when to either amp up your preparation for meetings or increase your extroverting during your meetings.

Let's explore some of the practical and actionable ways you can do this.

Do your homework about the meeting

Just as providing an agenda, being ready with a report, and having the correct and necessary equipment for setting up are essential steps in preparing for a meeting, there are other actions that could be viewed as specifically appealing to introverts that can also be taken.

Joyce Shelleman, PhD, an introvert and author of *The Introvert's Guide to Professional Success: How to Let Your Quiet Competence Be Your Career Advantage*, coaches her introvert clients around the three Rs of meetings. Designed to help us be better prepared and use our introverted nature to mutual advantage, the Rs are:

Lists
- ■ Research prior to any meeting
- ■ Rules awareness
- ■ Rehearse what you want to do and say

There are two problems potentially posed by meetings: we may get exhausted with extra time being with people and it is highly likely our thinking time is compromised. These three Rs will help dull this sword that cuts our energy and contribution.

James, an accountant whom Shelleman worked with, was not getting his voice heard in meetings. By studying the agenda he received, and finding out who would be there, part of his research set him up to know what will be discussed and what communication styles he will be working with during the meeting. In this research, he gives himself ample time to fully prepare his approach.

Rather than sticking with the rule of meetings that most people play by, James also creates and plays by his own rules. He might set up small one-to-one meetings before a larger one. Or, he might meet with people online rather than face-to-face. All this homework is what allows him to reshape the rules to fit his introversion tendencies.

Thinking about what we want to say in advance can really help us to ensure that our contributions in meetings are valuable. When we think things through, we can be confident that our message is on target. When we have already composed our thoughts ahead of time, we find it easier to contribute. It can also help us to better pace our style with the meeting.

This rehearsal of the three Rs is primarily helpful to contribution and going at our pace in two key ways: it allows us to contribute much more easily and to set the pace in meetings.

Being able to contribute more easily

The three Rs provide us with a structure or method that makes it easier for us to think things through and, as a result, boost our confidence when it comes to meetings. We may still find that there are some things we want to ponder, but if we know the agenda and the topics of discussion and have already met with some of the participants, we will at least be on the same level as them.

If an idea has been given time to percolate, it becomes much easier to communicate. Consequently, it is also more likely to improve the value of your ideas, as your contribution to a meeting should go up considerably if you give yourself time to think and prepare beforehand.

Meetings are frequently as much about one-to-one interaction as they are about communication within a group of people. Shelleman's three Rs offer a solid plan to make meetings work for us instead of against us, even when one-to-one.

Being the pace setter

Nora, another client of Shelleman's, had weekly meetings with her boss before the team meetings. She prepared a report of her activities for that week researched by looking back through her calendar. This allowed her the advantage of avoiding having to be defensive and helping her boss to stay focused on what she wanted to discuss to help boost her performance the next week.

In leading during the meeting in this way, which most if not all of us have the opportunity to do, she was able to set the rules for the meeting with her boss: her report became the meeting agenda, and rather than being thrown off balance with her boss wandering, she focused the discussion.

Her planning the researched report became her rehearsal!

A title is a title, and ours might often lead us to believe we cannot positively affect change. But each of us can be a tidal wave of change when we help our introverted style to be heard by understanding how to better use this often-needed time to think, which allows us to then express our best ideas.

Trust your instincts to contribute your way

Research suggests a meeting will be perceived as valuable if participants feel their participation is valued. One study by D. J. Leach from Leeds University Business School, S. G. Rogelberg from the University of North Carolina, Charlotte, P. B. Warr from the Institute of Work Psychology, and J. L. Burnfield from the Human Resources Organization, found involvement may be the most important factor in our rating of a meeting's effectiveness.

In Susan Cain's book, *Quiet: The Power of Introverts in a World that Can't Stop Talking*, chapter 9 is titled, "When Should You Act More Extroverted Than You Really Are?" Meetings, as I see it, might be one place to consider acting more introverted. We already understand the typical dynamic being talk, talk, and more talk. Playing to our quieter strengths and preferring time to think can help us be more confident to talk in the moment that counts the most in a meeting. At the very least, our contribution might give us a sense that a meeting was worthwhile.

Meetings, workshops, and seminars are all places to take the opportunity to be more extroverted. Next time, we can be more prepared. Considering technology has grown to include teleclasses, online forums, and social media, we might also include these different kinds of places where people gather as meetings.

But how can we be more involved in any kind of meeting?

Meeting Size

One thing that may be in favor of introverts, and one of the most frequently repeated suggestions from researchers, is that corporations and organizations hold smaller sized meetings. Smaller sized meetings have a number of benefits for introverts. First, this gives introverts a strong footing to maintain our energy for a longer period of time. And secondly, it allows us a greater opportunity to contribute.

Think about your own experiences in meetings. When do you feel you are able to get a word in? Is it a larger or smaller group meeting? And when are you able to more easily maintain more energy to make your contribution? When the group is larger or smaller?

In general, the size of a meeting can have a real effect on issues such as start time and attendee involvement. The larger the meeting, the more likely it is that a meeting will start late and involvement will include fewer people.

Moreover, research also finds that higher levels of involvement correlate with increased perceptions of the effectiveness of a meeting. As a result, meeting leaders who focus on putting in place as many meeting variables to encourage participant contribution – such as size, agenda, temperature comfort, and more – will find they get more people contributing.

If, in your role, you are not able to control the size, consider the preparatory work such as Shelleman suggests and create smaller preliminary meetings with key identified people attending the meeting. On a personal level, it will create the same effect.

Pre-meetings

Shelleman is not the only introvert authority suggesting preliminary meetings. Susan Steele, introvert blogger, comments about her corporate meeting experience in a similar way. When she was a project manager, she would sometimes have informal conversations with one or two key people on the team to figure out which way a discussion might go or anticipate where a problem might occur.

Granted, this can be more challenging if you are not leading the meeting. But this is one of the situations to act on your self-confidence and lead the way. Steele suggests this 'ahead-of-time' preparation is essential both for our comfort as introverts and, consequently, our ability to make a meaningful contribution.

Agendas

We have probably all heard or read about at one time that we should not have a meeting without an agenda. Agendas are essential for a meeting to be successful. Without one, all participants can have a difficult time.

An agenda is a multi-purpose document serving first to communicate housekeeping items such as location, date, and time. Then, secondly, an agenda serves to identify the topics of discussion, and third, maybe most importantly, serves to allow participants time to prepare their own contribution.

This third purpose of an agenda is useful for all attendees and, in particular, for the introvert. We intellectually know the purpose of meeting agendas. But when either there is no agenda or the agenda fails to do as intended, we have the introvert advantage to help improve the situation.

Meghan Wier, author of *Confession of an Introvert: The She Girl's Guide to Career, Networking and Getting the Most Out of Life*, frames the dilemma of not being prepared in a meeting as, "No one has patience for the person who doesn't seem to 'know' what they are doing." While extroverts tap easily into their spontaneity to appear charismatic, charming, and confident, the truth is we might more often come to be these things with some preparation. "Preparedness and the keen interest in knowing the topic will make them (introverts) better resources and better employees in the long run."

Wier says, "There is no room for introverts in the workplace to become flustered and unprepared."

Meeting agendas provide for preparedness. They are a tool to keep things on topic and even a standard to help judge meeting effectiveness. If you do not get one from the person calling for the meeting or leading it, ask for one in advance. If no agenda is planned, you should be proactive with a simple question before the meeting, like, "And what will the main topic of discussion or focus in our meeting be?" An introvert who asks a question like this will come as no surprise to a meeting leader working with them on a daily basis.

If we want our tendency toward preparation to help us with our meeting contribution, either without an agenda or with an agenda gone astray, we can enhance our presence by as small of an action as asking a question that puts the focus on clarifying the agenda. It helps us, it helps the leader, and it helps the attendees.

Meeting contribution

Julia Barnickle is an introvert specialist, admittedly more of an 'ambivert', who helps other introverts build an Internet-based business lifestyle. She brings her experience in meetings from a corporate and linguistic background.

Throughout her career, she found extroverts in meetings were typically the first ones to ask questions or make suggestions around a problem, often before even fully understanding the problem at hand. "In these situations, my introverted nature pays dividends, because I have the opportunity to size up the situation while everyone else is busy talking, and I can then ask a pertinent question once I have a clearer idea about the problem."

Our general tendency is to think before we speak. Just as Barnickle takes the time to use this thinking time to prepare to make the most relevant point about the problem, we too can relax in knowing our preference for thinking time can pay dividends. Often, our idea will take hold with other meeting participants and then be at the core of a solution.

When we learn to be comfortable with traits like our introspective nature, we can strengthen our confidence knowing that when we do make a meeting contribution, it is highly likely the idea will be more relevant.

Beyond the meeting

When we think about sales meetings, we very likely think about a motivational effect from the meeting leader. "Let's do it!" "We can get this done!" This kind of cheerleading is often followed by loudly spoken contributions by many of the sales team members. And of course, finally, cheers for the salesperson of the day, week, or month.

During my early sales career, I was the quiet one during such meetings. That is when I discovered meetings are not all they are cracked up to be. We still have goals to meet when we leave the rally.

As it is with sales, it is highly likely that with any other position in a company, your biggest contribution to your organization happens outside the meeting.

"If you build credibility one on one with the people with whom you work, they will turn to you in meetings for your observations and contributions," says Shelleman.

This is exactly what I have found whether I am working as a volunteer leader in a non-profit organization, as a salesperson on a team, or as an independent business coach. Everyday influence grows outside the meeting through my competence, my integrity, my focus, and other traits, so that by the time we finally are in a meeting, I have quietly become the go-to person.

If I can do it, you can do it.

While extroverts depend on their natural instincts to guide their behavior in any kind of meeting, when we use innate abilities, our involvement will be more widely appreciated. Our contribution will more often be asked for instead of us trying to find the opening to make it.

Bring your style into a meeting process

Most tips and strategies for more effective meetings focus on factors relating to the meeting process. Some of those are on the meeting personal assessment earlier in this chapter. And we are covering a good amount of these details moving forward in this chapter.

Is there an agenda? Do people have the agenda in advance? Is someone running the meeting? Is there a note taker? Is there a follow-up plan?

Attending to the process factors in whatever role we have in a meeting helps to keep a meeting moving, keep people to a timetable, focus the meeting conversations, and help elicit relevant contributions.

But a question we might want to ask is how can we stay in the process loop our way and still make a meaningful contribution? After all, business meetings are known to be a quicksand pit for productivity because of the difficulty of making the process work for the majority in attendance.

A review of some of our top innate differences as introverts and extroverts working together will add to the discussion:

Extroverts	Introverts
■ Prefer face-to-face meetings	■ Prefer e-mail (or online) meetings
■ Think while talking	■ Talk after thinking
■ Talks more	■ Listens more
■ More interested in people	■ More interest in ideas
■ Breadth of discussion	■ Depth of discussion
■ Distracted	■ Concentrates
■ Energized from others	■ Energized from self
■ Do many things at once	■ Be focused on one thing
■ Act then assess	■ Assess then act
■ Enjoys leading	■ Enjoys independence

Using our introvert nature is advantageous before the meeting in being prepared. Doing your homework will, as we have seen, put you on a solid footing, allowing you to be more confident in adding your voice to the discussion.

But what do you do once you are in the meeting and it feels like rush hour in Grand Central Station?

Do what you do best

A leader and a participant can work together towards more successful meetings, starting with acknowledging the purpose of the meeting. Some meeting purposes include:

> ➤ Informational, for example, training sessions or workshops, clarifying policy issues, performance reporting, or assessments

> ➤ Discussion of idea generation, including finding solutions/solving problems, consulting, and getting feedback

> ➤ Decisions for things like planning and crisis management

> ➤ Motivational; outside guest speakers may feature

> ➤ Goal setting

> ➤ Setting tasks and delegating

> ➤ Team building

There is no formal magic to make this happen, unless of course, there is no agenda. People know what the purpose of a meeting is. Depending on what the purpose of a meeting is, we want to do what we do best in our style along the way. Barnickle proposes it is helpful that extroverts tend to keep the conversation moving (breadth of discussion preference) in group meetings. This can give her time to listen, make her assessment of things, and finally offer her own strategy as an idea to consider for contribution (talk after thinking). Assess then act.

The downside of this less verbally involved approach, as Barnickle points out, might be, in particular in one-to-one meetings, that we could be judged as reactive as opposed to proactive.

This potential negative judgment is one reason again for a one-to-one meeting beforehand. Regardless of the purpose for a meeting, it is important to ask questions beforehand, as simple as, "And what will we be addressing in our meeting?"

On the whole, if we do our homework before the meeting and then balance it with our more contemplative side in a meeting, more people, in particular leaders, will appreciate our thoughtful approach, particularly when we can tie it to results.

Find your role

In any kind of meeting, someone may find that their personal style might be suited to a particular role within the meeting. Extroverts might shrivel up at not being able to talk, so why be silent? Introverts can more easily stay focused, so why not help everyone by doing what we can to keep the meeting focused?

In almost any temperament or type assessment, there ends up being a suggested synergy that can happen with a diverse team. More examples of how we, as introverts, can balance a team processes include:

➤ Introverts are needed to allow for contemplation to make words stick, whether in writing or reviewing aloud. While extroverts do what they do comfortably, keep the conversation going, we can help make the words stick.

➤ Introverts can take their time to piggyback on the most relevant idea while extroverts take delight in spouting off initial ideas. Introverts may end up with a more creative and robust suggestion from the broad offering of ideas usually given during a brainstorming session.

➤ Introverts can assess which of the numerous ideas that extroverts often go with and suggest which are worth talking about further in depth.

➤ Introverts can grab onto the scattering of ideas offered by the enthusiastic extrovert. Doing this, we can often concentrate on what we know to be most relevant to the purpose of the meeting and then steer more of the conversation that way.

> To bring in our general introverted preference of communicating in writing or one to one, we could suggest a follow-up via e-mail or notes. Extroverts will, it has been my experience as well, prefer meeting in person so we can suggest one to one when appropriate.

Each of us has a role and can contribute positively to a meeting by harnessing our preferred style and allowing ourselves to thrive on what charges us up. Part of what it takes to succeed at finding our role is recognizing and acknowledging our differences, honoring this uniqueness, and putting it into action for the good of the group.

Act as if

It is likely acting as if can help in many of the everyday communication opportunities we have. Why? When we act as if we are free to create what we want, we can redirect our lack of confidence into a confident contribution in an instance of communication.

When we tolerate the possible discomfort of being in and contributing to a business meeting, bringing our whole mind and body into the experience can reap really positive results.

Iris W. Hung and Aparna A. Labroo led participants through five studies to focus on using self-control to use immediate pain to have long term benefits. For our purposes here, the pain we want to gain from might be the need to attend a business meeting.

Experiment 1 considered whether firming muscles can make people attend to a disturbing and immediately aversive charity appeal by parting with their own money to help others in need. Other experiments were similar to tolerate immediate pain (how about put one hand into an ice bucket!), overcome food temptation, take unpleasant medicines, and attend to immediately disturbing but essential information.

One finding was that as long as our long term goals (for example, in regards to business meetings, to have ideas heard, or to be considered for future promotion) are aligned with what we really want, long term benefits are just within our grasp.

So, to act as if, firm your muscles to help firm your willpower and bring in some of those extroverting behaviors you might not normally take with you into a meeting.

Take time out

If we apply what we do best, including preparing with research, rules, and rehearsal, we may still find ourselves in need of some ways to recharge ourselves. After all, meetings are mostly about being surrounded with people, one aspect of life that drains our energy.

One-to-one meetings are likely the least energy drain for us. But regardless of whether it is one-to-one, a small group, or a large group, we want to be able to put our best into a meeting. One of the best ways of doing this is to plan to recharge.

Wier always plans a "meeting" after a meeting with herself. She might close her office door, or take a walk, or just sit in her car. Depending on the event and the duration she might need just a few minutes. But, she declares, "Sometimes... I need a nap!"

You may need some alone time before, during, or after a meeting. My preference is to do all three, particularly if I know that my day includes a longer meeting or a larger group event where there is likely to be team building, idea generation, or any kind of meeting, in particular in the preliminary stages of a project. This self-care acts like a warm blanket. To me, the comfort it brings in my professional life suggests that this approach helps me to work to the highest standard possible.

When we are in a new role at work, and maybe even new to understanding our preference to introversion, this kind of self-care might be incredibly useful. A time-out is not something we may see our more extroverted co-workers doing, and so the unspoken message might be that it is unacceptable. Even taking as little as a five-minute break to an area outside the crowded and maybe noisy meeting room could be enough for you to ground yourself and let those percolating ideas bubble up to be ready to contribute on your return. Let your own energy level be your guide if you feel you need to break away for just a few minutes.

Trust maturity and experience to lead you to know how to tune into yourself and recognize how much recharging you need. If we fail to do so, we may find we are leaving the best of ourselves out of the meeting.

Body language for confident communication

Seating language, the language of color, our body, and other people's bodies can provide us with lesser planned and instead more easily done things to help ourselves be able to contribute better to meetings.

Seating language

When I was a sales manager, one of my salespeople, John, called me to have a meeting with our boss, Mike. I recall that John wanted some help with one of his larger clients to resolve a possible customer service situation.

At the time, I was not fully aware of this seating language and how it would affect both communication and meeting results.

Because we were meeting in my boss's office, it was natural that he sat behind his desk. John and I sat directly opposite him. This is already a confrontational set-up, so I adjust John and my seats to be at an angle to each other forming a v-pattern toward Mike.

That worked up to the point where I started to understand the dilemma Mike was presenting more than supporting John, and subconsciously I changed the position of my chair to square off against John!

John let me know this in a direct fashion after the meeting in a meeting debrief. "Why did you change your mind on my proposal?" he drilled me.

"What do you mean," was my defensive reply.

"Well you had all the right words but when you moved your chair I knew you weren't on my side anymore."

It turns out that seat positions have their own body language, which can exert influence.

In the following image, let's look at a few of the positions around a typical business meeting table and how they affect a person's influence in contribution.

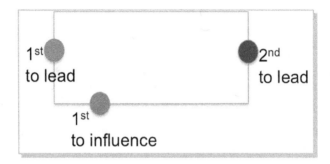

A power position at a rectangular table is at the head of the table if there are chairs there. Have you ever noticed how in the offices of political leaders they sit in this position? Or if there are no chairs, the center of the rows are leading positions. Short of these positions, when you are leading a meeting, sit directly to the lead person's right or left. In some cases, it would be their right; see the upcoming insider tip.

As you may have discovered in my story about John and Mike, sitting directly across from each other is more competitive. Do not accept this seating arrangement, in particular if you are meeting to negotiate or working toward collaboration. I learned this first hand, and now you do not have to.

Chairs in a circle encourage equal participation and collaboration. It is always best to influence by sitting as close to the meeting facilitator as possible. As a consultant coming in to assess an organization's problem situation, this is my go to position.

Several studies confirm that while they may be subtle details, seating arrangements affect the success or failure of communication in meetings.

Make a note

Insider tips to seating language:

Researchers at the University of Oregon suggest that we each have a best side in giving a presentation.

Our left side is our best, being in the other person's right visual field.

Depending on whom it is we have to influence in a small or large group meeting, keep that person or those people to our left so they can see us with their right side.

Color language

For years I wore pale, quiet, and soft colors. Pink, beige, pale green, and blue clothing were organized in my clothes closet. The year before I graduated high school, my father suggested with a gift of a red winter coat that he thought I would look vibrant in red. This was one of those turning points in my life, although I did not know what I was going to learn years later.

For about a year early on in my public workshop career, I worked as a workshop presenter with a color psychologist. Her expertise was how color influences our behaviors, whether we wear them or we see them.

In one of the last events we collaborated on, as I got ready to turn the program over for her next portion, she literally froze, looking at the audience.

Seeing no response, I asked "Nancy?", as she stood frozen in her last step.

I moved over from my side on the small stage to where she was standing. "Nancy, are you okay?" I asked more softly. This time, she looked at me. And the participants were moving their heads from left to right looking at each of us.

So I asked her again, "Nancy, I'm passing the next part of our program over to you, can you take it from here?"

"Uh, oh, no," she said, quite startled. In somewhat of a daze, I was able to keep my focus on being able to decide our next best move now.

While she physically looked almost normal, except for the frozen stance, I finally asked her if she wanted me to take over for her. She said yes.

That is when I learned the power of color, at least in some situations.

What she later told me, when the program was over and the participants were leaving, is that she had some kind of severe reaction where she was transfixed by the black and yellow outfit of a woman in the front row. It turned out when Nancy was a child she had a severe reaction to a bumblebee sting, and yellow and black going forward was an unfriendly color combination for her.

While I doubt everyone would react this way to that combination of color, you will find that color does affect us, whether they appear in our environment or we want to create a subtle affect for ourselves. Color affects our mood, feelings, and behaviors. I got to see all of that at once with Nancy.

Before this event with Nancy, my understanding of colors was limited. All I had in the back of my mind was a shift somewhere deep inside me going from furnishing my clothes closet with the pale light colors to the bright and often bold colors. This was triggered when my father gave me that lovely red winter coat as a gift. Wearing more bright and bold colors did change how I felt about myself.

As introverts, we might be attracted to colors that are quiet and contemplative, or even dark or light but which don't have so much saturation to them. Think about how green, brown, and dark red might appeal to us.

We also might like pale colors that are subtle and not overpowering.

Most color research is done under the banner of marketing and art, but there are findings from a variety of other areas as well. There are also cultural differences to consider when it comes to a broad interpretation. Even if the effects are only temporary, as they were for Nancy, there are still generalities you might consider to put into action.

Maybe you want to assure yourself that you will both be comfortable and calm in a meeting. It is possible what you wear can help you achieve that feeling. The action is an easy one. You do not even have to change your entire wardrobe to start. Adding a tie or a scarf or other little accessory can help you to get started with what could be a positive change for you.

One research study of color preferences affected by personality is reported by Carl Robinson of the University of Colorado. With 40 students, all wearing translucent glasses giving a uniform color when looking through them, Carl found that "a preference for the cooler (tending toward blue and green) or calmer color was considered an introvert response, while a preference for the warmer (tending toward red and yellow) or more intense color was considered extrovert."

➤ **Blue**: Think about a clear blue sky. How does it normally make you feel? If you think about lying down on a thick, healthy green lawn to look up at the sky, you likely feel calm and expansive. When worn in the cooler intensity, introverts would have a predisposition for something blue. Try wearing something blue, whether it is dark or cooler, to your next meeting, in particular if you do not normally wear that.

➤ **Green**: This is another nature-based color. Another calming effect color. Researchers have found green can also improve reading ability. Some students found laying a transparent sheet of green paper over a book or journal increased their reading speed and comprehension. If you are given a report last minute, and have available a green light or a green transparency, it might be worth trying to read it that way. But as simple as wearing more green, it could be dark or pale in intensity for those of us more introverted, which might again help reduce your anxiousness.

➤ **Red**: A study in the journal Emotion found that people act more forcefully when they see the color red. The researcher Andrew Elliot, psychology professor at the University of Rochester, reported because red can be seen as a cue for danger, it enhances our physical reaction. My experience with it comes from reporting once to Nancy. I often felt an energy loss if I had too many extroverting activities scheduled. She suggested I should try wearing just an accent of red color, like a scarf or a belt, even if it was under my clothes. While it was short lived, I did experience an energy boost. Try dark red to start if your preference tends to avoid the bolder and brighter.

➤ **Black**: Black is usually associated with death and dying; less than energy charged events. You could say it affects us negatively. Of course, we do not interpret this with a black tie event when men strut around in their tuxedos, predominantly black, and women seem to have their spirits lifted with their long, black gown. The point is, notice if black does anything for you the next time your wear it. If you have any sense that you are losing your energy or feeling somehow less than confident or any other state that keeps you from contributing, maybe try a different color next time.

➤ **Brown**: What comes to mind in nature? Tree trunks or earth maybe. That is one reason brown is described as bringing to mind being down-to-earth. In other words, it usually evokes security and confidence. If you find your introvert nature not being able to pull your confidence up before a particularly tense kind of meeting, brown is one of those more calming type of colors.

Think about the colors in nature that any of us likely find the same appeal to and then you can find research supporting such nature-born inspiration. For sure, more scientific research is needed in the area of color psychology. Even in the research reported, the effects on our feelings or moods are temporary. Given meetings are temporary, consider how the color of what you wear to a meeting might affect you or other participants.

Make a note

If you want or need some easy actionable ideas to boost your meeting effectiveness, start with a color tactic.

Color studies to determine a preference as a function of introversion or extroversion are both few and not always conclusive. The wisest choice you can make in using this body language tactic to help improve your calm and confidence might be to be contemplative about what colors you think make you feel that way.

The effects may be more subtle than profound. Even if we are the only person, we know something changed. This is going to contribute to part of us showing up more fully in meetings, and that little change in the color of what we wear needs to be one of our tools. We can only know the positive effect when we try a particular tactic.

As relates to color, we could ask ourselves when we look in our own clothing closet, "Why have I chosen these particular colors for myself to wear? Is it because of how they make me feel? Is it because I look good in them? Something else? Or a combination of all this?" Content with our answer, we can contemplate what the best outfit is for us to wear to any upcoming meeting that we might be anxious about.

Your power poses

Remember the power poses in *Chapter 3, Confident to Communicate*? Those can also work to prepare for a business meeting as they fall into the category of "Act as if."

Amy Cuddy, a social psychologist and associate professor at Harvard Business School, found that regardless of our personality, we can control those feelings of anxiousness or nervousness in those situations when we need more sense of power or positive wellbeing.

A meeting can be just that situation.

We may want to raise our testosterone, the hormone linked to feeling more powerful and generally more confident. Or we may want to ease our anxiousness and reduce cortisol levels, the stress hormone that makes us feel high anxiety and even 'brain fog'. Certain body poses, as described in Cuddy's research, help us naturally and quickly both raise what we need and reduce what we do not want.

Too often in meetings, because we are sitting, we sit in what is called a low-power pose where we make ourselves small behind a table with our arms and hands folded close to our body.

Ideally, what we want is to take one of several open poses, and only two minutes is required to get the hormone to rush in and out:

Lists

- **First pose**: Put your hands behind your head with your feet spread wide beneath the table.
- **Second pose**: Stand up. It's that easy. Add more to your positive feeling and lean into the desk with your hands on the table or desktop.
- **Third pose**: Sit with your arm spread out on the chair beside you. Remember, the idea is to help yourself be as big as possible.

Any of these three pose examples can be done during the meeting or in your own personal space before the meeting starts.

Given you might want only ideas for before the meeting starts, in the event you find you do not follow-through during a meeting with the suggestion, here are a couple more for your consideration before a meeting.

Lists

- **Fourth pose**: The Wonder Woman pose; feet shoulder width apart and hands on the hips.
- **Fifth pose**: The warriors pose used in yoga: commonly called Warrior II, start from a straight standing position. Then, raise up your arms and release them to where your right arm comes forward and left arm is toward your back. Then lower your right knee to bend over the right ankle. Your left leg will be behind you.

The warrior pose signifies just that, a fierce warrior. The main idea, whether we choose it or any of the power poses before or during a meeting, is to make certain we feel bigger and more powerful as opposed to how we might feel sitting down on a chair, often smaller and powerless. "Our non-verbals govern how we think and feel about ourselves. Our bodies change our minds," says Cuddy.

My natural tendency over the years is to get in the Wonder Woman pose. It is the easiest way I have found to make myself feel bigger—a bigger space and a bigger sense of self. It has become something I do naturally without any planning before I go on stage. If you need validation of how any of these poses make you feel this way, try one for yourself.

When we are feeling anxious or stressed about a particular meeting, and we want a technique that works quickly, we could remember to try one of the scientifically proven power poses until we find one that works for us.

Percolate to full steam

Using our general introverted preference to think things through can be an advantage, as long as what we are thinking moves us forward in meeting participation and helps us feel confident for our voice to be heard.

Sometimes, when we think of ourselves in the light of introvert myths, we can damage who we are naturally by tossing that thinking behavior aside or not perfecting it for the situation.

We have to stop sabotaging ourselves this way. One of the first places we can find positive results is to show up bringing the best of ourselves to a meeting.

Overcoming anticipatory anxiety

Have you ever found after a meeting you might have been anxious about that you left it saying to yourself, "Well that wasn't as bad as I thought!" I certainly have.

The unknown and something we might not have ever done can often take us to projecting thoughts and feelings into the future.

While we are thinking things through, we might be including what could go wrong, what might happen to prevent our ideas being heard, and other negative thoughts.

What most of us intend in any business meeting is that we and others are very comfortable and we communicate confidence in our expertise quickly. When we show up prepared and contribute, introverts will be considered for more opportunities in the workplace.

The extrovert, with their charisma, charm, and confidence, will nail these same situations with no problem at all. It isn't fair, but it is the truth.

Here is one approach to dedicating being in our heads so much to future meeting success.

Steele has found she is often needlessly projecting negativity into situations. It is called anticipatory anxiety. Studies have shown that imagining an event is going to go badly can actually make you perceive that it did go badly – even if it did not. Our brains are so action-oriented we might imagine every conceivable outcome so that we can be better prepared. Steele says even knowing this, she will "sometimes have to consciously pull myself back from the edge." When you find yourself having a negative projection, immediately stop and think of a positive projection. Instead of "I'm never going to get a chance to speak in this meeting", think "I'm looking forward to participating in this meeting."

Given we have reviewed different ways of contributing our strength to different kinds of meetings, get your anticipatory anxiety working for you positively instead of getting caught up in the negative. It is about letting your logical brain lead your emotional brain and not the other way around. Steele suggests we ask ourselves, "What other ways can I contribute? Can I write an e-mail? Speak to the meeting facilitator? Have a discussion with someone?"

These are ways to do what energizes us: preparation by thinking things through. When the preparation is positive, there can only be positive results. As Wier says, those of us more introverted will ultimately succeed.

The important thing going forward is to use any ideas in a way that prepares us to be able to contribute confidently.

The next actionable idea will help people want to listen up for your meeting contribution.

Eye contact

When I was first promoted to sales manager, there were more presentations to give in my role. Being the introverted type who likes to prepare as you may know, we might read everything we can to find out about what would often escape us in larger meetings. But what if in that preparation, we avoid eye contact in the delivery of our ideas?

It turns out there is a way to utilize both the length of the contact and where to put your eyes in meetings and presentations to get the most effectiveness. A communications analytics company, Quantified Impressions, reported in their findings of 3,000 people that while adults make eye contact between 30 percent and 60 percent on average in conversations, the ideal amount of time is 60 percent to 70 percent to create a strong connection. Less than this time and you reduce your credibility.

So put your mobile device away as step one to help.

One-to-one meetings usually have a natural flow. We usually listen with our entire body, leaning forward, using our eyes and even gestures to signal we are listening. Eye contact helps build and maintain rapport. Since introverts generally manage eye contact well while in one-to-one conversations, it is a matter of applying the same concepts when with more people. As a conversation continues, each of these body gestures like eye contact, learning forward, or even rubbing the chin, in part signals "I have interest" in the conversation.

Have you ever been at lunch with someone, absorbed in the conversation, then either you or the person you are with sees someone they know, literally out of the corner of their eyes? This then breaks rapport, and interrupts the conversation. After a courteous exchange with the person who just entered the room, you lock eyes again with the one you were meeting with at the start and the conversation flows again.

In larger meetings, eye contact can serve multiple purposes. It can communicate listening, confidence, and even action. Using the eyes appropriately is the most important factor for communicating effectively, at least as an academic study conducted by the University of Akron's School of Communication concluded.

I started out practicing eye contact in front of a mirror a day or two before a presentation. I let my eye contact with myself go longer and longer. From the mirror I moved to my dog for creature connection. Not too much to be considered staring, but just enough. This is important both for credibility and confidence. Too much more than the suggested time may come across making the other person feel uncomfortable rather than its intended purpose of maintaining rapport.

Think about the length of your gaze in this way: have you ever had someone stare at you? That would be likely 100 percent of the time of a look. And how did that make you feel? There you have it.

When you contribute an idea and then you drop your eyes instead of moving a steady gaze from one meeting participants' eyes to the next, like in sports, you have dropped the ball. Either people you are speaking with are not all that important or the idea you have is not relevant. So we don't really need to look away to avoid prolonged eye contact with any one person, we just need to look at other people as we talk.

We want to look at each person when we speak in a meeting to convey our appreciation of their listening as well as communicating we have a valuable contribution.

My learning took me from guessing how the initial 60 to 70 percent of the time really translates into time or something else tangible.

Make a note

My experiences in looking at people for what could be that recommended percentage of time is to express a complete thought (which would likely be about 5 seconds), and then move on to the next person.

How can you improve your eye contact to be sure that the value of what you are saying is communicated?

Follow the extrovert lead

There are extrovert business friends I have who often remark they do enjoy a little down time and they appreciate me talking about it. The truth, for us as introverts in quite often extrovert-friendly situations like business meetings, is that we are going to want to follow the lead of extroverts, as much as we are able.

Sometimes, we do benefit from that little bit of acting as if. Wier talks about how she was still working in the same job for a non-profit company after an extrovert who was hired got promoted. Stacy was good at being in front of the groups who attended their fundraising events. She appeared to be a natural. But because Wier and Stacy were friends, when Stacy became her boss, she showed Wier by example as well as helped her to push herself beyond her comfort zone. Today, even though her preparation is introvert-based for any kind of speaking to a group, Wier is able to be comfortable in these situations.

There is power in eye contact, so if you are not comfortable with maintaining eye contact, that would be an easy place to start. In a study, Business professor Gregory Northcraft writes, "Face-to-face contact yielded the most trust and cooperation while e-mail netted the least, with video conferences somewhere in between." Of course, we know that in those face-to-face settings, eye contact has an influencing role.

You could select a one-to-one in-person conversation to take note of where you are with your gaze with an extrovert friend.

Next, accept an invitation to an event that you might not normally say yes to, like a small networking group. Notice in your conversations at this event if you are within the 60 percent to 70 percent range for eye contact time. If you are, then be sure to take this ability into your next meeting. Or, notice in your next meeting in a small or large group, what is the eye contact percentage you give?

My own experience is to suggest that you only follow the extrovert to a degree on eye contact. Our eyes take in so much in understanding our environment. Because extroverts get their energy from people and events outside themselves, you are likely to notice that they break their contact quite often. Logically, we might have the advantage when it comes to eye contact because of our preference to focus on one thing at a time.

John Zelenski, researcher and Associate Professor of Psychology at Carleton University, found in one study that introverts are better off acting extroverted. The study he led suggests acting extroverted might produce more positive emotions and happiness. Regardless of personality, the people in the study who acting more extroverted felt better. But as we might be thinking, the researchers also asked if there are emotional benefits, and whether there are also costs like depletion of energy.

Knowing the energy drain might be a problem for introverts, they continued with the study to test this. Everyone was given a test afterwards, which required his or her complete focus. Introverts were still able to focus for the test, with positive results. Why? There are only theories right now, including when we act extroverted, it might elicit more of the neurotransmitter dopamine, which is what is natural for the extrovert. Or it may more simply mean because you think it, you act it, and then maybe you will be it.

Because you think you can add valuable contribution to your next meeting, act the extroverted way with your introverted preparation style and it is highly likely you will find yourself being the lead.

Summary

Do you think business meetings are on the decline? Neither do I. If anything, they might continue to change as technology changes. Regardless of the way that meetings are conducted in the coming years, in any interactive scenario, it is important that our voice is heard. We want to feel confident that when our voice is heard, we still stand the same chance of promotion, increased earnings, and success as anyone else.

On completing this chapter, you now:

- ➤ Understand your meeting participation effectiveness.

- ➤ Have identified actions you can take before a meeting.

- ➤ Can feel comfortable with contributing to different meeting components.

- ➤ Recognize meeting contribution is just a small part of your organizational contribution. Your larger contribution comes from applying your strengths to the best of your ability to the role you are tasked with all through the day.

- ➤ Comprehend how your style fits best into the varying meeting parts, and can select what you can most comfortably apply.

- ➤ Can distinguish between various body language helpers—seating, color, power poses – to use in upcoming meetings.

- ➤ Have practical ideas to choose from – preparation, eye contact, acting as if – to help you get on an even ground with extroverts in meetings.

- ➤ Can try acting as if you are extroverted. At the very least, it can only lead to positive feelings.

Thoughts to contemplate

Let's think back on the ideas presented in this chapter about your contribution to any kind of business meeting:

> ➤ Meetings do not run themselves, people do.
>> ➢ What role is the most comfortable for you in a meeting, leading it or being a participant?
>> ➢ What are you willing to put into action to be more comfortable in the one role you did not select?

> ➤ Choose just three of the actionable ideas you either discovered or were reminded of in this chapter. It could come from any of the range presented here, from the various rehearsals and planning ideas, to seating language or color influence, right down to eye contact.
>> ➢ Which one will you put into practice and initiate in your next meeting regardless of the size?

> ➤ Determine what upcoming planned communication events you might have, like a presentation or a sales meeting or a negotiation meeting.
>> ➢ Consider setting up an action plan for the next 30 days.
>> ➢ Include at least three ideas from this chapter.
>> ➢ Just as it is helpful to follow-up to evaluate results of any meeting, it is helpful to our growth to follow-up on ourselves and how new actions are creating more positive results. Plan to follow-up on your plan.

Bibliography

> ➤ Adam Grant, Wharton School of Business with co-authors Francesca Gino, Harvard Business School, and David Hofmann, University of North Carolina Business School, *Reversing the Extraverted Leadership Advantage: The Role of Employee Proactivity*, Academy of Management Journal, 2011

> ➤ Joyce Shelleman, *The Introvert's Guide to Professional Success: How to Let Your Quiet Competence Be Your Career Advantage*, http://theintrovertsguide.blogspot.com

> ➤ Susan Steele, introvert blogger,

> ➤ Meghan Wier, *Confession of an Introvert: The She Girl's Guide to Career, Networking and Getting the Most Out of Life*

> ➤ D. J. Leach, Leeds University Business School, S. G. Rogelberg, University of North Carolina, Charlotte, P. B. Warr, Institute of Work Psychology, and J. L. Burnfield, Human Resources Organization, *Perceived Meeting Effectiveness: The Role of Design Characteristics*, Journal of Business Psychology, 2009

➤ Meetings – basic rules and meeting purposes, `http://www.businessballs.com/meetings.htm`

➤ *The effect of personality type on team performance*, John H. Bradley and Frederic J. Hebert, East Carolina University, Greenville, USA, Journal of Management, Nov 1997

➤ *From Firm Muscles to Firm Willpower: Understanding the Role of Embodied Cognition in Self-Regulation*, Iris W. Hung and Aparna A. Labroo, Journal of Consumer Research, April 2011

> 6

Tape Measure Your Success for Powerful Presentations

"There are always three speeches, for every one you actually gave. The one you practiced, the one you gave, and the one you wish you gave."

–Dale Carnegie, American self-improvement lecturer

Are you one of those people who would rather die than speak in public? You do not need to fear presenting. You can present comfortably, confidently, and powerfully and have the presentation you give be both the one you practiced and wished you gave.

Similar to a tape measure, presentations are so common that almost everyone has seen one at some point in their life. Yet even though they are so common to see and hear, when we are the one who must present, a presentation can often be challenging.

There is usually a small group of introverts who love being on a platform. In planning for this chapter, my natural curiosity took me down a mental path to look at what point my confidence changed to empower me to actually love giving presentations. Being naturally curious, I wanted to think about whether this was natural for me or did it evolve? If it evolved, then how and when might it have changed?

Early in my childhood, my parents encouraged my two sisters and I to sing together for family gatherings. None of us were star material, but our family applauded us so we were encouraged.

In college I aced my public speaking course. It pulled up my grade point average since an economics course was weighing me down.

As an elementary school teacher, the third graders' natural curiosity for learning encouraged me to relax into the fun of teaching in what felt like a safe way on the platform.

After graduating with a Masters in Business Management, employment search firms encouraged me to go into sales because of how I presented myself. That could point to public speaking.

A sales associate I worked with early in my computer sales career once commented casually to me, "You just charm prospects into buying." This was a different perspective than mine, as I was more concerned with knowing the difference between bits and bytes.

There were many more specific seemingly mundane and possibly unrelated daily happenings, which might have either been building blocks or a turning point to actually being excited about giving presentations.

But the day likely to be the turning point was being awarded a training contract with our local American Society of Training and Development, and being selected among over a dozen applicants, including a Dale Carnegie instructor. It was the second year in a row when I was selected that this recognition fueled from outside myself planted a belief I was able to speak in public even as an introvert.

All of these situations, and more than we have time for in this chapter, added to a long tape measure of confidence and skill of presenting to audiences. Years later, I can meet a participant and they remember me and comment, "When you spoke at our company I was so inspired," or "I'll never forget your message at our conference." Becoming a professionally paid speaker did not happen by creating a presentation, having someone buy my service, and then showing up to speak. So be prepared for your success to be a path of success you too can measure.

Julia Barnickle, a Business Coach helping introverts build a business online, says her MBTI® profile is INFP. She is highly sociable and as a linguist is a good communicator. She believes she is just slightly an ambivert because when she has a longer exposure to people, she feels exhausted and has to recharge.

She describes herself as the kind of introvert who loves to have an audience, but isn't interested in being flashy. Instead, she says she aims to entertain while sharing what she has learned.

I also love to share what I have learned. Sometimes I will comment to an associate, "I speak because I love telling people what to do."

What about you?

Regardless of the type of presentation, are you enthusiastic in the sense of being able to take what is in your head and share it with others to help them in some way?

Maybe you are gifted and use your ability to present everyday in business, or maybe you have yet to tap into the power within you. Because this ability to present is within each of us, we are going to bring it out to where it shines for you.

Presentations are prevalent in business, and almost as much in our personal life. They are pivotal to more positively affecting our daily business interactions.

A tape measure will help you decide whether a refrigerator will fit between the countertop and cabinets. Your presentation success is measured by the improved techniques, a more effective application of abilities you bring to each daily presentation opportunity, and the results and response you get from your audience. Each is a measuring tool.

Make a note

Powerful presentations need planning, organizing, and of course our delivery. The key is to reduce and redirect our anxiousness around them into impactful speaking. By the end of this chapter you will:

- Assess your personal presentation competence
- Recognize how you can show up more like the introvert you are with a delivery that persuades, sells, or motivates
- Feel more comfortable, and less anxious, with presenting
- Understand and use our preference for one-to-one communication for better presenting
- Use the introvert strengths to carry your presentation with your passion
- Recognize that sometimes we will use visual aids, and at other times they will not be appropriate
- Either learn or tweak your storytelling to engage people
- What to do before, during, and after your presentation to bring your best self to your audience no matter the purpose
- Have actions, ideas, and practices available to better plan, organize, and deliver any type of presentation

Now let's start to turn our tape measure on edge to improve our presentation ability.

Presentation assessment

Think back to any of your last presentations: whether you last presented giving an elevator pitch at a networking event, or gave a report in a team meeting, or rocked the house on the platform talking with a group of a thousand people.

Stop and answer the following statements with just one of the words in the Scale of Words. Remember, the more honest your answers are the better understanding you will have of your presentation skill level. This will allow you to make the best choices of actions to take to improve.

Powerful presentation assessment

	Never	Rarely	Sometimes	Often	Always
Planning					
My preparation included an audience assessment					

	Never	Rarely	Sometimes	Often	Always
I visited the room and space I would be presenting					
My point of contact discussed the meeting objective with me					
I used the meeting objective to guide my presentation					
I practiced, not memorized, the content					
CONTENT					
My opening was strong enough to break the audience preoccupations					
When I concluded, I called for action					
I used a specific type of organizational method					
I supported my points with relevant examples					
Delivery					
I was able to present in a poised manner					
I used humor when possible					

	Never	Rarely	Sometimes	Often	Always
Visual aids					
My visual aids supported my presentation, instead of being it					
My content spoke to the visual, auditory, and kinesthetic thinker					
Body language					
My body language was congruent with my message					
My body movement was fluid, using up space purposefully					
I used the right amount of gestures					
I used appropriate eye contact with participants					
My facial expressions were appropriate for each point					
Vocal power					
My tone of voice, volume, and pitch fluctuated					
Instead of "um," "uh," or other filler words, I simply, paused					
I remembered to stop and breathe as needed					

	Never	Rarely	Sometimes	Often	Always
Command					
I was able to handle problem or difficult situations					
I used a variety of techniques for appropriate audience participation					
I stayed within the time scheduled for my part					

Score interpretation

Score the words you identified with each statement:

- ➤ Never: 2 points
- ➤ Rarely: 4 points
- ➤ Sometimes: 6 points
- ➤ Often: 8 points
- ➤ Always: 10 points

The higher your score, the more effective you are in your presentations regardless of the setting. The lower your score, then you want to examine when to either amp up your preparation for meetings or increase your extroverting during your meetings. We cannot ignore the reality that presenting to a group regardless of the size is an activity that is built for extroverts: presenting focuses on delivering a message to an audience.

With so many practical, proven, and actionable ways we, as introverts, can make any presentation we give one that we enjoy giving and the audience benefits from listening.

The vote is in – introverts make natural public speakers

About seven years into my computer career I was promoted on a Friday from top salesperson to sales manager that next Monday. It was only then I was given the opportunity to learn about being an introvert, and all the surrounding misconceptions. Discovery was part of the management training offered about half a year later when taking the MBTI®, Myers-Briggs Type Indicator, assessed me as an INTJ: introvert, intuitive, thinker, and judger.

In going from presenting to potential customers to leading staff from administration to technicians to salespeople, presentations still play a part.

Are you anything like me? For years, it was my understanding that as an introvert, we are to fear and be poor with public speaking.

My advantage, which I hope to make yours as well, is that public speaking is nothing for us to fear, and that we can be exceptional at it in spite of being more introverted.

Leading a monthly meeting to a staff of 55 people must have some similar traits to bring in from winning presentations to hundreds of customers. My thoughts and feelings about sales success helped to boost my confidence, and steer me to a successful outcome as a top sales manager.

What we, as introverts, want to recognize is there are several traits we have that make us natural public speakers.

Bob McIntosh, CPRW, `www.thingscareerrelated.com`, is more of an introvert as assessed several times with the MBTI®. He talks about leading a workshop at an urban career center for the first time, on Twitter. This was for participants in a social media certificate program at one of the local community colleges near his home. The reason he chose the topic was because of the newness of this workshop and the sense of calm he had going in.

He had no experience leading a Twitter workshop, other than being on Twitter for approximately two years and sending a rash of tweets to authorities he followed. They gave him some great ideas, but most importantly was a message to him that, Twitter is not rocket science.

While he was concerned about a more advanced level of participants it turned out, they were mostly beginners.

He felt successful because he felt he "rocked the house," feeling it was one of his best workshops ever in terms of delivery and interaction.

But the participant evaluations were not as good as his self-evaluation mainly because the participants were overwhelmed with the information. He learned that workshop participants are looking for guidance and a better grasp on what they are learning.

Was he successful since his own evaluation was better than the participants? Of course he was. He knew the material and engaged participants in activities such as tweeting, setting up their profiles, and creating hash tags for their own discussion.

But McIntosh also tended to internalize his failures more than his success because of the introvert's reflective nature. Getting the negative feedback and internalizing it is actually consistent with research about the anticipation of public speaking that different personalities have: introverts expect more negative evaluations from the audience and show greater fears of a negative opinion of themselves from some audience members. If it is believed it can become a self-fulfilling prophecy, just as McIntosh may have discovered.

My experience with the self-fulfilling prophecy, maybe because of my lack of understanding of what an introvert is supposed to be, took me from successful presentations in selling to leading many inspiring meetings with my staff.

As part of McIntosh's recovery, he quickly began to prepare for his next Twitter workshop incorporating his introvert preferences into what he learned:

Lists

- Be better prepared by knowing the knowledge level of your audience
- With a diverse group in terms of knowledge, cater to each group the best you are able to
- Internalize the success; strategize how to improve next time for any failure

Preparation, personalization, and being "in our head" (often reflective), is a comfortable introvert plan.

Introvert innate and preferred qualities such as these are helpful to recognize as adding strengths to our presentation presence.

Let your listening help you

Speaking in public allows us the chance to observe and listen. It takes longer to write or read about this important ability then to take what we see and hear and then make a conscious decision of how to continue or which direction to go with a well-planned presentation.

What are we looking for? What would it be helpful to see or hear?

Before we present, we can scan the room and get a feel of it. Notice things such as room temperature and acoustics. Pay attention to the energy in the room. Are the people present in a positive or negative kind of feeling and being state? Think about whether people are happy, amused, excited, something else positive, or frustrated, angry, or otherwise negative?

McIntosh claims, "Introverts tend to be more attuned to the needs of the needs of their customers, in this case the workshop participants. Extroverts do not necessarily hear their customers as well as they tend to talk on autopilot."

In my experience, this is not exactly the situation. Instead, introverts are more attuned and therefore are usually the first to hear their audience. Still, extroverts talking on autopilot do hear their customers but often make the adjustments later. It gets down to a timing issue to adjust, determined by style.

During speaking we can also use our eyes and ears to assess how engaged our audience is. Are they taking notes, nodding their heads, or asking questions?

With our intuition, we want to give ourselves permission to listen to and observe the reaction of the audience to know if and when to make a presentation adjustment. Take that second or two to go inside your head, which introverts are so wont to do, and think about what to do. Then if you find that you need to change something, do so.

How is it we will be able to adapt a presentation if our listening tells us we are on the wrong track? We can do this with the help of one of our main preferences in all things we do: be prepared.

Be prepared

On my office bookshelves are three books purchased my first year as a professionally paid speaker. Even though written in 1988, I find myself referring to any one of them every three or four years. The content is timeless.

Powerspeak, by Dorothy Leeds, starts out *Chapter 3, Confident to Communicate*, "Of all the ways to banish fear...one stands out: simple, thorough preparation."

If there is one thing we can count on for ourselves in our preferred ways of working and doing, it is that we, as introverts, enjoy the act of preparation. It has a comfort to it like an old worn shoe. It is part of what we carry with us without any burden of weight.

We can do ourselves a favor continuing to cultivate this trait. Our audience will appreciate us for it because they will hear and see a confident, relaxed, and prepared speaker.

When you know what the objective of your presentation is, it can help you in part, decide the type of outline or structure to follow. When I was still a sales manager working for a corporation, I joined a local chapter of a national woman's group. I learned then that we can prepare even for the situation when we are called on in an impromptu style to speak.

Whether we find we have to be more basic or we have to share more advanced ideas, be prepared to share valuable content for the participants' different levels of understanding.

Value yourself

Be yourself; have you ever heard this piece of advice, whether in giving a meeting presentation or maybe going for a job interview? How can you be yourself, or just be you for a presentation?

In most instances, when we are giving a presentation being ourselves means first to value ourselves. What do you think about yourself? How is your self-esteem? Valuing ourselves is about the mental self-image we hold.

How do we speak to others one-to-one in particular, when we value our self? When we identify what we do in that more comfortable type of conversation, we can transfer it into almost any kind of presentation, even in front of an audience of hundreds.

When I value myself, I stop trying, and instead I become present and mindful. The thoughts that might be relevant for a presentation go from my head, through my heart, and to my voice. If it is a more robust presentation there was likely some research that is at my fingertips. I have thought about what the most relevant information in all of this that needs to be said.

There is an expression that introverts think to speak, and extroverts speak to think. While we think about giving a presentation we can help both ourselves and our audience by focusing on how we speak confidently and with ease in one-to-one conversations.

The process of speaking one-to-one or to a larger audience isn't actually that different. It is simply that there are more people in front of us—but of course, it is a larger audience that can be daunting.

It is when we treat the audience as if we are speaking to one person that we can begin to locate ourselves in a more familiar and comfortable scenario.

When we work with who we are, we can trust ourselves more to know what we are speaking out.

Here are a few specific suggestions that might help:

Action Point

Start with what you are wearing; does it make you feel good about yourself? Does it make you feel comfortable? *Chapter 5, Your Head Band Light – Succeeding in the Business Meeting* has some suggestions for this in terms of color and its effect on ourselves and others.

The words we use are powerful. If it helps you be yourself, speak names of people who you know in the audience. Instead of saying, "Some of us here today understand the importance of..." change it to be personal, like we introverts like, and say, "Some of us, like Bill and Marty, here today understand the importance of...".

We know we like to take time to think. Guess what? People listening to a presentation also welcome a pause. Whether you are presenting soft skills or scientific research, our brains regardless of our temperament often need time to let things sink in.

We can bring these suggestions from who we are in everyday one-to-one conversations, into any presentation to help us be more like ourselves. This lays a solid foundation for us to be able to continue throughout a presentation to ease our anxiety and release our personal power.

Getting the butterflies in formation

Business presentations happen whenever we communicate information and ideas. We often find ourselves presenting to a group, giving a status report, delivering training, making a sales presentation, or being in a job interview. There are many forms of presentations.

How can we then get those natural butterflies we might experience to fly in formation for us? Maybe we are to deliver one of those everyday business presentations. Or we are designated with some company bestowed recognition and want to speak graciously to thank those people who helped us to achieve. Regardless of the presentation situation, how can we deliver our message with poise and confidence?

Research and preparation

We are once again going to reaffirm our confidence in ourselves by one of the things that comes naturally to us. One of the things we love, as introverts, is behind-the-scenes research. It gives us the opportunity to go deep in trying to understand a certain topic or issue.

Our preference to do behind-the-scenes research can immobilize us from saying to ourselves, "I'm ready." What might help us to move into action is to have some measurement to know what is enough time to research and prepare compared to how long your presentation is to be.

The research I do for an hour long presentation, including finding relevant stories and quotations, practicing, and preparing any materials for attendees can take me about three hours. The benefit a speaker and trainer has is that often this presentation is used again, and then tweaking it around the edges to freshen up the message and personalizing it will take maybe about only about an hour.

If you find you welcome the research and preparation but know it may keep you either physically or mentally and emotionally stuck at that stage, make a mental note of this.

Make a note

The typical ratio is for one hour of presentation, allow about three hours of initial preparation. Using the presentation again, it's likely only one hour is needed to tweak it

---

When McIntosh, who leads workshops at a local urban center, realized the customers of an urban career center at which he works needed more advanced workshops, this gave him the perfect opportunity to do what introverts love, which is researching and preparing material. The first workshop he remembers designing was an advanced résumé writing workshop. He recalls how many of the more advanced customers were shaking their heads at the simplicity of the more intermediate workshop on résumé writing. "I thought the workshop was fine for mid-level jobseekers, but the upper management and even CEO's needed something more," McIntosh says.

So he attended a conference at which one of the premier résumé writers spoke and listened to a résumé writing webinar before he got to work on laying out the material that was required for this workshop. He also realized he needed more visuals for his new workshop. He scoured the Internet for examples of "effective résumés today" and took what he learned from the speaker at the conference, as well as the webinar, and accumulated examples of more advanced résumés. He also wrote examples of performance profiles and accomplishment statements that would be part of his presentation.

Researching the workshop and preparing to deliver it for the first time was the easiest part of going "live" with it. He would have to face a live audience and sound like he knew what he was talking about. "For the first workshop," he says, "I was nervous as hell. I mean here were a bunch of high-level jobseekers all expecting something from an advanced résumé writing workshop. I couldn't fail them; that's unacceptable to me."

The workshop went well, not great, the first time around; and subsequent ones fared better. Now this workshop is one of the best workshops offered at the career center by McIntosh and his colleague.

Since designing this workshop, McIntosh has researched and designed approximately six new ones and redesigned many others. Like most introverts, he enjoyed the design process more. So every once in a while he'll get into research mode and redesign the workshops he created.

People who either have to listen to you or want to listen to you in any public speaking venue want to know the speaker knows what they are talking about. Most of us are not appreciative of a speaker who wings it.

Whether it is a business meeting, a job performance review, or a department presentation, our colleagues want us to be prepared.

Balancing some of what charges us, research and preparation, with the actual art of speaking, will bring the best of us to our audience. They are counting on us for this. Preparation goes beyond research.

The best butterfly catchers

One of the best presentation butterfly catchers is preparation, followed by planning.

Whether we are presenting to inform, motivate, or persuade, what we say in a presentation we want to say clearly, directly, and appropriately for our audience. To communicate this way means anxiousness or nervousness has to be at a minimal.

Practice, practice, practice

When I first started as a public speaker I used notes in a brainstorming outline. I used it to practice with as well as refining my notes for the live workshop or speaking event.

Practice helps us to become comfortable with what we have to say, which reduces anxiety. It may even be, as in my case, something that helps you to refer less to notes and more to what is in your head. Practice is one of the most effective ways to convert nervousness into positive energy.

Almost all experts include practice, not memorization when presenting.

Snowden McFall, President of Fired Up, a professional speaking, authorship, and coaching company, believes the more we practice the more relaxed we become.

Anxiousness is normal, McFall says, and if someone claims they are not nervous on some level they are lying. She quotes Mark Twain as saying, "There are only two type of speakers; those who are nervous and those who are liars." As a speaker for over 20 years McFall always feels her nervousness is a sign of her interest in wanting her audience to enjoy and learn from her presentation.

Beth Buelow, introvert coach for entrepreneurs and author, says practice is how to set our self up for success. Besides preparing your talking points, it is a must to practice them out loud. While Buelow finds it silly to practice by herself, even in her car, I find it is by practicing by myself and even in front of my most trusted audience, my dog, that my practice leads to boosted confidence and improved performance.

Practice is not memorization. But you may wonder if there is any appropriate time for memorization? In my experience there is.

Memorize only your opening

It would be remiss of me to not share this tip with you, which I read in the 1992 book *Presentations Plus*, by David A. Peoples, and have put into practice ever since then. It is one of those books I mentioned earlier that is still on my bookshelves in plain sight.

Whether it is a board meeting, a workshop, a speaking engagement, or a sales presentation, approximately the first 10 percent of what I have to say is either so well rehearsed or used over time, a person hearing it for the first time receives it as if it is new.

That first impression is powerful. People remember most what we say at the beginning and the end. People who might be in the audience, or the meeting, or giving the job interview, are preoccupied with other things in their life. Even we might have that tendency so this is a particularly powerful action.

Consider, depending on what the presentation mode is, memorizing that first two minutes. This way you will guarantee yourself to be on the way to a powerful presentation and calm your anxiety as well.

Arrive early

This idea of arriving early if our presentation is in a particular room, as well as practice and minimal memorization, are usually comfortable for the more introverted of us who like to prepare, prepare, and prepare.

What do we do when we arrive early and what purpose does it serve?

We want to have enough time to take a number of preparation steps:

> ➤ From the position of where we will present, visualize our audience.

> ➤ Actually say our memorized opening or first two minutes.

> ➤ Check any audio-visual that we might be using.

> ➤ Meet with, shake hands, and have some casual conversation with others who might arrive early.

> ➤ Identify people who we know. This can help during our presentation when we want a familiar face to land our eyes on.

Anyone who we present to wants us to do well. Like in the television reality shows where a group of judges hold up a rating card, our audience wants to hold up a card rating us a perfect ten.

Suzy Kedzierski, Marketing Communications professional, says it the way one of the product managers advised her in her article, *10 Secrets to Powerful Public Speaking*.

When she asked him his secret of seeming to relish being on the platform, he instead asked her "What about public speaking don't you like?"

Kedzierski said she only knew that she felt like she might freeze up, forget what she wanted to say, or in some other way screw up the presentation.

When the manager expanded on his answer of the audience is rooting for you, he said, "Think about it," he said. "Most people feel their time is valuable. Don't you? So when you listen to someone give a presentation, aren't you behind them all the way, hoping they're going to be good and that you're going to come away feeling that your time was well spent?" If we can arrive early and consider some of the benefits from using this as preparation time, then our anxiousness will drop away.

We owe it to our audience regardless of how many people to give our best.

Stick with water

Avoid any kind of vinegar-based food before you speak in public or make a presentation. From personal experience, when I was a keynoter, while the coleslaw side served with lunch was delicious, it seemed there was not enough water to drink to keep my mouth and throat moist. These types of foods can cause us to pucker our lips and all the water we drink will not help with to keep our mouth and throat loose and moist.

Room temperature water is a presenter's friend. Cold water is as bad in constricting our throat. This lubricates your throat making it easier to speak and keep your throat open.

My friend McFall also advises sticking with drinking water when giving a presentation. Her main message is to not drink coffee, tea, and even soda with caffeine, as these cause our throats and mouth to go dry. These kinds of drinks are counterproductive. Her advice is to stick with hot water with honey if you want something sweet.

Water and appropriate food is about having the right fuel to allow your enthusiasm to be that secret sauce to fuel your presentation.

Owning the space

Arriving early is one concrete example of how we can help ourselves to own the space. When we do take this step, we have already begun our presentation and become comfortable with everything being in place. The physical space helps us to fully "own the space", which otherwise might be only in our head.

"Owning the space" by doing more of what we can do to infuse our confidence, increases our knowledge that we have the ability to communicate our message and what we will communicate will be helpful, inspiring, or interesting for all.

It will be worthwhile for a few different examples of owning the space so we can decide on specific actions as individuals that we want to take, in order to take this vital step in helping any anxiety to subside before a presentation.

First, think about one of your favorite bands or singers. If you have ever been to experience them live then think about how they took the space, walked in it, and maybe talked with the audience. Even if only seen on television, the best of performers can make us feel they are talking directly with us. What they are doing early on is warming up to entertain the audience by making themselves comfortable in their own space.

Here is another perspective of owning the space. Have you heard the golf, tennis, or other ball sports expression, "Keep your eye on the ball?" That kind of coaching from an instructor reminds us to give our complete attention to what we are doing, and what we want to achieve. It might also be called focus. The other piece of this is to be cognizant of other things around us to allow us to successfully hit the ball where we want it to go.

If our presentation is in a boardroom, own the space. If we are speaking from the stage, own the stage. If our job performance review is in someone else's office, they likely feel they own the space.

What we want to have happen in all types of presentation environments is for the space, which is perceived by us as comfortable, communicate our confidence to our audience so they feel comfortable.

A study from Karolinska Institutet in Sweden has shown that neurons in our brain 'mirror' the space near others. Published in the scientific journal *Current Biology*, psychologists and neuroscientists have suggested an answer to the long-standing question about how the brain represents other people and the events that happen to those people. "We perceive the space around other people in the same way as we perceive the space around our own body." If we get our perception of our own space feeling safe and comfortable, how do we get the presentation space the same for our audience?

This research is important to find a way to own our space. If we are uncomfortable, our audience is as well. If we own our space our audience will perceive the same. An example might help clarify how to get to this point of owning the space.

Early in my public speaking career, maybe a dozen presentations before this one, I accepted a contract to speak to a group of pharmaceutical representatives for an after lunch meeting to inspire them for the rest of their day. As normal I arrived early while the late morning part of their meeting was coming to an end.

My friend, author and introvert Beth Buelow, describes it perfectly when she described one such similar experience she had as, "The obstacles existed primarily in the space, which was about as un-introvert-friendly as you can imagine."

What I found myself in for this event was an open courtyard. People were both sitting at round tables being cleared of dishware by the servers and also mulling around the courtyard in small groups. There was no actual stage, which for a speaker brings up fears. It can mean distractions and no central point to return to on a stage like a stage actor does.

When it was time, the event planner asked everyone to be seated. This did two things to the space: indicated to me the best options for standing, moving, and grounding, but kept me stuck in the middle of the group while talking with him.

As he left my side I had to make a decision about the best way to move, to feel my own space. Because as of that moment, I was in every one else's space.

Thankfully with a memorized opening, the time allowed me to both begin my delivery, and while looking at some friendly people, find an anchor location to speak and move from.

While it was not one of my best performances, more than any other platform presentation, it allowed me to understand the importance of owning the space. With preparedness and self-confidence walk up to the podium, or sit at the table, and own the space.

Making a presentation like a one-to-one conversation

Most authorities would agree that when it comes to one-to-one relationships and communication, introverts excel. We listen more, we focus, and we enjoy diving deep into a conversation. We can take actions like this, which come to us naturally in these situations and put them to advantageous use in any kind of presentation.

Some of the characteristics in a chart in *Chapter 5, Your Headband Light - Succeeding in the Business Meeting*, are worth returning to as we explore how to, in making a presentation more like a one-to-one conversation, become more at ease and successful. Here are the characteristics in that chart most germane to this discussion of improving our presentation poise and presence:

Extroverts	Introverts
■ Prefer face-to-face meetings	■ Prefer e-mail (or online) meetings
■ Think while talking	■ Talk after thinking
■ Talk more	■ Listen more
■ More interested in people	■ More interest in ideas
■ Breath of discussion	■ Depth of discussion
■ Distracted	■ Concentrate

Just because extroverts are more energized by other people does not equate to them being better presenters. Yes, extroverts would be more likely to enjoy any public speaking opportunity and even raise their hand if asked to volunteer to give a talk or report. While in the beginning, introverts may not find this as enjoyable it is, they will once they get going.

Public speaking or giving presentations can mean as an introvert or an extrovert doing the task, to do it successfully. When we are overly conscious to what we and our audience are doing it can inhibit our ability to present effectively.

Because extroverts are enjoying being in the moment of the event it is highly unlikely they will be in their head like us introverts. That is what we are going to do—become more in the moment, but from a different perspective than how an extrovert might.

What we want to take action on are things that will make us more at ease, carry on a conversation, and be able to help our audience with the information we want to share.

We are going to take our skill in one-to-one conversations and have them work appropriately as well for almost any kind of presentation.

Use stories to engage people

Telling stories is often used as content in presentations in part because stories help deliver our message in any setting to any audience with results.

Michel Neray, an acknowledged shy introvert even as a young child, hosts MoMondays once a month in Toronto, Canada. It started off as a one-off event, as a forum for people to practice speaking. Now with locations throughout Canada and entering the United States, this personal transformation even attracts a large number of speakers, coaches, trainers, event planners, and people with personal stories who contribute in hundreds of different ways.

Neray's MoMondays bring in speakers of all levels. Professionally paid speakers often attend and actually love presenting in a total story mode. It is a forum for many to practice their material to a friendly, supportive audience.

One of the speakers commented to Neray that while often their reputation is to be a valuable content presenter, he loved MoMondays' atmosphere of being able to share stories. The first time he spoke, it was a highly personal and never told before story of leaving home at age 17, where the first night he was sleeping in a stairwell. Then he fell in with a bad crowd. His life took shape from that but he turned it around. He went on to have a most successful career.

The audience was moved. The professional speaker realized from this environment how powerful the personal story is. Presenting strategic or technical information on its own leaves out what only personal human stories do: connect emotionally. It is the emotional component that inspires each of us to take action on those strategic and technical ideas.

Purposefully sprinkle in some storytelling

If we think about being in conversation, just our self and a good friend for example, it is highly likely we naturally filter storytelling into our conversation.

Have you ever talked a co-worker through a situation they did not know how to work through, with an example of how you handled something similar?

That is, in effect, storytelling. Effective stories are what people remember in most presentations.

Neray believes we all do something so well that we just cannot see it because it is easy for us and we do it naturally. That is what makes hearing stories valuable for others who find a certain situation or action challenging.

While public speaking may not be what we do naturally or comfortably at first, the knowledge, our life situations, and challenges we have faced, all come from a place that we do know. It is that place that can help us release our anxiety and present confidently, and is often worthy of a story.

If we can tell a story in a one-to-one conversation, we can do the same in presenting to a group.

For introverts, having a good practiced story to open any presentation serves to break the audience's preoccupation with other things on their mind, but more than that, calm ourselves.

We can find stories anywhere but here is an example of one I often use in my public workshops about using networking effectively for business results. So often, people network without a plan, without indicators of what is working for them, and what is not. In my workshop opening I want to give people an idea of how the presented information will help them.

Years ago, when my son was about 10 years old, my husband offered to take him for a ride in an airplane we owned. My husband got his pilot's license a few years before extending the invitation so it was apparent from my son saying, "Sure," that he was feeling comfortable.

What I was told is that on arriving at the hangar my husband and son pulled the plane out to do the pre-flight check. My husband is highly organized and had previously laminated his pre-flight checklist, which most pilots have. My son followed him around the plane as he checked off tires inflated, fuel line clear, no birds caught in the propeller, and so on.

Once complete they each took their respective seats in the plane. My husband started up the engine. As he did, he told my son to put his headset on as they were going to talk with the air traffic controller. My husband followed his own instructions but noticed that my son was not following. "Chris," he asked. "Did you hear me? It's time to put our headsets on."

Holding the headset firmly, and now turning to be sure my husband could hear him, my son said, "Dad, if you have to read about flying the plane, I think I want to stay on the ground instead of fly with you while you are still figuring it out."

This story always gets some laughs and chuckles. The laughs break the preoccupation and I have their attention.

The point relates to the topic, and I move right into my program with this, that just like a pilot has a checklist, someone who networks for business needs a checklist of sorts so they know they are attending the right events, meeting enough people, and even meeting the right people. The purpose of the session is to give you both the checklist and the way to get your networking off the ground.

The story helps bridge the gap between what might be a question in people's mind about what they are going to hear and the beginning of the presentation.

Here is a way we find stories from our lives:

> ➤ Think about a past event in your life that could give you a story. Just a two to three minute story will be enough.

> ➤ Ask yourself whether it could help open an upcoming presentation. If not, think through small events in your life until you find one. We all have them.

> ➤ Make notes of a few stories that come to mind.

> ➤ Find a past story that will be relevant for you in the next presentation.

> ➤ Now, practice, practice, practice, and give it a try.

An opening story can build rapport, relax the audience as we put ourselves on even footing, and even get a laugh.

However, an opening story that does get a laugh or a few chuckles is not to be confused with using a joke. People often wonder, should I and when do I want to use a joke in a presentation?

To joke or not to joke

One of my LinkedIn connections Joe, e-mailed me for some advice about humor. He qualified his e-mail communication as "a fellow introvert" needing advice in the dating area.

After some details of his situation he asked, "Can you offer some advice on how I can have more of a sense of humor being just me and not allow my introvert nature to limit my sociability amongst others in both business and in life?"

The first thing to come to mind was in thinking about my extrovert husband. He listens to a lot of humor. He always has found humor in many life situations.He makes mental notes these days around jokes and funny stories compared to years ago, when he actually carried written notes around with him. He makes all our friends laugh, and with more than jokes.

Many introverts come across in communication as serious-minded so there might be a mismatch between our introvert nature and adding humor when presenting or speaking in public. When I began my speaking career humor was something I had to practice and practice. It is not I felt my sense of humor was lacking but, instead, for the platform it lacked polish.

The main place in a training program or association presentation that I started to use humor was in the opening. If I could find a relevant joke or story that was humorous, it would be my opening if and only if someone who I practiced it with found it funny.

My rule has always been to make someone laugh with my funny story or joke in a one-to-one conversation would be useful on the platform. Using personal experiences are best in particular when they are relevant to the situation. If we are not comfortable with humor we want to practice on people we know well. My husband does this with me too.

Using tested humor both relaxes us and breaks the audience's preoccupation. Of course, now that we have a connection we will also want to keep the rapport as we go along.

The key idea in using humor in a presentation effectively is to refer to a situation that every one or most people can relate to. This helps people feel connected to us. Most of us can find light-hearted humorous situations in our lives. The key is to use a humorous story that is relevant to your topic and are either self-deprecating or at least noncritical of others.

Bob Stowers, a clinical professor of management and leadership communications at the Mason School of Business at the College of William & Mary, writes about whether we should start a presentation with a joke.

Stowers says, "Too often, jokes simply are not funny. Your audience may have heard the joke before. It may not be relevant to what the speaker intends to talk about, or the joke may be offensive. A joke should not be told if it would be offensive to anyone who hears it, a test that may be too high for almost any joke to pass."

My personal experience is that relevancy and personal are key. This translates to a three-way test: if the joke fits, if it is not offensive, and if it makes people laugh, you should be confident using it. Ask yourself "Do I use humor effectively in my one-to-one conversations?" If you can answer yes, then using humor is worth considering for an upcoming presentation. If you answer no, then ask yourself whether you can find any personal funny situations that could be relevant to an upcoming presentation.

Carrying passion naturally into a presentation

We want to tap into our conviction for our topic or the points we want to make so we can be as passionate as we can. People listening are hoping for a speaker both with relevant information and an enthusiastic presentation. Not the "jump up and down" kind of enthusiasm, but instead our passion for the information.

How do we tap into this passion or enthusiasm so we communicate it during a presentation?

Speaking is not extroversion

Often, we think of the gregarious extrovert when we think of presentations and public speaking with passion. Simply because a person gets their energy from outside themselves and in particular from other people, does not suggest that speaking is for the extroverted.

Many conversations on the Internet often bring up celebrities who appear to be more extroverted because we have the association like, "public speaking" is for extroverts. In face these people are often introverts.

Famous actors who are introverts include Glenn Close, Grace Kelly, Julia Roberts, Clint Eastwood, Steve Martin, and David Lettermen. When you consider the business world we can find similar names of people who are introverts who we might mistake as extroverts: Richard Branson, Al Gore, J.K. Rowling, and Steven Spielberg, for example.

In an interview with The Guardian, Journalist and author Malcolm Gladwell tells Sarfraz Manzoor about his experience being a shy public speaker. My guess is Gladwell is more introverted. Early on in his career, he says he would just read what he wrote and then realized that it did not work. The way we speak means a higher standard for clarity, he says.

The way Gladwell believes he has become outstanding is through telling his stories over and over again. It is a role he inhabits when he is on the stage although he is not chatty at dinner parties. This approach might give us some insights on our natural habits that could be good for introverts. What habits do we want to examine, and possibly change, to bring our enthusiasm into a presentation?

Bring in feelings then voice

Our conversation skills, as introverts, can give us a foundation of things to infuse our authenticity in a confident way into any presentation. When we are in one-to-one conversations with people we know we highly likely skip the PowerPoint slides. We use our confidence in the knowledge of what the topic or issue is to pull our enthusiasm into our conversation.

We know many people feel passionate about politics. Maybe you can relate to this?

We also know that people can be passionate when speaking about a recent medical diagnosis that may change their life. Do you remember Steven Jobs speaking publicly about his cancer diagnosis?

If so, then we have an understanding of the fervor of belief around ideology or enthusiasm for an idea.

Think about times when you speak about something like politics or some other issue you are passionate about. It is likely that during such conversations the intensity of our voice changes. One popular study found that about 55 percent of our communication connection comes from the tone of our voice, which includes the range, the pace, and the volume.

We want to avoid a monotone voice in a business presentation if we know we normally speak that way. One year, I hired a voice coach to be able to understand my voice. The one exercise I remember he gave me to do for range is to start a sentence at the high end of my range and end it at the bottom of the voice range. It is like a rollercoaster going from high to low.

We also might want to change the volume of our voice. Many introverts are considered soft-spoken. To be heard, it is partly a matter of where our voice comes from and not appear as we are shouting, which can damage our voice.

The main tip I remember from my voice coach is that I was not bringing in enough breath. The idea is to take in a deeper breath into our lower belly and moving out from there. If we do think about where our voice comes from, most of us bring it out from out throat. That will not get us volume. Speak from the bottom of your belly.

It can take years to perfect our voice, which would be important to us if we were an actor or a public speaker. But for our everyday success in business presentations, find what makes you passionate when in conversation with friends and then use different elements of your voice to help communicate your presentation better.

Shift focus

Words are so important in life. They shape the way we think, which in turn affects what we believe, then directs our actions and this all creates our results. Words also affect our ability to communicate our message passionately.

When I start out any of my presentations or workshops, my memorized opening often helps me to shift focus from myself to other people. The act of storytelling does that, and we can use any kind of opening to do so when we choose the right words.

The right words include "we" instead of "I", and something like "meeting" instead of "presentation". Most introverts do not like the focus on ourselves and to add to the dilemma, external stimulation from others around us compound what might already be making us anxious. Using words like "I" and "presentation" merely reinforce what might already be making us anxious.

According to author Anne Miller, she too believes in the power of words, which because of her ground-breaking work on using metaphors in selling is not a big surprise.

For years, I have followed an online newsletter from Anne Miller, and in interviewing her for this book I discovered I have been on the right track for years not knowing this is an actual tactic to use for those of us who might have their anxiety get in the way.

When using the word "I", in particular, as an introduction to our presentation, it puts the spotlight on us. As introverts, we know this is not as much of a motivator for us as it might be for our extrovert friends. It may even add to our anxiousness.

A simple change to make would be instead of saying something like, "I'll be presenting today about ...", we could say "We'll be ...". The one word change can, just like power poses, change our entire body language to bring our passion into the presentation through this other language.

Additionally, Miller suggested avoiding the word "presentation" if it is used in the introduction. Instead of saying something like, "Today in our presentation, we will be ..." change things to "Today we will be discussing..." or "Today the information we'll be getting into...".

Just two word changes can shift our focus from allowing anxiety to get in the way of our passion coming through.Our voice is our instrument in any presentation. When we strengthen how we use it we both increase our confidence and let the passion come out.

Let our strengths add to the tape measure

So far, we have focused on innate characteristics we have as introverts to help us boost the effectiveness of a presentation of any kind. Sometimes, using a particular presentation skill requires use to either change our perspective of the trait or take the trait and use it differently.

For example, maybe preparation including practice is not an apparent strength but instead it is something considered as a must for better presentations.

Also, taking the naturalness of enjoyable one-to-one conversations and directing some of those characteristics into a presentation may not be something considered previously as fitting into more comfortable presentations.

We do have preferences that energize us, which can add to a confident, comfortable, and effective presentation.

Use statistics

Whether we give a meeting debrief or open up a presentation to a group of two hundred people, there are keys to use statistics to make them more meaningful to the listener. As relates to helping us as introverts, many of us are comfortable with research that helps us to find relevant statistics. The very task puts us on strong footing.

Use statistics sparingly. If we use PowerPoint, one way that points to the often used expression "Death by PowerPoint," is to have a slide full of numbers. This can be distracting and put people off from paying attention.

When we use words in presentation slides, people may or may not spot a misspelling. While misspellings are unprofessional, this kind of error is not as egregious as making a mistake with statistics. Whether intentional to support a position, or unintentional because of a typo, statistical errors can lead to inaccurate conclusions. Misspellings demonstrate lack of proofreading or being a poor speller.

The statistic that 20 percent of salespeople get 80 percent of sales carries with it the understanding that fewer salespeople get more sales. It allows speaking further to the point that it is the better salespeople that get those results. And then, what makes a top salesperson?

Reversing the statement to 80 percent of sales people get 20 percent of sales results, while it may sound the same can lead us to find a cold and intimidating conclusion and water down our points to what makes a top salesperson.

Opening up a presentation with a startling statistic helps us to build the audience's confidence as well as quickly gain their attention. A starting statistic is simply something unexpected. I remember hearing a representative from our local chapter of the American Heart Association open with one, "42 percent of Americans are expected to be obese by 2030." Wow; that is quite unexpected and startling.

The first source to go to is your own research in your field. Then, we can find government websites and even the Pinterest social media website to offer many statistics to consider for an upcoming presentation. Boost the statistic with context, relevancy, and even visuals to increase the audience connection.

Rest a bit with props

One year I was sitting in on a time management workshop and the speaker pulled out a big glass jar. It was filled with large rocks. He asked, "Is the jar full?" Most of us answered yes.

Then he took out a pail from behind the podium, and he showed us it had gravel sized rocks in it. He poured them into the jar and they filled the gaps between the large rocks. Asking again if the jar was full, most of us caught on and said, "No."

One more time he reached for another pail, this one filled with sand. As he poured the sand into the jar he said, "Consider these rocks, gravel, and sand like our things to do. What do you think is the point?"

A few people offered some points such as do the big things first, act on the important things first, and so on.

"Yes," he said. "Put the big rocks in first." Many speakers use this prop act so you too may be familiar with it. Some people credit it to Steven Covey.

One benefit of us using props as introverts is that props always put attention on the prop and the message, and divert it away from the speaker. If you feel you do not want to be in the limelight, consider a prop or two in an upcoming presentation to help redirect the attention.

When you choose a relevant prop it serves the dual purpose of emphasizing your point with words using a visual, as well as shining the light on the message in a creative way.

Being that props are also concrete, it is one more way we can get out of our head of focusing on our self, our anxiousness, or worries in the present message. While we touch a prop, use it, or feel it, it adds to the reality of the moment.

The reason I like props is they often have a surprise to them and in demonstrating this, I am clarifying what could be information not as immediately or clearly understood.

Any prop used needs to be relevant to the topic, just like all aspects we have been discussing. A prop can either be a thing, a good graph, or even a metaphor. The key thing to ask yourself before you use a prop is does it add value? If you can answer yes, then use it.

Ask your questions, listen to theirs

"It is better to know some of the questions than all of the answers."

–James Thurber

Questions are an introvert's friend. We use them often so why not make them work for us in a presentation?

There are our questions and the listener's questions to consider.

Adult understanding is enhanced with participation. Questions encourage participation. Personally I use questions as I go along. Some public speakers, and depending on the presentation purpose, questions can be called for at the end. Timing is more of an individual preference.

Unless your presentation is very short, maybe three or four minutes, relevant questions will let the participants participate, even if it is merely to get a show of hands, so be willing to use a few as you go along.

Many people have questions for even the shortest presentation! As most introverts like to be prepared, include thinking about questions that might be asked during your next presentation. You can think about it and you can ask friends what they might ask.

If someone asks a question, take time to repeat it aloud. This makes sure we understand the question and do not provide an answer that takes us down the wrong trail. It also can buy some much welcome thinking time if we find we are going to need to take many questions.

The important thing about questions is to be ready to ask them and to answer them. If we do not know the answer to a question, the best thing to say is that we do not know but would be willing to find out and get back with an answer.

If it is a question relating to a specific individual problem, offer to have a private discussion later. This will prevent the possibility of having a "side tracker" create a difficult situation.

Reference quotations

Robert Cialdini, Regents' Professor Emeritus of Psychology and Marketing at Arizona State University, refers to quotations as social proof.

Quotations offer support to our own ideas when making a presentation. As an opener, it could be a strong confidence booster to our audience if we used this effective technique. In order to work this way using someone famous or often quoted lends this authority to us.

Besides using quotations we can use them to make a strong ending. We can also use them to support or emphasize a point. If possible, we want to acknowledge the quotation. Sometimes this will be a person's name or a statement such as an old Irish proverb. If you use PowerPoint to present, then having a quotation on a slide as we talk is also effective.

As with statistics, props, and questions, quotations to use are those that are relevant and add support to what we say as the presenter.

Eye contact

When first promoted to sales manager, there were more presentations to give in my new role. Being the introvert temperament type who likes to prepare, as you may know, we often read and research everything we can to find out about what would often escape us in larger meetings.

But what if in that diligent preparation, we avoid eye contact in the delivery of our ideas? Eye contact can be used to both alleviate our anxiousness and get people involved. Remember many people who are in our audience are introverts like us. We do not necessarily like to raise our hand to contribute. When we are the speaker part of our role is to help people feel like we are talking with just them. Eye contact is equally important in presentations as it is in business meetings.

In *Chapter 5, Your Headband Light - Succeeding in the Business Meeting,* on business meetings, I referenced research from a communications analytics company, Quantified Impressions, who reported their findings of 3,000 people. The research found that while, as adults, we make eye contact between 30 percent and 60 percent on average in conversations, the ideal amount of time is 60 percent to 70 percent to create strong connection. Less than this time, and you reduce your credibility.

Rather than guessing what 60 percent to 70 percent of the time equates to, a reminder is to look at a person for whatever time it is to speak a complete phrase or thought. This turns out to be about five seconds.

Because as a presenter all people's eyes are on us, we might find ourselves tempted to look at the table or down at the floor.

Wrong. Do not do this! Our eyes speak to people and just like how we look to our posture to portray and instill confidence, eye contact plays as significant of a role with a group of people. The only difference with eye contact with a group is we move from one person to another by sections in the audience.

Lift your head and look them in the eyes. If you use PowerPoint, the degree to which we master eye contact will lessen any tendencies we have to read from PowerPoint.

PowerPoint presentations

It took me having a ten-year client who called me for management training workshops one year to ask me to use PowerPoint to move into high tech. I still avoid it. Why? Because I learned early on that people sitting in on a presentation are there to listen and often learn from us. They are not there to hear, those of us who fall into the spell of PowerPoint and life tools, watch us, and listen to us as we use it as a crutch.

Here are some key things to consider as an introvert using PowerPoint or Keynote or whatever your choice is for presentation software. If you are using PowerPoint to boost your confidence, do not. Use other tips, techniques, and strategies to do this.

When we think or say, "use PowerPoint to boost confidence," it often means falling into the dark pit of death by PowerPoint where we put almost every word we want to say onto a blank slide. Or, when we read directly from the slide we prevent ourselves from making personal eye contact.

A few years ago, one of our local military commands hired me for an all day workshop on conflict management of different styles of people. This was before that long-term client pulled me into PowerPoint. It turned out to be a good thing. What I discovered was that the base commander disliked PowerPoint so much he banned the use of them.

Follow another's lead

There are extrovert business friends I have who often remark they do enjoy a little down time and they appreciate me talking about it. The truth for us, as introverts, is that there are many things we can learn, tweak, and borrow from the more extroverted.

Tips to polish the presentation before, during, or after the event

A presentation is a highly extroverting activity that includes other people making it an activity that uses high amounts of personal energy. As introverts whose personal energy comes from within, we will find it more necessary than with other business activities to plan purposefully to recharge. There is no one right action or time to manage our energy. Be willing to experiment with different ideas and find what works best for you.

Breathing for energy to minimize anxiousness and raise energy

Take deep breaths, letting air out slowly. Part of the issue with being anxious is that we usually breathe too shallow when we are speaking. Then, by being anxious we are letting our energy escape us as in a slow leak in a balloon.

McFall has a specific breathing tactic if we find we are not sure how to get to our diaphragm instead of staying in our throat. Breathing in a way that relaxes us is valuable to act on before we present. We would likely want to do this in our office or a nearby restroom before heading to the meeting for the presentation:

Tip

- Find your lower belly. This is the part of your stomach that is the most bulging.
- Take a deep breath, deep enough to fill up your lower belly.
- Hold the breath for two to three seconds.
- Then let it all out with a "whoosh" sound.
- Repeat this sequence three times.

Now you have relaxed enough to regain some energy, reduce your anxiety and pull all presentation practice into the moment.

Into and out from your body

Many of us more introverted tend to make ourselves physically smaller either when presenting in a meeting at a table or speaking from the stage. I feel fortunate being of Italian descent because being around many Italian conversations growing up allowed me to bring in some physical gestures to the stage or any presentation to be a visual aid to emphasize and support important points.

Our anxiousness is going to take us more into our head and out of our body. That does little to ground us in the present moment. We will be likely thinking about all the things that can go wrong. Take specific action to ground yourself.

Power poses

Think back to the power poses we explored in a couple of the previous chapters, which were researched by social psychologist Amy Cuddy of Harvard Business School, then remember that a power pose like Wonder Woman or Warrior is one of the easiest and most helpful things we can do.

Deep breathing

Using any kind of deep breathing technique that is either mentioned in this chapter or that you might know of, which is going to bring you into our body.

Purposeful gestures

Also, if it is anxious energy then we can think about and then move our breath into gestures. Gesturing with our hands for important points in order to emphasize them can move that anxious energy out from our body. Think about it this way; energy is usually moving. If we hold in anxious feelings what happens to the energy?

It stays within us. If it is anxious energy it will affect our presentation negatively.

Moving our body, breathing properly, and using appropriate gesturing moves the energy out. Then we can focus on saying what we practiced to make our presentation effective.

Keep people from dozing off

Have you ever been a presentation participant and found yourself dozing or acting in ways that indicated boredom? The last thing we want as a presenter is for people to go from dozing to dying. My goodness this will only add to either other people's misconceptions or the common myth that introverts are not interesting. We know this can apply to any temperament style speaker so let us lead the way.

First, understand that this dozing off and lack of attention is prevalent in presentations and meetings. In our preference to be thoroughly prepared we can put at the top of our mind some things to easily do to interrupt or minimize it.

Verizon recently created a white paper from a study commissioned and conducted by InfoCom in Greenwich, Connecticut.

One finding included that nearly all meeting attendees (91 percent) admit to daydreaming during meetings, while over one-third (39 percent) have dozed.

If you are the presenter for such a meeting, consider what you can do to shift this to people being more focused and alert:

Make a note

- Start the meeting with a question. Wait for a response!
- Speak with "you" and "we" statements.
- Use peoples' names.
- Use eye contact.
- Use questions that require any kind of response.
- Get people to help you with something.
- If you are asking for solutions, use round robin.
- Use a flip chart to capture comments.

Hopefully these suggestions are ones we can practice as well. In your next presentation practice, consider trying to double-up on any of these ideas.

For example, sprinkle in peoples' names that you know will be in attendance, as you ask them a question.Or, as you capture comments on a flip chart or easel, thank people for their contribution by name.

What are you willing to double-up on?

Handling difficult situations

Depending on the interactive nature of a presentation, there can be a number of difficult situations the presenter wants to be ready to manage. The key in being able to do this is to be prepared enough to be flexible with options to try.

Picture this scenario I found myself in during an early year in my public speaking career.

The manager who hired me was excited about customer service training for her department. However, she withheld the truth that some of the participants were hostile about this idea.

Imagine how uncomfortable this situation was when I found out the truth about their discontent when just after she introduced me, one or two people started a highly emotional discussion in the group about their feeling of the uselessness of the upcoming four hours.

In their expressiveness, they started to ramble into areas outside the focus of the training into issues we were not going to address.

As I listened to their complaints my thinking started to shift. Intuitively, I knew my planned and memorized opening would be ineffective, and even fall on deaf ears. Drawing on another opening seemed like the best approach; one that allowed a controlled but further airing of discontent. The next best thing in my assessment was to both use a different opening, and change a couple of the beginning activities to be able to move in closer to the direction of what would meet the decision-maker's intention for the training.

Handling difficult situations hinges on being over-prepared, if we can imagine that! Yes, difficult situations are perfectly aligned for the prepared introvert.

There are many known and common situations that can rear themselves with people in almost every presentation:

> **The rambler**: Participants like the people in the above example. After what seems like an appropriate question or statement, someone starts to talk or complain about issues outside the purpose of the presentation.

> **Unresponsiveness**: A person who tends to not participate.

> **Side conversations**: Two or even three people may be involved with this.

> **Know-it-all or controller**: The person thinks they know everything about what is being presented.

> **Idea shooter down**: The person who argues about almost any idea presented by you or someone else.

To be flexible instead of being thrown off course when any of these situations occur, consider being prepared with a variety of actions to take at different times in a presentation. Each presentation is different and may not warrant every particular approach to minimize difficult situations.

The key to flexibility is an awareness of the fact that there are several options available. Consider these as a starting point for your toolkit:

> **Before presentation**: Discuss the guidelines or meeting ground rules when all or most people are present. If you are familiar with participants' typical behavior, maybe there is a small group known for side conversations, phrase the guideline in a positive light like, "Rather than share your thoughts in a side conversation, share it with the group."

> **During presentation**: Since this is when flexibility counts most, here is an idea for each type of situation above:

>> Listen for a pause in speaking from the rambler and take that as a cue to take back control. Often a thank you or a summary statement for them allows a transition to the next part.

>> Consider that unresponsiveness can come from a variety of reasons. As an introvert, often I do not look like I am participating but as we know we introverts often think things through. To check in with the unresponsive, it may be a simple statement like, "Do you have any thoughts you want to share about this idea?" It makes it okay for them to say yes or no.

>> Most groups dislike side conversations and are hoping the presenter can control it. This subtle approach works: as you are speaking to your point, walk toward the offenders. Then stand by them as you continue. Let your eye contact go from that small group to others in the larger group. This is often enough.

> ➤ Sometimes ignoring someone like the know-it-all who controls the questions or answers, might be appropriate. It's better to address issues as they happen. Take advantage of a break and speak to any specific individual one-to-one about the issue. Offer a suggestion or ask to find a solution together. With the know-it-all, sincerely acknowledge their expertise. Often getting this kind of positive attention is what they are seeking.

> ➤ The people who shoot down ideas are best handled with an acknowledgement and specific request for the good of the group. "I appreciate that we are going to disagree. The thing is that others here do want to consider this to understand it better." Then move back into your presentation.

> ➤ **After presentation**: Direct a conversation to specific individuals, like a person who shoots down ideas, in particular if you know they will likely attend a presentation that you give again.

The key to being able to handle situations that come up is to be flexible, and being flexible means to have a variety of options prepared, which can be put into action. The important thing to remember is that the audience as a whole is on our side in wanting to turn any negative situations into a positive one.

Make a note

Often, the group as a whole will take care of a difficult situation. If the group is small, and you know some of the members consider allowing them to help. Be open to turning some situations, like someone who wants to tear down others ideas, to the group with a simple question, "What does anyone else think?"

Get back up again, quickly

In my first year as a public speaker there were many invitations, both fee and non-fee. One in particular was a total failure

With 300 people finishing up dessert and refreshing their wine or other alcohol, as I looked at the sea of faces from the platform, it felt like I was drowning.

When I left the platform 20 minutes early I immediately sought out the event planner for damage control. "This was a total mismatch. As I suggested to you, while I can be entertaining, I am not an entertainer. Clearly, with drinks after dinner your client wanted entertainment. Please do not charge them and do not pay me for this evening, and let's remain in touch."

Clearly, my intuition to decline was right, and the event planner, well, her assessment of the fit was wrong. Still, the experience was devastating and replayed in my mind a few times before I could release it.

The next week having to speak to a local civic organization pro-bono, I was right back on my feet. Talking things through with a friend helped. The program went splendidly, several attendees purchased my book, and a couple of people asked me to contact them about doing a similar program for them.

It was early in my career and it allowed me to use the lesson to redirect my marketing and focus. After any damage control we can do, like mine in a failed presentation, the next thing to do if you find yourself in an unsuccessful presentation mode is as Buelow says: "Give yourself credit for getting up there and doing something most people—even extroverts—don't want to do!"

In between a presentation failure and your next time at the table or on the platform, we can do what we benefit from often as introverts, and reflect. This reassurance we give ourselves might need some time, space, and discussion with friends.

While we do want to examine what went right and what went wrong, accept that not every presentation is going to bring the audience to their feet with wild applause.

The more effective action to take is to think about successes in presentations and build on them. So while you take time to reflect on any particular presentation, learn from the poor ones and build on the successful ones going forward.

Summary

Presentations can be three minutes or even three hours. Regardless of the time, it takes personal energy to deliver effective presentations, which both meet the intended goal and satisfy the audience. After completing this chapter and before upcoming presentations:

➤ Be clear on your presentation goal before planning it

➤ Practice is your best preparation for improved performance

➤ Vary using statistic, props, quotations, and questions to engage the participants in your presentation

➤ Identify specific actions you will take to reduce anxiety

➤ Acknowledge your introvert style brings some natural tendencies to presenting that can make it comfortable and successful

➤ Assess your one-to-one conversation strengths and appropriately apply what works in a group presentation

➤ Let your vocal quality help to bring passion into presenting to fuel your energy

➤ Over-prepare what to do before, during, and after a presentation for certain difficult situations to maintain or improve flexibility

> ➤ Revisit the personal presentation assessment for any particular area you want to approve and find a chapter tip to take action

Thoughts to contemplate

There are presentation opportunities in business everyday. With the ideas and actions in this chapter, we are now ready to let go of any misconception that being an introvert means your public speaking will be awkward. Instead:

> ➤ How and what you can do to relax more? It is in relaxing about delivering a presentation that our authenticity shines through.

> ➤ Do you acknowledge the smallest a step forward, or focus on things you did not do well? If it is the latter, let that be the next thing you change.

> ➤ Consider starting with what you consider small changes to make for future presentations. First notice how you feel with the changes about your delivery. Then, think about whether feedback from listeners tells you others noticed the change in a positive way. This could be simple, such as "Nice job," which you might not otherwise hear. Then try new actions that cause you to step up to a bigger change. Listen to yourself and others' feedback.

Too many quiet voices do not get heard and too many valuable ideas go unspoken because of fear of public speaking. Many of our natural introvert preferences and traits are an asset to public speaking and presentations. Let us use those and then build up any extroverting to make every next presentation our best.

Bibliography

- Julia Barnickle, Business Coach helping introverts build a business online, http://www.thequietentrepreneur.com

- Bob McIntosh, CPRW, http://www.thingscareerrelated.com

- Michel Neray, Speaker, Founder of MoMondays, Consultant on Differentiation; www.neray.com and www.MoMondays.com

- Beth Buelow, www.TheIntrovertEntrepreneur.com, Insight: *Reflections on the Gifts of Being an Introvert*

- Snowden McFall, President of Fired Up, a professional speaking, authorship and coaching company, http://www.firedupnow.com, *Fire Up! Your Presentation Skills* audio program

- Bob Stowers, clinical professor of management and leadership communications at the Mason School of Business at the College of William & Mary

- Anne Miller, Presentation and Sales Specialist, author of *The Tall Lady With The Iceberg: The power of metaphors to sell, persuade & explain anything to anyone*, http://www.annemiller.com/

Do You Have an Axe to Grind? Use a Positive Approach for Workplace Conflict

"If we manage conflict constructively, we harness its energy for creativity and development."

-Kenneth Kaye, American Psychologist

If you have ever been scheduled to fly only to have your flight canceled, it can, particularly when you are stressed and tired, lead to conflict with airline staff. It may not be easy dealing with feelings of frustration but the airline staff is doing their job the best they can to get you where you want to go. On a particular flight that was canceled I recall observing the tactics of the person ahead of me to find a new flight; watching the scene unfold before me, I believe I discovered a better way of heading off a potential conflict.

As a people-watcher, I observed that some of the over one hundred people around me were angry, others were frustrated, and some grateful to finally know the status of things to be able to move on with their plans.

After some time, the person ahead of me finally reached the airline agent; my focus then fell on the interaction between the passenger directly ahead of me and the agent.

The customer started his approach with loud and uncomplimentary phrases like, "You idiots," and "How dare you!" and "Well what are you going to do for me?"

I was shocked at how quickly the conversation escalated to anger and aggression. While I could not hear every word after those choice remarks, what I could see was a total mismatch of a highly animated upset passenger and an agent reigning in gestures and speaking in soft tones.

While there was certainly something to complain about, was it really necessary to be quite so aggressive? It seems absurd to expect a positive and agreeable outcome from such behavior. My approach was radically different.

Immediately, I let the agent know that I understood the overwhelming nature of their task, given there were over one hundred passengers inconvenienced.

I then confirmed in my behavior, and words, that "I would be patient," as they found my next outbound flight availability. I discovered later in the evening this win-win approach paid off with more make-up gifts than most people—free hotel, free transportation to and from the hotel, free dinner and breakfast, and a complimentary round-trip ticket to anywhere in the United States in the next twelve months.

Some of us might see conflict as bad or wrong, but this view can sometimes cause arguments to escalate as we may believe we have an axe to grind. Conflict happens because of opposing needs, wants, goals, or values. Often what comes from conflict resolution is a more ideal solution.

In the workplace, conflict is simply a fact of life; the issue is how we deal with it. If we handle situations of conflict effectively we will be able to get a result that should at least have some positives for us. Moreover, handling conflict effectively will also mark you at as a strong leader and someone who is able to deal with tricky situations, earning you the respect of your peers and those above you.

Make a note

Workplace conflict is not that dissimilar to conflict with people outside of work. However, there are some unique aspects. The causes vary from poor communication, different values, disparate interests, vying for the same resources, and personality clashes. In this chapter you will:

- Assess your personal understanding of conflict
- Understand specific workplace conflict causes
- Be able to decide whether or not to confront a particular conflict
- Understand and be able use assertive communications in conflicts you choose not to ignore
- Be able to identify different styles of conflict management we use
- Recognize our introvert strength of thinking things through can give us a better position
- Learn some techniques to be able to better manage your energy depletion from conflict stress
- Discover how you can benefit from workplace conflict

It is time to put away the axe and instead find better tools to bring to everyday workplace conflicts.

How do you manage conflict?

Whether you are a manager managing a conflict or someone caught in a conflict situation, it helps to have a variety of skills and options to manage these situations.

Think back to any recent conflicts: maybe you could not finish your job because someone else did not complete theirs, or you have been approaching your work creatively but it has not received as you had hoped by a target driven manager, or your educational background and life experiences are not being tolerated by a co-worker.

Keep these disagreements in mind as you answer the following statements with only one of the words in the Scale of Words. The more honest you answer, the clearer your understanding of how you generally approach conflict will be and more options for the future.

Conflict management understanding

	Never	Rarely	Sometimes	Often	Always
I understand conflict is natural					
Everyone's viewpoint is valid in conflict					
I listen to understand each co-workers view in a conflict situation					
I stand up for what I believe being best for all					
In resolving conflict I am respectful of others but not intimated					
Conflict situations are not equal					
Different conflicts require different handling					
In conflict it is best to focus on the issues					
Conveying blame is one of the least helpful ways to solve conflict					
A creative and best solution for all can come from conflict management					
Ignoring conflict does not make it go away					
Conflict can be emotional and bring up ill feelings					
Working collaboratively helps in reaching a mutually acceptable resolution					
Listening and asking questions is important to get resolution					
Unresolved conflict can cost in productivity, stress and escalation of the issue					

Score interpretation

Score the words you identified with each statement:

- ➤ Never: 2 points
- ➤ Rarely: 4 points
- ➤ Sometimes: 6 points
- ➤ Often: 8 points
- ➤ Always: 10 points

This assessment is to give you an awareness of your understanding of conflict. This understanding is the first step in developing your skills and improving the way you handle conflict. It is not complete, certified, or representative of any validated instrument.

Put the score you chose for each item on the appropriate numbered line below. Each style indicates the statement numbers associated with it. Then add up each scale.

My total score = _____

High conflict understanding (120 to 150)

Some conflict understanding (90 to 120)

Minimal conflict understanding (60 to 90)

Need to at least complete chapter (30 to 60)

Higher scores indicate that you understand that conflict is normal and often a necessary component in change and development in the workplace. Lower scores indicate that you may need to increase your knowledge of what workplace conflict is and how to manage it more effectively.

Some of our introvert tendencies such as thinking things through, listening more, and talking after thinking, may put us in a strong position to deal with conflict more effectively.

In addition, thinking things through can help us decide when one style might be better than another in a conflict situation. Finding a resolution to most conflicts is easier with an understanding of the causes, and deciding how best to confront it. It is in this type of planning that we can also be sure to design and include ways to manage our energy.

What causes workplace conflict?

During my seven years as a sales manager in the 1980s, I saw more conflict than my previous seven years as a salesperson. It might be someone claiming someone else stole an idea they had. Or it could be the technician staff claiming too much demand on their time. Sometimes retail salespeople would clash over who was to greet the next walk-in customer.

Whatever the conflict, I would speculate about all possible causes; it could be communication, or maybe a clash of personalities. It might be the sales pressure, or even that more conflict was happening because I was new manager.

A 1996 study referenced in Leadership Quarterly showed that 42 percent of a manager's time is spent on reaching agreement with others when conflicts occur. A later one in 2005 reported in the Washington Business Journal stated it another way: one to two days every work week a manager is dealing with workplace conflicts.

Employees spend about 3 hours a week dealing with conflict. As you can imagine, this results in lost productivity, poor relationships, and can even escalate to litigation in some instances.

As a manager needing to address conflict, when a disagreement surfaces among staff I would sort through possible causes with them to identify the root of the issue and then take action on how best to handle it.

Fortunately for us in the early 2000s, psychologists Art Bell and Brett Hart identified eight causes of conflict. Knowing the type of conflict is helpful, whether we are a manager or an employee, before we decide on a resolution approach.

The eight causes of workplace conflict, according to this valuable research, are as follows:

> ➤ **Conflicting needs**: In my canceled flight story, the inconvenienced passenger needs to get to a destination, and the agent needs to rearrange the flights on the schedule for every passenger. It is often helpful to see things from another's perspective to be able to discuss better or more solutions. Conflicting needs can include resources such as office space, a meeting room, and help from staff or supplies. Often, when multiple people need a particular resource there can be conflict.

> ➤ **Conflicting styles** : Our introvert and extrovert styles have central differences in approaching people and tasks. It can be an issue such as all staff working in a bullpen-like office environment where the extroverts usually thrive from the conversation and the introverts usually clam up to reserve their energy for the most important tasks.

> When you understand your own style it can help you better understand someone else's. This acknowledgement of differences will enable you to either be more flexible or to find a more effective way to better communicate your position.

> ➤ **Conflicting perceptions**: Different perceptions can cause office politics. My extrovert husband unwittingly sparked a power struggle when he brought in an associate with as much of an ego as his own to help with a new need of an established client. His perception was that she could help; her perception was an open door to taking control of a new client for her. Introverts might take more time to think through different options. When my husband and I looked back, he decided he did not communicate as fully as he might have with the associate. A pre-discussion might have solved a big part of the problem. Everyone looks at life and situations from a different perspective; the best way to deal with conflicts that arise from different perspectives is through discussion and effective communication.

➤ **Conflicting goals:** As a sales manager for many years, my goals often conflicted with the marketing manager's goals. My staff had sales goals to meet and her goals included using advertising dollars from manufacturers, which might not be offered again if left unused. Often, conflicting goals are difficult to reconcile when the goals are both a priority. Anyone in different departments, both accomplishing a goal, can have differences.

➤ **Conflicting pressures**: People are responsible for separate actions with the same due date. The operative situation is that there is either a due date or an urgent need. My experience as sales manager was wrought with conflicting pressures affecting many groups of staff. We had retail salespeople and outside corporate and government salespeople. Often, their sales demands would collide and put the technicians and installers in conflict as to who comes first.

➤ **Conflicting roles**: We either might be asked to complete a project outside our normal job or we may get assigned to a different job handled by another associate.

This is often closely related to the point above about conflicting perceptions, as evidenced in my example of my husband and an associate. Clearly, when someone is asked to work outside their normal responsibilities it can cause power struggles.

➤ **Different personal values**: Midway in my coaching career, I was working with a young woman who felt enormous conflict between her personal value system and some tasks her boss was asking her to do. She both felt the conflict, and he admitted he was aware of the underhandedness. She was struggling with having a conversation with him to set things right for fear of further conflict and the possibility of losing her job. There is a big difference between knowing the right thing to do and actually doing it. Values are as different as each person and in our context, differ for introverts and extroverts. Regardless of whether we're more of an introvert or extrovert, when we are asked to take on tasks that conflict with our values conflict can escalate.

➤ **Unpredictable policies**: Companies may change their policies for many reasons—sometimes good, sometimes bad. Whatever the reason, being caught between old policies and processes and new ones can lead to confusion, and, indeed, conflict. Even workplace policies that are inconsistently applied lead to confusion and conflict. Policies that are fair and consistent help to keep harmony in the workplace. Knowing the causes of conflict is helpful in sorting out more important issues and understanding effective solutions. While we cannot prevent all conflict in the workplace we can have tools readily at hand to be prepared to manage and reduce issues.

As our focus remains on helping those of us more introverted to be able to better deal with workplace conflict, which is diverse with personality types. We can devise some better strategies in four conflict causes in particular:

➤ Needs
➤ Styles
➤ Perceptions
➤ Values

When is conflict worth confronting?

"The truth is that our finest moments are most likely to occur when we are feeling deeply uncomfortable, unhappy, or unfulfilled. For it is only in such moments, propelled by our discomfort, that we are likely to step out of our ruts and start searching for different ways or truer answers."

-M. Scott Peck, psychiatrist and author, The Road Less Traveled

Have you ever had a situation that went from bad to worse and as you thought back on it you said to yourself, "I knew I should have said something?"

In some situations silence speaks loudly. In other situations, future problems are avoided when a problem is dealt with at the beginning. In my experience, avoiding conflict is rarely useful to anyone or any situation.

For many years I served in a leadership role in one of the oldest women's networking association in the USA. For two terms I was Vice President of Membership, increasing the membership about 25 percent in my first term and then maintaining steady growth in my second.

It was time after that to be a Member at Large and serve on the board in a less time-consuming capacity. While many younger women were taking leadership roles, they spoke to me about wanting members with knowledge of the organization's history to continue to be active in the decision-making. That of course translated to a board position.

Towards the end of my second year on the board as a Member at Large, some of the members started changing things around. Some things were of less consequence—the location or the time of the monthly meeting, or whether to have only networking or a speaker and networking, for example. But some things were major—the logo, the mission statement, and the vision.

In the meeting with the 16 members that this discussion came up in for the third time, the president called for a committee to start the work. My introversion trait of thinking things through was in full gear. I had three months to consider what good and bad could come from too hasty action.

For an organization guided by a mission statement and vision for 35 years, my thinking was that it would not be wise to undertake this in a few board meetings so I decided to speak up against this as my next step. If you think ever think it is uncomfortable to confront just one person, think about the whir of anxiety with fifteen sets of eyes on you.

There was a conflict between newer members and longevity members. Newer members wanted to move ahead quickly with changes. There were immediate opportunities they wanted to attract with the changes. Longevity members wanted to know the why, what, and how of making such changes. They wanted to be certain that things were thought through for the long term. This was a conflict of both perceptions and possibly changed policies.

What resulted were evaluation, planning, and a strategy for several meetings. Instead of moving to make the changes, send a request for proposals for the logo design, and rewriting the mission, I challenged them to consider the bigger picture.

This led to a series of facilitated meetings, open to the entire membership of about 150 women, to come and discuss what the organization meant to them and how they were benefiting or not.

Out of that the board discovered their strengths and weaknesses. Those were prioritized, committees were formed, and women became focused and energized. This was going to mean the possibility of membership growth.

While I was unable to attend the annual meeting when the new mission, vision, and logo were unveiled, I heard from many members. They thanked me for speaking up. They were grateful they had not acted hastily and that I confronted things to give them the better course of action. Members were ecstatic with the new direction of things.

Many of us are uncomfortable with conflict and want to avoid it. The truth is, and if you consider the many causes, then conflict is going to happen. There will often be discord with people because of different ideas and opinions. But by addressing conflict early on we can avoid major affects it is proven to have on productivity and morale.

Is the conflict worth confronting?

One of our introvert traits to think things through can be helpful in conflicts where immediate action is not necessary.

We know that spending time alone, whether related to problem solving or conflict, can give us the time we need to reflect. This allows us time to strategize the next best steps for the situation.

Thinking time can include asking more questions. A variety of questions are useful in conflict. Some might be fact-based questions like, "How will ignoring this be helpful?" or the opposite, "How will speaking out about this help?"

Other questions can be more open-ended or exploratory questions like "What are some different ways to resolve this?"

Once you have focused your own thoughts, another useful and comfortable approach preferred by introverts would be to take the opportunity for in-between group meetings to have one-to-one meetings. During these more intimate conversations, we can discover all individual ideas, and get a broader picture to help you decide on the worthiness of addressing the situation or not. This is helpful to be more prepared to flush out our own approach if we decide confronting is the best option.

By asking questions of yourself and others, and then listening to those answers, we discover how to create a win-win conflict situation.

What is the cost of confronting or not confronting?

Confronting conflict is never comfortable. It is one reason, at least in the United Sates, that government often gets little done on big issues. All parties are reluctant to anger their constituents. But quite often the constituents are negatively affected by this behavior.

Ignoring a conflict is useless. Just like ignoring spurting and spurring sounds in a car, ignoring a bad situation only gets worst as time goes on.

If you think your frustration with a situation is spurting and spurring louder and gunkier, it is likely that others are affected the same way.

We may find other questions to ask before we make a decision if it is worth addressing a particular conflict.

The key is that as an introvert, let's take a stand to reserve our right to think things through before we act in those situations that are not as immediately as crystal clear.

In my example above, the results of confronting the conflict were positive. The conflict was resolved by finding a better way forward for all concerned.

The president was receptive. Even some members who wanted to act more quickly were not disappointed with the results.

You must remember to say what you think, provided you deliver it in a constructive and forward-thinking way. It is only through open dialog that a consensus can be reached. This may sometimes require compromises but it will nevertheless help to reduce the chance of conflict happening.

Styles of conflict management that can work for an introvert

My primary style of conflict management is often identified as a collaborator. It is a style I developed in a couple of decades of work experience and general life experience. This is a style that balances both assertiveness and cooperation. This "I win, you win" general approach takes more time and relies on trust and clear communication. Not every situation calls for this style and not everyone has it as their primary style.

If you or your company has access to one of the validated instruments such as the Thomas-Kilman Conflict Mode Instrument, the Rahim Organizational Conflict Inventory, or the Emotional Intelligence Test, it would be worth the time of about 30 minutes to more fully assess your conflict dominant tendency.

Over the years starting with Blake and Mouton in 1964, various studies have analyzed a popular five-style approach to conflict. Then in the 1970s Thomas and Kilman reinterpreted this initial work. Today, this popular conflict management tools is called the five styles conflict: competition, avoidance, accommodation, collaboration, and compromise. Most corporate conflict management training uses this five style model, which measures the degree of two dimensions of a person's level of assertiveness and cooperation in conflict.

It is because of this two-dimension balance often described as characteristic of the extrovert (assertiveness) and introvert (cooperative) that this five-style model is most appropriate for our purposes of making those of us more introverted more comfortable and competent in conflict management.

Research using the MBTI, Myers-Briggs Type Indicator®, shows that individuals who tend to be introverted are more likely to try and avoid conflict. Introverts prefer to observe a situation and hold back their thoughts and feelings. This is different than the extrovert preference to often talk things through until the matter gets resolved.

For those of us more introverted, after thought and deliberation we may be ready to act. But we are not so inclined to spontaneously assert ourselves in, or to initiate any conflict.

Because we know introverts who avoid conflict can be labeled as weak, our learning approach will take advantage of not engaging in conflict until the situation is right and we are prepared. We are not going to withdraw but instead we are going within. Then we can come back and address the issue and solution.

Dr. Christine Bacon, communication expert, seminar leader and radio show host, summed up the importance of bringing your strengths into conflict by saying "In today's modern society basic human respect and civility are becoming rarer and rarer and people often focus on our differences as if they are weaknesses and not strengths. Conflict between introverts and extroverts can serve to take advantage of the strengths of each and foster substantial growth in both."

The following sections explore some ideas on how to make conflict work for our introvert style in each of the five styles as briefly assessed above in this chapter.

Competition

The conflict style of competition can be a win/lose proposition. It tends to be high on assertiveness while low on cooperation. If you have ever been in a meeting where someone tries to be argumentative or disagreeable with a basic and even previously determined point, this is the competition style. It might sound like, "Let's get down to the real issue."

Make a note

When using a competing conflict style, weigh the pros and cons, listen with openness to possibly change your mind, and be willing to evaluate all options. Then decide and act.

One morning on arriving to work as a salesperson with a computer retailer, I walked into a lot of hustle bustle. There was a fire in the store the night before and the majority of staff was just getting to work. People wanted to be helpful but our manager saw it another way: safety comes first. This was a situation where a quick decision was needed and safety was the top priority. Formal authority often gives this competing or forcing style the advantage. Even though many people, including me, were disappointed, our offer to help in some way was rejected, the style which showed up as "Everyone leave and let me and my manager take care of things," was likely to be the better approach.

Avoidance

An avoidance style is the least helpful as it does not confront the conflict and cannot satisfy either person's concerns. It is both uncooperative and unassertive.

It has its place in the workplace when the issue is so simple that actually confronting anything just wastes time.

It might be a comfortable approach for an introvert if we believe that the best approach is to buy time by waiting which gives more angry people time to cool off. As introverts, we are more likely to observe both the situation and our own thoughts so we can be more confident before we act. It is not a passive effort unless you do not come back to confront the situation.

Make a note

When you want time to think things through, or let a hot head cool down, agree on a future time to revisit the situation.

We may not react to a conflict situation or provoke it unless the given situation has some sort of meaning for us, such as having a stake in the problem at hand. However, be sure that as an introvert we are not either suffering from "paralysis from analysis", or struck by fear and anxiety. Sometimes there is an advantage in waiting for a situation to develop before acting or speaking, but whatever the nature of the situation, let's be sure we are able to get a positive outcome.

According to Christine M. Bacon, most often "An extrovert is not going to give the introvert time to think through the issue because history has shown them that, if they do back off, the introvert will rarely come back to talk about the issue." She is an extrovert and it is what she believes.

My tip for this is to end your request to revisit the issue by suggesting a date to reconvene and to state that you'll both focus on this issue at that time.

Accommodation

The accommodating conflict style is low on assertiveness and high on cooperation. The focus is more on being a peacekeeper of a relationship rather than getting a specific result. It involves listening more, something introverts do naturally. Using this style means satisfying the other person's concerns at the expense of your own.

Make a note

Use your thinking things through preference to balance attention on both the relationship and the issues before deciding to either keep the peace or defend your position.

Sometimes introverts express that they feel as if their ideas go unheard. Maybe you have reasons about why you deserve a corner office, or why you want to take the lead with a new client. Before you accommodate, as introverts are frequently inclined to do, consider the effect of all parties involved.

Collaboration

As I mentioned earlier, my conflict style falls here on assessments. When faced with a workplace conflict I tend to behave in a manner that is both assertive and cooperative. I act in ways to seek a win-win and often, a win-win-win. There are often more than the immediate parties affected. A triple win means satisfaction for me, the direct people involved, and stakeholders outside the key people, for example customers or another department.

Make a note

This is a primary conflict style for many people. It encourages creative problem-solving, which will help them move towards a win-win outcome.

When I was a sales manager, the CEO made a decision to change salespeople's compensation. Fortunately he and I realized this might cause unnecessary conflict if we did not involve the sales members before a final change went into effect. In this particular situation, we got ahead of the conflict and averted it by collaborating in advance.

Our approach included the announcement to revamp the commission structure with the input of the sales team members.

A collaborative approach often involves meta-discussions; discussion about the discussion. That is just what happened. We held a larger meeting for all to attend and then met with individuals who wanted one-to-one attention. These typical actions are healthy either as an advance strategy to avert conflict, or to act on in a conflict.

Introverts may have less chance to be embarrassed using a collaborative style because creativity is more collaborative and we do not have as much chance in losing in the ultimate decision.

Compromise

Neither assertiveness nor cooperation is high; instead the conflict is settled with partial satisfaction for all people. It often is the result, which we can sum up in the expression, "agree to disagree."

Make a note

If you have a tendency to make pragmatic decisions, this might be the most viable style. If you are more concerned about the people affect from a conflict and feel stress from the situation, a compromise, even if it feels like a loss, can stable the situation so you can move forward at a later time.

This style will work best when we can be objective with our assessment of where differences lie as well as being able to bring in facts to the decision. The type of resolution from this style required each party to give up something to reach an agreement.

Recently, one of my family members was taking in a new tenant in their rental house. The tenant had no previous experience with rental agreements. There were many requirements my family member wanted, not considered abnormal to most but certainly to someone who never rented before.

One requirement was a security deposit. This was something my family member wanted to be able to help get the house ready. The potential tenant did not understand this, even after an explanation of the purpose of a deposit.

But the tenant's reason was because of a financial burden. Even though my family member wanted the security deposit all at once to ease their burden, they decided instead to compromise, and ask for the deposit over three months. An agreement was reached to get the signed rental agreement.

What is necessary to get to a compromise is communication skills that will help you get to the root of the issue, willingness to meet some of the other's needs through cooperation, and standing firm on anything that would compromise your own integrity. In this example, each party was willing to cooperate with the other to get to a mutual agreement.

Acknowledging our preference

When my work as a sales manager changed to more of sales and marketing role, I approached my boss with a request for both a change in title and a raise in salary. We did not see things in the same way. It was a conflict that led naturally to a negotiation. He did acknowledge a change in my role and so getting the title was easier for him to agree to, at first. Initially, I accepted this splitting of the difference because I knew I would have future facts to more strongly support a negotiation for the salary increase.

Each approach has its strengths and weaknesses for any particular conflict situation. Additionally, we will each have a natural tendency to act on one style over another. The key to choosing effectively is to know the stakes of the situation, to acknowledge what strengths we bring to conflict and to understand we have the ability to choose to use any one of the styles.

Emotional Intelligence (EQ) for better conflict management

The 2002 research of E. Michael Nussbaum, University of Nevada, How Introverts versus Extroverts Approach Small Group Argumentative Discussions, rolled two studies in one report and included eight 6th grade students and sixteen service teachers, with college juniors and seniors enrolled in a college course.

Three of the conclusions from the totality of the study were extroverts prefer the excitement from the give and take in arguing, which lessens their concerns about winning or losing, introverts prefer constructive arguments versus conflicts because of the intellectual stimulation, and introverts prefer more cooperative modes of argumentation.

These findings juxtapose an inner thinking approach against a feeling one. Thinking and feeling are at opposite ends. Feeling usually happens as a response to our thoughts. In business, we can use our feelings to help guide our thinking. For example, if we think we have a chance of winning in a conflict, we can feel good about ourselves and our approach, even if it is in the give and take of arguing. If we think we could lose in a conflict, we might feel frustrated, at a loss of what to do, or prefer a more substantiated approach. While as introverts we may prefer an inner thinking approach to conflict, eventually resolving it in any model leads us to act on tactics outside us, outside our thinking, and between us and other people.

Conflict brings up negative feelings and emotions. Feelings like stress can bring up emotions of confusion or over the longer-term even stress.

Knowing something intellectually is not a guarantee we will be able to manage our emotions in situations of conflict. Being intellectually stimulated on its own is ultimately not what will win in disagreements. It is when we use that intelligence to know what and how our emotions affect a certain situation that we can better manage a resolution.

This ability to identify, control, and express our emotions, as well as understand and respond to the emotions of others, is Emotional Intelligence, EQ.

In my later years as a sales manager I felt shocked when one of my top salespeople who I thought I had a close relationship with confronted me in a manner about a particular issue. I discovered he first broke protocol and went to my manager and then he finally spoke with me. The situation caused me to be emotionally angry. If you have ever been angry you know it takes a lot of energy to be angry. I could manage my shock of his approach more easily than I could manage my anger.

I had to acknowledge my feelings and emotions. Often the response to our feelings can be quick since we are immediately in touch with them. But our emotions might take time to surface and identify. But it is only then we can know whether a conflict situation is worth confronting.

This situation with my sales person took both understanding my feelings and being able to consider a structured even cerebral approach like the five-style model of conflict.

For decades, using personality assessment such as the Myers-Briggs Type Indicator® (MBTI) have been used for personal development, leadership development, and team building in the workplace. Then studies in the 1980s and 1990s showed less of a correlation between IQ (intelligence quotient) and career success. One result in the late 1990s was to give more attention to examining the effect of emotional intelligence and improving it on a personal level.

Workplace conflict, being interpersonal situations, can often be difficult for an introvert to manage because we tend to be more effective in the intrapersonal, knowing ourselves, including our emotions and feelings. Our preferred interpersonal relationships are for more intimate and smaller groups, and not wanting to spend so much time in anything of a large group nature. But because we are highly self-aware from our preference of time alone, we usually have more of an understanding of our own inner processes. This distinction is in line with Carl Jung's personality typologies in the popular book, *Psychological Types*.

In a situation of conflict, there are multiple people with emotions surrounding the issue to be resolved. As introverts we might have the tendency for intellectual introspection and self-evaluation of our emotions. But it might be those of us more introverted who can also practice and be more diligent with exercising both IQ, intelligence quotient and EQ, emotional intelligence, to bring in a fuller response to conflict situations.

We can use our EQ to help

A possible dilemma is that we may be able to easily acknowledge our thoughts, emotions, and feelings, but we may not be able to express or display them. Additionally, we need to understand and acknowledge the emotions of the other stakeholders. Think of resolving a conflict situation as needing the use of two muscles: our intellectual muscle and our emotional muscle.

Our Emotional Intelligence provides the balance to what we likely have already discerned through our intellect of the situation, so let's strengthen it too.

Emotional Intelligence is a term usually attributed to the original 1985 research of Wayne Payne as well as the 1995 book Emotional Intelligence by Daniel Goleman. Today, Emotional Intelligence evolved to be abbreviated as EQ. It is knowing and using our feelings in a way to motivate others and ourselves to managing our communications and relationships.

How can we combine a cognitive model, which our personality preference may tend toward, with our emotional handling of conflict?

We are whole

There is no correlation that EQ can predict IQ or vice versa. But experts do agree that our IQ, usually established in our mid-teens, is not flexible. Our EQ is changeable and can be improved during our lifetime.

Our personality, including the trait of introversion, is a result of preferences and some theorize brain pathway differences, and is stable over our lifetime.

Whether we are an introvert or an extrovert, whether we have a higher or a lower IQ, we can all change our EQ.

Why consider EQ? According to Travis Bradeberry and Jean Greaves in *Emotional Intelligence 2.0*, "EQ tends to have a wide-ranging, positive impact on our life."
It is the foundation for a host of critical skills, such as conflict management.

How our EQ can help in conflict

One of my administrative people on my sales team was a relatively personable, although quiet, young woman. After a poor sales year, when people were expecting an annual raise in salary, I was not able to give as generously as I wanted. One day, totally taken off guard, the woman's husband came in to our offices and asked to meet with me. He verbally unloaded what were his and her feelings, without her presence, about being treated unfairly with the compensation increase.

My initial focus was to allow him to "let it all out" while I listened to get all the information. This helped me understand how I wanted to react: ask him to leave. He was not even an employee after all.

I was able to manage my initial reactive thinking and start to focus on my awareness of what was happening. They were young, no doubt in love, and he was the knight in shining armor for her distasteful situation. He did not have all the information. He did not know I went to bat for her but my boss turned me down.

It was up to me as the perceived cause of the conflict to manage the situation. When the husband seemed finished, and I did ask if he had anything else to add, I moved toward talking about how to remedy the situation, without being able to give her an appropriate raise.

Any conflict causes feelings like anger, confusion, disappointment, worry, even fear, to arise in us. Conflict is both emotional and rational. Managing conflict is relationship management as well as recognizing our own emotions and thoughts about the situation.

Today we can reference and even assess our EQ, with the EQ model. There are four skills that make up EQ that essentially create balance to effective conflict management:

➤ One part of the balance includes two personal competencies of the intrapersonal nature: self-awareness and self-management

➤ The other part of the balance is two social competencies or interpersonal skills of social awareness and relationships management

Because intrapersonal skills are focused on our inside thinking and feeling awareness introverts may be more predisposed to put them into action effectively. It is a focus on us as individuals rather than our interactions with others.

Extroverts may possess stronger interpersonal skills as their personality is, as the word suggests, focused on what is outside of themselves. This competency focus is on other people and their moods and behaviors.

Those feelings cause us to behave in a certain way when dealing with conflict. While this is often under the surface and subtly permeates our thinking, it is, most importantly, through the actions we take that we affect the outcome of a given situation.

With most everyday workplace conflict, listening alone is not as effective. We need to use our listening to then get involved with and work with the other person or people in the conflict to move toward resolution. Take steps in your next inevitable conflict to balance your listening with using what you learn to manage the relationship. This effectively can combine our personality while improving our EQ.

Managing your energy depletion from conflict stress

Conflict, whether in the workplace or in our personal lives, is stressful. Conflict can bring up strong emotions and even create body tension.

Stress can come from the frustrations and anger around unresolved conflict. We want to be able to manage our unpleasant emotions during conflict to be able to respond positively. If we let stress take its toll then we will find ourselves with little energy or positive emotion to bring to the situation.

To be able to manage our energy is to be able to more easily resolve the conflict while taking care of ourselves.

Control what you can

Stress limits our ability to think and communicate clearly and reduces our awareness of our feelings. It also prevents us from listening and engaging with others as effectively as we can, which may lead to more problems.

Rather than making conflict a choice between winning or losing, make the priority a creative and mutually beneficial resolution.

When we focus on a mutual win we can find better ways to respond and be sure whichever style we choose to put in action is one we have thought through.

Work on your self-confidence

In *Chapter 3, Confident to Communicate*, we considered our self-confidence in a wide range of situations, including conflict.

Being quiet and calm in uncertain conflict situations, can allow us to bring cohesiveness to a noncohesive situation. This gives us time to more clearly identify the problem and propose something mutually agreeable, even creative, in the end.

Keep this trait at the top of your mind to strengthen often weakened confidence, which we might take into a difficult situation.

Acceptance of conflict as normal

Like we can count on rush hour every day, conflict is going to happen in life and in the workplace. There are causes for it, times to walk away, and times to confront it and then turn it into an opportunity for growth.

When we want to think through the best ways to respond to a conflict, instead of talking a solution out loud, stress will put the brakes on our effective response.

As an introvert I have found that I am in touch with my thoughts regularly and this puts me closed to being able to express even my negative feelings without too much yelling or shouting. When a situation turns up the heat on my frustration or anger, I might back off yet only to clear all that wispy gray smoke out of my head for a clearer perspective.

Bacon suggests when possible to incorporate the 24-Hour Rule. The 24-Hour Rule says this: if there is conflict and one of the parties is not ready to deal with it, then that party holds up a timeout signal.

Both parties then walk away to process the issue their own way. However, at some point within the next 24 hours the person who called timeout is responsible to come back to the issue.

This is helpful for introverts because it gives them the realization that there is an issue, what the issue is, and time to process it internally. This is also helpful for the extroverts because they have time to calm down, flip over from their brain's emotion center to its logic center, and then process the issue externally by talking it through with another party or by writing the issue down.

It is important to manage our stress from conflict because general occupational research shows this is related to work dissatisfaction, depressions, absenteeism, and physiological measures such as heart rate and blood pressure.

It is also reasonable from this research to accept the theory that different conflict styles can cause different levels of stress. If it true that our general introvert tendency is to retreat from conflict, the nature of this action being the ambiguity of whether a problem is solved or not, will often create more stress.

Can you benefit from workplace conflict resolution?

> *"Successful leaders manage conflict; they don't shy away from it or suppress it but see it as an engine of creativity and innovation. Some of the most creative ideas come out of people in conflict remaining in conversation with one another rather than flying into their own corners or staking out entrenched positions. The challenge for leaders is to develop structures and processes in which such conflicts can be orchestrated productively."*
>
> *–Ronald Heifetz and Marty Linsky, authors, The Practice of Adaptive Leadership*

Given people have different needs, styles, perceptions, and values, many times we have to expect conflict. But we can also resolve the conflict in a healthy way. When there is no resolution and feelings fester or when the resolution is disagreeable in some way, it cannot be called healthy.

Healthy conflict resolution can benefit individuals as well as the organization.

Improved self-knowledge

Growing from conflict is inevitable. For every situation I have been part of my awareness of my effectiveness becomes clearer. More options open up. Yes; we are able to present facts and data and be convincing about things. But we can also be aware of how emotions and feelings can affect the situation and know how to steer things. It is in the end up to us whether we stick with our normal style or challenge our self to a different level.

More cohesion

Neither introverts nor extroverts can claim corner to effective conflict resolution in the workplace. Ignored or poorly managed conflict leaves space for friction between employees, possibly even affecting the customers. It is by creating space for all parties to be focused on a more collaborative, win-win approach that the space opens for resolution.

Increased creativity

By using conflict resolution skills we can pool our knowledge and styles to come up with the best, often most creative, solution or decision. With more willingness to listen to all perspectives we get to go deeper in alternatives. This kind of meta-discussion before big discussions allows minimum work disruption and for the introvert preserves energy.

Increased understanding

When we move outside of our intrapersonal thinking to more interpersonal relating, we move beyond on own emotions. Learning how our colleagues feel and think allows us in the process of solving the conflict to grow in appreciation of different needs, styles, perceptions, and values. As we grow in understanding we increase our ability to put the axe down for most conflict and instead collaborate better.

Stress management

Stress is a known contributor to workplace absenteeism and turnover. Because unresolved conflict increases stress, when we bring the best conflict management style to a situation, we indirectly decrease stress as we work better together for a solution. This benefit is invaluable for the introvert who is more sensitive to energy depletion brought on by stress.

In a 2008 study of workers in nine countries, research by CPP Inc showed that 81 percent of workers in the US and Brazil, where conflict training is common, report more positive changes from workplace conflict. Countries such as Belgium and France, where there is the least training, speak to the least amount of positive outcomes. There is a link between training as a catalyst to better affect conflict.

When we take steps to build conflict awareness, whether it is training in a group or by investing in time for our own personal growth, we all benefit.

Summary

When conflict is approached in a thoughtful and constructive way, we each benefit and the workplace environment is improved. By knowing our general understanding, the causes and the different styles to use, at the end of this chapter we:

> ➤ Know our natural tendency to manage conflict

> ➤ Can more easily identify a specific workplace conflict causes

> ➤ Can be more thoughtful in determining whether or not to confront a particular conflict

> ➤ Can identify different models of conflict management to use

> ➤ Recognize our introvert strengths of thinking things through and listening more can give us a better position to apply EQ, Emotional Intelligence

> ➤ Have a variety of techniques to be able to better manage your energy depletion from conflict stress

> ➤ Discover how we can benefit from workplace conflict

Thoughts to contemplate

➤ How do I personally feel about workplace conflict? Do I see it as helpful, disruptive, or neutral? Why do I believe this?

➤ Think of a recent conflict situation. What was your role? Was the outcome positive? Would you handle it the same of differently if you had to deal with it again?

➤ Consider this approach, given there are opportunities to manage conflict everyday:

>   ➤ Think of a conflict you might be having with someone at this time.

>   ➤ On a piece of paper head up the paper with a title representing this conflict.

>   ➤ On the left-hand side, write down your conflict style in action.

>   ➤ On the right-hand side write down all the facts about the issue.

>   ➤ As you look at the style you are using, and weigh it against the facts of the situation, assess whether you are using the best style and be willing to change to a more appropriate one if it is determined so.

Conflict in the workplace will always exist. Just because as an introvert you may have the tendency to withdraw when it surfaces does not mean you have to choose between fight or flight. Ineffectiveness at conflict resolution can improve when we are willing to put new thoughts and actions into place and let our voice be heard.

Bibliography

➤ Dr. Christine M. Bacon, marriage expert, speaker and radio show host of Breakfast with Bacon: the Relationship Doctor, `http://super-couple.com/` and `http://BreakfastwithBacon.com`

➤ *What Goes Around Comes Around: The Impact of Personal Conflict Style on Work Conflict and Stress*, Raymond A. Friedman and Simom T. Tidd, Vanderbilt University, Steven C. Curral, Rice University, James C. Tsai, Vanderbilt University, The International Journal of Conflict Management, 2000

➤ *How Introverts versus Extroverts Approach small group argumentative discussions*, E. Michael Nussbaum, University of Nevada, The Elementary School Journal, 2002

➤ *Workplace Conflict and How Businesses Can Harness It to Thrive*, CPP Global, Human Capital Report, July 2008

➤ *Linking Emotional Intelligence with Jungain Typology*, Jo Maddocks, Bulletin of Psychological Type, Volume 29, No 3, 2006

➤ Thomas, K.W., and Kilmann, R. H. *The Thomas-Kilmann Conflict Mode Instrument* (Mountain View, CA: Xicom and CPP, Inc., 1974)

8

On the Level to Negotiate with Success

"The capability of negotiating... is something that means you not only have to understand fully what you believe and what your national interests are but in order to be a really good negotiator, you have to try to figure out what the other person on the other side of the table has in mind."

–Madeleine Albright, United States Secretary of State (1997 - 2001)

Imagine you are walking through a department store. You glance at items in the household items department. A salesperson watches you and then on approach says, "We have a terrific sale on whatever you want to buy today! How about it? What would you like?"

This is fiction; or is it? Not everywhere.

A Turkish bazaar is much like this fictitious department store. In it, we find a market consisting of street after street lined with shops and stalls. In Istanbul's Grand Bazaar, there are over 5,000 shops and 60 different entrances. You can buy anything from bread to shoes to leather coats to diamonds. But you better be prepared with your negotiating savvy.

The merchants of any Turkish bazaar are going to set things straight with you because they want you to buy. Just like a carpenter's level, everything needs to be aligned to move forward with a negotiation.

As you revel at the products lining the street, you may not notice each merchant who gazes at you. At each shop a merchant smiles at you, all the while warming you up to consider his wares. "We have a great deal on leather coats today. Would you like to buy one?"

Except for the product, each merchant has a great offer. You avoid his eyes, but cannot ignore his hands stroking a leather coat he holds. Still, you tell him no. He moves closer, not crowding your space, and he questions, "But why?". You mumble some reason and pick up your pace as you pass this store. You hear him ask again, "But why?". And the scene repeats itself shop after shop and street after street.

In this environment, you have to negotiate; it is part of the fun. And besides, if you don't, it's an insult.

On one particular trip when my son traveled with us, he was the better negotiator of all of us. He got a Turkish drum, which was originally $35.00 for just $17.00.

As I recall each of the conversations, the merchants are sincerely interested in hearing your answer to the question, "Why?". This gives them reason to ask you another question or direct your attention to another product or in some other way get you involved. They ask, or tell you to hold the drum, the pipe, or the shawl that you are eyeing.

Whether you visit Istanbul's bazaar to look for shoes or gold jewelry, or it is a day-to-day negotiation between colleagues, between an employee and a manager, and between an employee and a customer or even a vendor, there are a number of effective ways to negotiate.

As introverts there are some things we are going to do well naturally, and still other things we may have to learn when negotiating.

How do you negotiate?

Conflicts are often solved through negotiation. Two or more people who have a disagreement come together and negotiations ensue to reach a mutually satisfactory solution. However, not all negotiating in the workplace is to resolve conflict.

Often we will negotiate to establish a salary, organize priorities, get a vendor's best price, or even decide who will take telephone calls on a day the receptionist is off sick.

Negotiating can take place through any communication channel whether that is in person, on the telephone or by email. Each situation lends itself to more of one than another.

Think back to any recent negotiations: you and another person in your company were perhaps vying for similar resources in a tight budget year, or maybe you and another colleague wanted the same vacation dates.

Keep these events in mind and answer the following statements with only one of the words in the Scale of Words. Your honest answers will give you a clearer understanding of how you generally approach negotiating.

Understanding of negotiation

	Never	Rarely	Sometimes	Often	Always
Having a clearly defined outcome is the key to success					
Decide your personal bottom line, the least acceptable outcome					
Be sure you are talking with the decision maker					
Know as much as possible about the other party					
Preparation and planning before negotiating improve results					
Bring in what you learn from negotiating outside of work					
Silence is powerful in negotiating					
Personal comfort and confidence with negotiating improves outcomes					
Listening and asking questions are essential to success					
Start with the mutual agreed points					
Negotiations can trigger emotions and shape the skills we use					
Over enthusiasm can cause the other party to avoid concessions					
It's important to know how to bring negotiations to a close					
Negotiated agreements are best in writing					
Negotiation is a skill we can learn					

Score interpretation

Score the words you identified with each statement:

- ➤ Never: 2 points
- ➤ Rarely: 4 points
- ➤ Sometimes: 6 points
- ➤ Often: 8 points
- ➤ Always: 10 points

Knowing what the key points of negotiating are

Put the score you chose for each item on the appropriate numbered line below. Each style indicates the statement numbers associated with it. Then add up each scale.

My total score = _____

High negotiation understanding (120 to 150)

Some negotiation understanding (90 to 120)

Minimal negotiation understanding (60 to 90)

Weak negotiation understanding (30 to 60)

Higher scores indicate that you understand the negotiation process and you do what is necessary to get better results. Lower scores indicate that you may need to increase your knowledge of what negotiation is and how to bring in your strengths to have more confidence and more consistent outcomes.

Some of our introvert tendencies such as being prepared, thinking things through, listening more, and being quiet, may put us in a strong position.

Let's look at how we can preserve our energy through a process that calls for us to bring our best to the situation.

What does our energy have to do with negotiating?

Imagine your feelings in this situation: new on the job, no results to bring to the table, no understanding of sales, and you want to negotiate an assigned territory to give you the best chance of success.

Are you looking forward to this or do you want to avoid the negotiations?

When I first entered sales in the computer industry, it was a male dominated industry. This was an influencing factor in my success from the beginning.

In my first sales job, we were assigned specific lines of business. Each year, if a salesperson was not effective in their assigned lines, those target customers would be reassigned. The manager would call us in his office by overall sales results.

But in my first year of sales, without any company sales results, I was to negotiate my assigned lines of business with a different approach. It would be about a year later when I could use my position of being a top salesperson to get the better lines of business.

Waiting for a year is not a controllable factor. Energy however can be renewed and redirected in a positive way.

As a new first year representative, keeping calm to deal with a less than ideal situation instead of expressing disappointment or anger would likely enhance any outcome. Such kind of negative emotions might force someone to concede in negotiating, or be interpreted as being in the weaker position.

It is more effective to keep calm as uncontrolled or even fluctuating emotions can affect our personal energy to that same degree. The benefit of managing this process is we have clearer thinking and better responses.

This is important for the introvert who can often, even under the stress of a particularly high negotiation, be outwardly rather non-emotive or emotionally consistent. By bringing positive energy and steady emotions into a negotiation, we enhance the experience of it. With the more introverted of us normally being emotionally consistent, it may give us an advantage in feeling some control as well as the other party being willing to make some concessions as we go along.

One research study in *The Journal of Experimental Social Psychology* found that when feeling little control over the outcome of a negotiation, people are more susceptible to another's influence in particular with the fluctuating emotions of anger, happiness, and disappointment.

If we keep our personal energy in check when the other person is not, then we benefit two ways.

First, we can respond more thoughtfully and not react quickly whether possible inconsistent emotions from the other party are natural or purposeful.

Second, we can stay true to our introvert nature and keep focused on the objective. This is ultimately important to help us make and take time to think and prepare instead of just reacting.

Our best approach in negotiating is to be less guided by emotional reaction and instead manage our energy in a way we bring the best of our emotions to the negotiations. Our comfort will affect our confidence and the higher this is, the greater likelihood of a mutually satisfying agreement.

How do you negotiate when anxious?

If we feel stressed, then our energy is drained emotionally and physically. It knocks the carpenter level off balance. We can be weighed down with worry, anxiety, and fear.

A key point for those of us who are more introverted: do not negotiate when feeling anxious. Instead, direct this in a productive way to overcome those negative feelings.

This is when we can use our introvert preference to prepare and plan. I directed my efforts to talk with the more senior sales people to find out their experiences with different lines of business. Were the prospects receptive? Did they ever end a year with prospects who had still not bought? What geographic ground did they cover?

I also took time to research a couple of other branches of the same company about their sales results in some of the only remaining lines I would have the choice to select. But most importantly, researching gave me more confidence no matter what the outcome.

When we are stressed, it can show to others. We might assume being worried may impair our negotiation results. But researchers have found this is only true for some and that we can direct our behavior in a different direction if this happens.

Various research studies point to the harmful effects of anxiety in negotiating—the lowering of expectations, making lower offers, responding too quickly to counter offers, and even not taking enough time for a negotiation. In one study by Alison Brooks and Maurice Schweitzer, both of The Wharton School of Business, findings were that negotiators can improve their performance by boosting their self-perception and making negotiation situations a part of everyday business life. There was also the finding that mild amounts of anxiousness can improve a negotiator's result by improving attention, memory, and problem solving.

What happens is that there is more thorough preparation. Preparation is something introverts do with ease quite naturally. Pre-meetings and direct questions give us information to know as much as possible about the party across the table from us.

Reduce heightened anxiety early

Like most introverts, Julia Barnickle, a business coach who helps introverts build businesses online, likes to avoid confrontation wherever possible. When one of her corporate IT jobs meant working for an aggressive manager, she tended to keep her head down.

She was working on a project to deliver an ITT (Invitation to Tender) that had a short deadline. She was also due to be called for jury service in two weeks' time, which added an urgency to finishing the ITT before jury service started.

Her manager was the sort of person who liked to give the impression of doing a lot while actually doing very little. One day, when a colleague and Barnickle were discussing what they would do if they won the lottery, her manager said he would not give up his day job. Instead, he would turn up every day and do nothing until the company fired him. She and her colleague exchanged glances, knowing that we were both thinking: has he already won?

While she continued to work all out on the ITT, her manager kept tasking her with distractions, for example, phoning the regional offices to ask about progress, when he could easily have done so himself. Especially as he would phone them anyway, after I had reported back, to tell them they were not working hard enough.

Eventually, Barnickle told the IT Director that her manger's attitude was preventing her from completing the ITT. He suggested she speak to her manager. She did not.

The next day, her manager took her to task about something petty. That gave her an opening to tell him it would be helpful if she could focus on the ITT. They argued, in an open-plan office, for the next two hours. Finally, when it was time to go home, her manager said "let's ask the IT Director what he thinks."

Unfortunately, the IT Director was unavailable. However, the following morning her manager announced he had decided she should concentrate on getting the ITT finished, so it would be ready by the time she went off to do jury service.

It felt like a hollow victory because it was so pointless. It seemed logical to Barnickle to focus on the most important and urgent task, rather than being distracted by tasks that her manager could have done.

One mistake she made was not mentioning this to her manager sooner. She did not do this partly to avoid conflict, and partly because she assumed they would have the same opinion about priorities. When we feel worse about a situation, we will not have enough energy to approach it in the prepared and thoughtful way that we might under a situation without the negotiation stress.

Whether negotiating a new sales territory or negotiating a conflict, we can view it as either positive or negative. A key point for those of us more introverted: instead of thinking, "When I'm less anxious I will negotiate," think, "When I negotiate, I will be less anxious." After thinking things through and planning our approach, we can begin to shift our energy to be confident about negotiating.

Our quiet skills advantage

> *"Never forget the power of silence, that massively disconcerting pause which goes on and on and may last induce an opponent to babble and backtrack nervously."*

> *–Lance Morrow*

In my first fifteen years in sales it was naturally easy to follow the rule, "He who speaks first loses," during a final negotiations with a client. I was comfortable with silence in helping my customers buy. My confidence was intact as a high performing salesperson.

I recall one time with a competitor in hiring mode, when I broke the rule and I lost.

The company I was with was rumored to be closing. Many employees, including me, were networking for possible work. One of our competitors was one I would consider working for. Rather than using the recruiting agency to secure an appointment for me, I telephoned Doug the owner.

It was just an introductory call for me, but it became an exploratory call for Doug. I was speaking confidently answering his questions.

Power of small pauses

I would often speak with some gaps between what I was saying, rather like going through a proposal with a prospect. State one point and pause. These smaller gaps of silence allow the other party to break in and either ask a question or make a comment. Everyone, introvert or extrovert preference, benefits from pauses when speaking. If we do this in negotiating, we are not heading down a rabbit hole with unnecessary information, but instead the prospect leads us.

The conversation was moving smoothly and Doug did jump in by asking me when I wanted to come in to talk.

I answered with a date because after all, that was what I wanted, an appointment.

But, I let go of the rule. It was as if my anxious balloon burst and I continued to talk about myself, why I would be a good fit and selling myself before it was really time. It was the worst thing to do.

There was silence after running my mouth but it was too late. In negotiating for anything, including something like an appointment for a job interview, silent pauses make the conversation more effective.

Doug did not answer as I was hoping for him to either confirm the date with some times or give me some alternative dates.

Instead, after some silence finally, he said, "Let me get back to you."

It is human to want to fill silence but usually for introverts, silence is a welcome part of many conversations. Saying too much all at once can undermine our position in negotiating when we are anxious or stressed.

In my workshops for selling and presentation skills, when we get to the hour section about listening, I let people experience the feeling of silence. You can experiment with it if you want to in a one-to-one conversation.

The next time you are in conversation with someone you know, ask for a time-out. Explain to them you want the two of you to experience silence together for 60 seconds. Ask them whether they would play along with you. Let them know you will time things and speak when the 60 seconds is up. When ready, look at your watch and signal to start. It may feel awkward or uncomfortable. That is one of the goals—to help you be aware of your comfort level.

In selling, where negotiation is common, silence is a tape measure of success. Research supports that when asking questions or making a statement requiring an answer, most people take 8 to 10 seconds to respond. Let the silence be in the space of your conversation and hear your negotiating become more effective.

Silence changes the next move

Gaps of silence make us slow down and listen a lot more carefully and, subsequently, more constructively. It was not necessary for me to continue to "sell" myself as Doug was already asking me to meet with him.

When we are quiet we give the other person time, which most introverts relish, to think through what they want to say. They then get to decide on their next move.

If we break silence in negotiating, as I did because of letting anxiousness take hold, we can end up talking to ourselves, and even miss out on an opportunity.

Most of my experience with using silence as an effective tool in negotiating is that while remaining silent is not always easy, the results outweigh what can happen when you fill the gap with your words.

Preparing the elements for a successful outcome

A search for "negotiation" in books on Amazon.com yields about 23,000 results. A similar search on Google finds 22,400,000 results. Within all these results and in a variety of courses, we can find three, five, and seven or eight steps to the negotiation process. Regardless of the number of steps involved, many of them are suitable for our introverted nature. In general, these are the negotiation elements:

- ➤ Preparation
  - ➢ Have a clearly defined outcome
  - ➢ Decide your personal bottom line, the least acceptable outcome.
  - ➢ Be prepared with questions

- ➤ Engagement
  - ➢ Start with the mutually agreed points.
  - ➢ Ask for what you want.
  - ➢ Be prepared to justify your request.
  - ➢ Listen to what the other party wants.
  - ➢ Cooperate and collaborate to reach an agreement.

- ➤ Agreement
  - ➢ Bring negotiations to a close.
  - ➢ It's best to get things in writing.

We will follow a situation that Meghan Wier shared with me to see some of these steps in action.

Creative preparation

Meghan has admitted to me that she watches Pawn Stars on the History Channel to watch the art of negotiation in episode after episode. No doubt some of this influences her negotiating style. Decide what will help you prepare. It might be something like writing out these steps or re-reading this chapter and then getting all your ideas out of your head onto paper in note form.

When Wier was in a job negotiation situation, she was concerned that she would push too far or possibly seem greedy. She did not want that because it is not who she is, and she wanted the employment opportunity. Meghan started out prepared—and she has a clearly defined outcome.

Start engagement with agreed upon points

She knew what she wanted and was humble. She told the hiring manager she was thrilled with and grateful for the opportunity. Meghan lead the conversation with mutually agreed points, which needs to happen early in the engagement. She was talking about her understanding of the job and getting the manager's agreement about her understanding as she talked. This was an active way of building rapport through agreement.

She also told him she was hoping for some changes to the offer. She told him what her ideal offer was and then backed it up.

Justification

In preparing for any negotiation, it helps to influence the other party if you can support what you are asking for with any facts, figures, or examples. This is a logical reasoning approach, just one way to back up your points. But regardless of how you back up your requests, it is believed that having a reason for each request improves the chance for successful negotiations.

With Wier's offering justification for her requests in an engaging manner, she was more likely gaining agreement as she went along for a "yes."

Ask for what you want

For example, she said she would need to leave early some days because of family obligations, but she would work later those days from home and spend that time working on projects that required more dedicated "quiet time." She guaranteed that he would never meet a more loyal and hard-working employee. Meghan was prepared with her personal bottom line.

She also told him why she felt that the position required a different job title. She made the case that the responsibilities were more in line with a "Director" position rather than a "Senior Manager" and backed that up. She made a compelling argument, but she was not confrontational.

Listen to what the other party wants

Then she got quiet. Meghan was indirectly opening the door to cooperate and negotiate an agreement. It also helps when we get quiet to ask a question of the other party. Something like, "I'm wondering what you think of how you could be fair for us with my request?

She admits, as an introvert, that the whole situation was uncomfortable. It brought attention to her. It involved direct and candid conversations with a stranger—but a stranger with whom she was hoping to build a strong and long-term relationship.

Introverts tend to favor fewer, stronger relationships and she was concerned with damaging a relationship with her potential "new boss" before it began. However, she also recognized the value of being seen as someone who would stand up for themselves in a way that was professional and confident.

Bring negotiations to a close

Wier got the job, and the salary she wanted. Everything was sealed in writing.

With Wier's anecdotal example, do you see most of the more commonly espoused negotiation steps in use?

Before you step up to a bigger negotiation such as employment, which Wier successfully negotiated, practice negotiating in everyday situations. Or watch people around you who negotiate. Either will more fully prepare you for the future.

Practice in everyday situations

One of my friends works the night shift in a hospital laboratory. She negotiates regularly for vacation time.

Often, where we sit in a meeting might be quickly negotiated.

With friends, we might negotiate where to have dinner.

When planning a weekend of entertainment, we might negotiate with a spouse to go to theatre or comedy club.

In online social media, to move conversations forward, it can mean negotiating with a new acquaintance to meet face to face at a preferred meeting place or via something like Google Hangouts online.

I once negotiated with a dentist office for a better price for my mother's dental work by paying cash.

My husband calls me a tight wad so he leaves it to me to negotiate with home contractors. Needless to say, I get to practice negotiating regularly. When we take advantage of every opportunity to negotiate, we develop greater confidence, which we can take into higher stake opportunities.

A few years ago, when trading in my car as normal for us every three to five years, practice served me well. We have been with this particular car dealer for more than 20 years and in that time, only one sales representative and one manufacturer.

What shocked me when my husband and I went in to discuss the car options and price is that the representative interrupted our scheduled meeting to handle two or three other walk-in customers. Neither were urgent needs and there were at least three other car salespeople available to help.

This fact of being needlessly interrupted during a scheduled appointment was observed as well by my husband. Neither of us liked it.

We walked out with a proposal but doubt around several issues surfaced.

Did he remember we were buying, between the two of us, our eighth car of this make?

Did he actually account for the options I requested?

Were we missing anything?

After processing the situation and then discussing things with my husband, for the first time we agreed to shop another dealer. Taking time to realize my sense of doubt was founded, I was feeling confident about a more positive outcome elsewhere.

In the end, what we negotiated was for the General Manager of the same dealership to be our contact person, and about a $3,000 lower price. In the process, we cut out the salesman who gave us another lesson in negotiating.

What we can be assured of as an introvert who likes to be prepared is that using everyday situations to help us learn this skill will serve us foundationally to be able to have confidence and knowledge when needed in the workplace situation.

When we develop our negotiating skills to the degree it becomes a power tool, we will have more confidence to know what works as well as knowing when to walk away when someone just is not being fair.

Most of us do not know how to negotiate. Most schools do not teach it and unless our parents are in sales or other positions where their negotiation experience is common dinner table talk, we might just fear it.

When we welcome everyday or regularly occurring business or personal situations for negotiating, we can use them to be more prepared, more confident, and more effective in times where the stake is higher. Take some time now to think through everyday situations that might allow you some practice.

How to use a collaborative conflict style to negotiate

We can view negotiation as either competitive or collaborative. But in reality, negotiating is more like a tide with ebbs and flows. As the process flows, we will have to flow with it.

There are advantages introverts have in negotiating when we recognize certain traits we have and step them up to use in our everyday business negotiations. *Getting to Yes*, by Roger Fisher, William Ury, and Bruce Patton, is possibly the most referenced book for anyone who wants to negotiate in a collaborative way. *Getting to Yes* identifies a collaborative type of negotiation, with four specific points to use to best advance this kind of negotiation. We will explore these now.

People – separate people from the problem

After being a retail store manager for three years, my responsibilities and role changed. The two managers I reported to never addressed what this meant in terms of the next steps or even compensation. After almost three years in my first managerial role, with more tasks, more staff, and more responsibilities, it was time to raise the particular position I was in.

In general, many introverts tend to be humble in relationships, and making lasting relationships takes energy exertion. Extroverts do not always appear humble in their gregarious, often outspoken nature. Neither do they have to work to establish relationships since they are energized from everything around and outside themselves.

A possible advantage we have when we look more at the root of the problem around the issues than people involved is to consciously distance ourselves from people. Once we have some distance, which can minimize emotions, and we can bring in our typical analytical approach to come to an agreement. We can be more effective in focusing on the intricacies of the problem than thinking that the people are the problem. Sometimes our emotions surrounding others can cloud our thinking about the problem. When we make this separation, we can more easily focus on the best way to communicate with the people in the problem.

After thinking things through to take a more objective view of my work situation, the time allowed me to detail all the additional work in my area of responsibility, and strategize how to approach each of the two managers in a meeting of the three of us. By removing any emotionally charged issues, good or bad, with the people involved, a clearer plan with both supporting facts and knowing our acceptable bottom line can emerge more easily.

Interests – focus on interests instead of positions

My approach included stating facts about my contribution, the positive effects including an increase in sales better than in previous years, establishing a training program after the requests of many staff, and an overview of how redesigning my role would contribute to the entire organization and not just my location.

Most introverts are known to prefer listening instead of talking. In our approach to listening, we also usually have more questions than answers. Questions can uncover interests. Fisher, Ury, and Patton suggest particular questions to further the understanding of the issues instead of a person's position about them. Remember the Turkish bazaar merchants question to keep the negotiations moving? You remembered it correctly: Why? And why not? Why forces us to think more deeply. It can clear up the issue sooner because assumptions are removed and the root of things is exposed.

Because I worked for an introvert and extrovert husband and wife team, an innie-outie couple, during this time, focusing on the interests of the organization as a whole and the salespeople as a team allowed me to position my requests in a broader context with my presentation. The "why" questions helped to dissolve any concerns they had.

Options – be creative when identifying options for a decision

A combination of confidence that I could "sell" my idea and the self-acknowledgement of the stress I would continue to feel unless things changed pushed me to consider my options, without leaving the company. One high stake option would mean a complete organizational change. That was most desirable option for me and would allow me to take on the real goal: to build the organization to the top 10% in the nation as the one location was. A smaller stake option would be to bring on an assistant. Even smaller still would be changing hours and either cutting out or changing tasks.

Our preferred introvert world is one of preparedness and the world of ideas. It is highly likely anywhere from two people to a group will find themselves brainstorming for solutions to problems. Everyone will have a stake so it makes sense that ideas will come from everyone. While we may have to participate in some brainstorming, something we do not excel with, we can piggyback onto ideas.

Negotiating means being willing to open new ideas for consideration. Whoever contributes, allow us to offer more options to the discussion.

Use objective criteria

As you may conclude from my approach, focusing on concrete, objective data allowed me to both more easily communicate with a husband and wife innie-outie, introvert-extrovert, couple as well as integrate my approach with them in the most comfortable way for my style of selling.

Many times in negotiating, people get caught up in the emotions that surface because they believe that "I have to win and someone has to lose." Putting objective, factual, criteria into the discussion are going to be independent of anyone's position about an issue. This of course takes preparation, maybe even research and usually this favors the introvert tendencies.

In my negotiating situation, my bottom line was for my position to level up from a store manager to a director of sales. The criteria presented, was difficult to debate: this would allow the organization to grow, to focus people's skills with certain niche clients, and in the end lead to increase sales. After three meetings, we changed the organizational structure, my time was freed up to grow sales with a larger sales team, and my salary was commensurate with the work. This objective criteria type of approach is a genuine introvert approach taking the focus off ourselves, and putting on the benefits and other people.

About two years later my bosses told me the change was the best thing they ever did.

Getting to a win-win

Negotiate stems from the root word *negotiari*. This Latin word means to carry on business. This is important to keep in mind because negotiations can often be perceived in a negative light as being combative or someone surrendering to something. But most negotiations require us needing to continue to work with a customer, co-worker, manager, or employee.

It is not about "how can I get everything I want." It is about reaching an agreement that is mutually satisfactory to be able to continue to be in that relationship.

Most introverts are known to be more cooperative than assertive, which can firm up the win-win approach, but we can also learn some subtle approaches to negotiations from extroverts to ramp up our negotiating skills.

Cooperate on the little issues

After a few years of pushing myself out of my comfort zone, I have become connected with some high profile speakers. This helped to serve me in a joint venture later on when we wanted to invite people like Bob to be a guest on an entrepreneurial telesummit we were hosting. It was a multi-party joint venture where everyone would benefit in growing their online presence and share in the revenues.

He excitedly and graciously accepted my e-mail to talk via the telephone about the details.

The first thing he did not like was having to participate in the one and only call where we wanted to have each speaker introduce themselves, and give a teaser about their topic. He was not convinced this was the best use of his time. I took his lead and we negotiated it to only interviewing him for his hour-long portion. Maintaining the relationship and having him be one of the participants were more important for a win-win negotiation.

The next thing he did not like was a piece in the contract. It was simple in our mind with some administrative as well as financial pieces. Bob did not like having to promote the number of times we requested to his followers and since his reasons were sound, it was another small concession we made.

These negotiable small issues were something we were willing to give on. The main goal, our defined outcome, was to have him onboard as a speaker whose name, with hundreds of thousands of online followers, would draw a large audience and help build our prospective listeners.

We focused on the little issues, the big issues, and our relationship.

Since relationships are exhausting to initiate for most introverts, our vested interest to maintain a relationship might make it easier to keep the relationship as the focus. Then we can work on the issues without that concern. This then allows more of our preplanning to go into the issues.

Initiate negotiations

While we know not to initiate a request with someone for a favor during a difficult time they might be having, there are times being the initiator is helpful to negotiations. This might be a time an introvert could benefit from what some might believe is something more characteristic of someone more extroverted.

A client of Johnny Bravo, blogger and an extrovert, was in the process of re-negotiating their contract and lead the due diligence to look at other options. Bravo had only been their account executive for a couple of months so he was still new to them and they were new to him.

Although he was just "the next rep" to them he wanted to prove he was like a partner. That he was their champion, and that he truly had their best interests in mind.

As they discussed the options available, short or long term and relative to the competition, Bravo could relate to how they felt. That the weight of risk was more heavily on their shoulders no matter what their decision was.

During their conversations, Bravo came up with some great options for them in particular because they believed their old agreement was severely outdated. Not only did he have a chance to be their hero but to keep them as a long-term partner.

So when it came time for the actual negotiations, he came prepared. He had multiple conversations with superiors to understand not only the client's current agreement, but also what concessions his company was able to offer to continue the partnership.

He knew that they wanted to stay them with and that they felt cheated by their old agreement. Bravo came to the table with a few options to help make their decision as easy as possible.

There were shorter-term options that reflected some of the more recent standards for contracts of that kind, and of course longer-term options. The longer-term agreement allowed Bravo to offer more favorable terms on his end. Lower pricing, smaller increases, reduced add-ons, and more opportunities to make sure their employees are trained to use the software to its fullest.

They were well on the way to signing a long-term agreement based on what Bravo was willing to give. And in return they were willing to give Bravo's company a longer-term agreement. Sometimes we have to be the initiator, even with new relationships.

What we might need to work on

"There is nothing good or bad, but thinking makes it so."

–Shakespeare, Hamlet, Act II, Scene II

Our natural traits and preferences as introverts such as listening more and being curious to get many details and innuendos clear, lend themselves to successful negotiations. With negotiating being an activity that may come more naturally to extroverts, we must acknowledge that we will have to consciously use more extroverting behaviors.

While we may have certain preferences about how we interact with other people, it is the very nature of social interaction that we may sometimes have to act in ways that are contrary to our preferences. We must be willing to get out of our comfort zone. Over time, interacting in a more extroverted manner can become more comfortable. Often when speaking to an association or organization about how introverts and extroverts can collaborate in the workplace, people will comment to me, "There is no way you are an introvert!".

This comes from both their mistaken understanding what introversion is and being able, over time to learn enough extroverting to use as needed.

> ➤ **We want to keep emotions from escalating**: Allow ourselves to both feel and acknowledge any anxiousness. If we do not know what we are feeling when negotiating and we ignore it, we will undermine a chance to break and recharge. When acting as a consultant to a small team of managers who were struggling with conflict, I assumed the role of a mediator. As I observed and listened to the feelings that were on the surface, it was apparent that no one took the time with each other to express their feelings before they rose to this level of anger. You may have heard the expression "what we resist persists." It is actions like this that can exhaust an introvert if during a negotiation we pay little attention to this.

> ➤ **Stay the course**: Research points to the need for extroverts to seek additional stimulation more than introverts. Because of how our brains are wired differently in this regard, we are not going to thrive in negotiating. We may even want to avoid it. However, we need to overcome this feeling if we are to be successful. Preparing for the actual negotiating engagement will give us the ability to manage our energy. Take some time in between negotiation meetings if appropriate. Follow-up via e-mail or telephone. The energy we will use in lower levels of direct interaction will sustain us through the extroverting engagement.

➤ **Assert yourself**: It may feel energy draining to do so but consider asserting yourself like acting. It is not about being dominant. It is more of taking the facts related to a situation, anticipating the possible resistance, having questions to increase awareness, and then having the confidence in what your position is to let the process work for you. We have already planned thoroughly for our position and the least acceptable outcome. During the actual engagement is when we will have to draw on our confidence to allow us to stay the course.

➤ **Extroverting is acquired**: Yes; extroverting is a verb too. We extrovert all day long when we are give a presentation, engage in a debate, or attend a staff party. Any activity, which turns our attention outside our self, is considered characteristic of the more extroverted. We may feel when we say something spontaneously, such as during a brainstorming, that we either speak too slow or deliberately, or that not having the time to think something through we can say something we really do not mean. Saying something we might regret is not an issue reserved for the introvert. This is something everyone has felt at some point in their lives!

➤ **Extrovert tendencies may not be an option**: Even if we select a company position that suits our temperament like being in research, or writing, or customer service, position and roles are ever changing. It is not about giving up our preferences as an introvert. It is about understanding how to integrate more extroverted tendencies when the situation, like negotiating, calls for it. Negotiating is a complex issue. While it is a process, it evolves. While there might be identified steps, they are not always followed sequentially. Think about bringing your introversion strengths into the workplace to successfully manage negotiating like using a level. Sometimes we are going to feel a strong sense of contribution and appreciation from our listening, questioning, and subjective analytic approach. At other times, we have to tap into more extrovert tendencies and in doing so, possibly feel less confident behaving that way. In any negotiation, we level the situation because we are able to navigate the introvert and extrovert behavioral continuum.

Summary

"In business, you don't get what you deserve, you get what you negotiate."

–Dr. Chester L. Karrass, pioneer of seminar Effective NegotiatingÒ

Negotiating is commonplace in all aspects of our lives. Knowing what we are worth, knowing the issues and being able to communicate these into a win-win negotiation is essential in our business success.

The more we understand about negotiating, we find that it is a comfortable blend of introvert and extrovert traits to balance for higher and lower stake situations. We no longer have to retreat. We can stand up for ourselves, and what we desire, in our way.

We can use lower stake situations as practice so that when it comes to negotiating our salary, or a promotion, or even preferred parking space, we can develop our negotiating confidently.

In our work life, whether it is compensation, benefits, work hours, or a corner office, we have many of the skills quite naturally and might need to develop others. But we can learn the how to's if we have to negotiate as if our life depended on it.

As we end this chapter, we can:

> ➤ Understand the necessary balance of introverting and extroverting in negotiating.
> ➤ Reducing our stress and keeping our anxiety in check can help improve our outcome.
> ➤ Pauses and silence can give us an advantage.
> ➤ Identify three or ten steps of negotiating which is a fluid process.
> ➤ Use everyday situations involving negotiations as stepping-stones to confidence and more successful outcome in higher stake situations.
> ➤ Use our preference for preparing to help us be more comfortable engaging in the actual talks.
> ➤ Know how to use a collaborative approach to get to win-win negotiations results.
> ➤ Discover how we can benefit as equally as those more extroverted from being better at negotiating.

Thoughts to contemplate

Introversion is not an all or nothing trait. Neither is negotiating solely dependent on this one trait. Because each of us falls on a continuum of introversion to extroversion, we can choose to adjust and bring in the necessary more effective introvert and extrovert traits as negotiating ebbs and flows.

> ➤ How comfortable am I negotiating in everyday situations with people outside of work? If I am effective, can I find what to bring into work that I do well?

> ➤ Can I put personalities aside and focus on the issues to search for agreement?

> ➤ In preparing for a negotiation, do you use a win-win approach?

Negotiating successfully happens when we collaborate so that all parties walk away with a mutually beneficial agreement. It is a leveling of various skills, some of which introverts are naturally predisposed to and some of which we have to be willing to learn, practice, and apply. Negotiating can be learned.

Bibliography

> ➤ *Can Nervous Nelly Negotiate? How Anxiety Causes Negotiators to Make Low First Offers, Exit Early, and Earn Less Profit*, by Alison Wood Brooks and Maurice Schweitzer, The Wharton School, University of Pennsylvania, January 2011

> ➤ *The advantages of being unpredictable: How emotional inconsistency extracts concessions in negotiation*, by M. Sinaceur, A, Hajo, G.A. Van Cleef and A. D. Galinsky, Journal of Experimental Social Psychology, 2013

> ➤ Julia Barnickle,Business Coach helping Introverts build a business on-line, http://www.thequietentrepreneur.com

> ➤ Meghan Wier, author: *Confession of an Introvert: The She Girl's Guide to Career, Networking and Getting the Most Out of Life*

> ➤ Johnny Bravo, *The Sales Pro Blog*, http://salesproblog.com, blogger and extrovert

> ➤ *The Introvert Advantage*, Marti Olsen Laney, Psy. D, Workman Publishing Company, 2002

> ➤ *Getting to Yes*, Roger Fisher, William Ury and Bruce Patton, Penguin Books, 1991

9

Power Tools of Influence, Persuasion, and Selling

"Everyone is a salesperson whether they realize it or not. You may not be selling a product or service for money, but in our daily lives, each of us are in situations where we need to influence and persuade other people and affect their decisions in favor of our position."

–Jerry Bruckner, author

If you are an introvert, you may have ruled out sales as a career path. However, rather than thinking of selling as a specific line of work, for certain types of people, if you acknowledge that selling is something we do in everyday life in a range of contexts – similar to negotiation – you will begin to see that selling isn't such a difficult task for those of an introvert persuasion.

Whether we are selling an idea for a company to implement, or a proposal for a department to undertake, or a product for the exchange of money, we all sell something. The fact is that in the process, there are as many opportunities for the introvert as there are for the extrovert to step in and excel.

Selling, influence, and persuasion

Have you ever interviewed for a new job or promotion? That is selling.

Have you ever created a plan for some form of organizational change you wanted and then stuck to it? That is selling, selling yourself to just do it.

Have you ever asked to have a meeting with someone one to one, and they accepted? That is selling.

Selling happens every day using influence and persuasion.

Selling in commerce occurs with the intention of a buyer exchanging some money for the seller's goods or services to solve a problem or serve some form of need.

Persuasion has a similar objective: to change either a person's thinking or behavior.

Influence is something that works subtly; but both the power of persuasion and selling require a diverse range of skills including presenting, conflict management, and negotiation.

If we are in business, we are always selling, but not necessarily always for the exchange of money.

Successful selling in commerce is about helping the buyer to make a decision that what you and your company offer are what they want to buy.

However, as well as any kind of exchange of goods for money, there are other instances in which you will utilize the skills that are essential for selling, such as interviewing for a promotion, or making a presentation to ask others to act on your ideas. Without the exchange of money, we might ordinarily consider this to be persuasion—however, it is interesting to see that there are some very real similarities between the notion of persuasion and what we are trying to achieve when we sell.

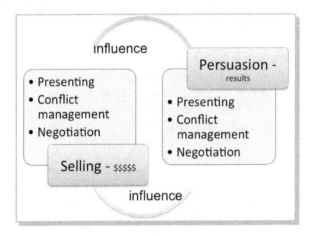

Today, traditional methods of selling (think of the typical image of the 'door-to-door salesman') have all but disappeared. In its place are tactics that are aimed at influencing and persuading the modern buyer. Whether we are introvert or extrovert, we find at the root of the new ways is an old selling philosophy often found in larger type sales. It is called relationship-focused selling.

Just like power tools need to be used with caution, often influence, persuasion, and selling can be used in a manipulative way. If we have ever experienced buying something and walked away thinking, "Gee, I was sold," we know we have been manipulated.

It is the process of selling that involves those skills of influence and persuasion; it is, moreover, by paying attention to the process, that the buyer will be satisfied with their purchase. Selling success is not just about the sale—it is also about a happy customer or client.

We are selling all the time in the workplace, for example, when we have an idea for the company or department to take on, or we want new furnishings for our office, or when we want an increase in salary. These are all situations we can influence to get results that are mutually beneficial. It is called the art of selling because it combines influence and persuasion. By the end of this chapter, you will:

➤ Assess your understanding of influence, persuasion, and selling.

➤ Empower yourself to be a successful seller and influencer as an introvert.

➤ Use online social media effectively if you are in sales.

➤ Drive results by developing your skills of influence and persuasion.

➤ Be able to identify how to mix and balance our introvert style with extrovert behaviors.

➤ Recognize and find ways of using your personal introvert preferences to become an effective influencer.

➤ Understand some techniques to be able to know what to do next in a high stakes sales situation.

➤ Discover how you can make selling work for you.

There are plenty of books with a chapter about selling, and likely even more books devoted to the entire art and science of selling.

But there is little offered with specific angles and strategies to help the introvert appreciate that they are, contrary to received wisdom, a natural for successful selling and persuasion.

Introverted traits can, in fact, be extremely useful for selling. That is what this chapter is about—introverts as natural and effective sellers and persuaders.

Are we all in sales?

"Power lasts ten years; influence not more than a hundred."

–Korean proverb

Think back to any recent situation where you felt required or were compelled to persuade someone on the merits of something: a disagreement escalating to conflict, dealing with senior management, expressing what you believed was a money-saving idea that was quickly ignored, you wanted a promotion, your new cross-functional team is dysfunctional, or your company has been merged with another and you want to keep your job.

Keep any of these situations in mind as you answer the following statements with only one of the words in the Scale of Words. The more honest you answer, the clearer your understanding of how you generally approach conflict will be and the more options you will have for the future.

Understanding sales, influence, and persuasion

You may be someone in sales or recognize that persuasion works to similar end results. In the end, they are about changing someone's behavior or mind, except persuasion can be without the exchange of money.

This assessment includes behaviors in, elements of, and the general process of sales and persuasion, each using influence.

By assessing your understanding of what we might call higher-level softer skills, selling and persuasion, you will likely raise your recognition of how they are one and the same in a more concrete way.

	Never	Rarely	Sometimes	Often	Always
Selling, like other roles at work, revolves around goals					
I plan, know, and act on priorities					
A first impression is a good impression					
Using positive and affirming self-talk is crucial					
Enthusiasm helps to sell					
Research the "prospect" before contacting					
Qualify the decision maker and know you are talking with the right person					
A follow-up process needs to be in place and acted on					
The use of telephone, e-mail, and in-person is used					

	Never	Rarely	Sometimes	Often	Always
Asking more questions than telling leads to greater success					
My presentation is more "you" than "I" oriented					
My presentation is geared more to what the other person wants, not my offer					
I pay attention to non-verbals					
I use my voice tone and non-verbals with my customer in mind					
I recognize buying signals					
I'll test a prospect's interest as I go					
My focus is on benefits and value, not features					
I communicate to my customer's style, not my own preference					
I realize rejection is not personal					
I am creative about contact with others					

Score interpretation

Score the words you identified with each statement:

> ➤ Never: 2 points

> ➤ Rarely: 4 points

> ➤ Sometimes: 6 points

> ➤ Often: 8 points

> ➤ Always: 10 points

This assessment is designed to help you to gain an awareness of your personal understanding of selling, influence, and persuasion. It is provided as a road map to help you discover where your understanding is and where you might want to develop it.

Put the score you chose for each item on the appropriate numbered line below. Each style indicates the statement numbers associated with it. Then, add up each scale.

My total score = _____

High selling understanding (120 to 150)

Some selling understanding (90 to 120)

Minimal selling understanding (60 to 90)

Barely aware of the terms selling, influence, persuasion (30 to 60)

Higher scores indicate you understand the components and attitudes essential for successful influence and selling. Lower scores indicate you may need to increase your awareness of situations that we are in that are actually selling or influence opportunities.

Some of our introverted tendencies such as listening more, preparation, and talking after thinking may give us a strong foundation to allow us to more comfortably utilize extroverted skills when needed. Each of the primary introvert and extrovert skills used in selling is where we will begin to raise both our confidence and skills awareness.

Actions for effective influencing

"The truth isn't the truth until people believe you, and they can't believe you if they don't know what you're saying, and they can't know what you're saying if they don't listen to you, and they won't listen to you if you're not interesting, and you won't be interesting unless you say things imaginatively, originally, freshly."

—William Bernbach, Advertising Director

Influence is often about big issues and situations, but it is also about small things that occur everyday in business. Our virtual world is opening each of us up to a much more global perspective, where we encounter a diverse range of cultures and people. We can use our more introverted nature and those behaviors we are comfortable with to more easily find the success we want in business.

For one thing, cultures you may now be in contact and communicating with may also be more introverted than your immediate environment. This will mean more common ground with behaviors like thinking things through before speaking.

How important is it when you want to ask for an increase in salary, that you influence your manager about how much value you bring to the company? Or when you want to raise prices, how you want your customers to remember the value of your products and services to keep buying?

The quality of your life may rely on your ability to influence your request in your daily business interactions.

Let's focus on influence in a similar kind of situation, as we consider three effective influencing behaviors. These particular ideas will appeal to most introverts because of them leading with logic and then moving on to be more relational.

Logical persuasion

Persuasion can involve an appeal to either reason or emotion. The best forms of persuasion involve an appeal to both. It is a form of influence and is not to be confused with manipulation. Persuasion, while a process of guiding people toward a possible different view or action, should result in mutual benefit. Manipulation however is using persuasion to guide someone to make a decision not in their best interest.

When I was seeking a change of employment early on in my computer sales career, one company I interviewed had already attracted a former boss who I admired and worked well with. I asked him to give me the logic behind making the move. During the interview, I could feel the positive emotions of knowing our past relationship pulling on me to say yes to the offer. He wisely told me, "You're going to make your decision based on emotion, not logic."

That is what successful selling encompasses. As a buyer, as someone being asked to take on a new approach, as a decision maker, we make our decisions based on emotion. The logic we might either have presented or requested justifies our choice.

In asking for a raise or an increase in prices, we might take the approach of building a case of why this is deserved, who else it can help, and the rationality of doing it. This often includes the strategies of talking about benefits.

Benefits act as justification

When we spotlight the benefits of taking a particular course of action, we put things in a positive light.

Here are the key elements to assure our success as we continue to focus on our continuing example of either asking for a raise or informing customers of our raising prices.

When I was given a new position, I remember waiting about three months or more to ask for a raise to go with it. I focused my request on the benefits that my manager could gain from my role change.

For example, since I was already familiar with the tasks, and we had quickly achieved some short-term goals, he would not have to bring an unknown person into unknown territory. Also, having already done some research, I suggested he would save money with the raise because other people he might want to consider would ask for more.

Saving money was particularly important to him, which I knew as a result of his continuing focus on expense cutting measures during our management meetings.

Because he agreed that my results were on target and my familiarity with the tasks was a plus, he was justifying my request for himself. He also knew by comparison of what other qualified people might ask for, that I was being fair in my request.

While a contrary stance might be possible, when we take the approach of focusing the light to what we know to be most important to the other party, it will generally overwhelm any objections.

The key to speaking to and presenting the "right" benefits is to use the ones that the other person is interested in. To know this, we identify these in our conversations with the person, and not necessarily just a conversation around the area we want to have our idea accepted.

This approach, which requires thorough preparation, is something that would be particularly attractive to an introvert. When we couple our listening and questioning skills in our conversations, we discover the best benefits to position for a greater chance of successful influence when we finally do present our request.

Social proof

Social proof is a psychological term for a type of conformity. In business, testimonials and endorsements for a product or service are a form of social proof. Positive comments about your company point to trustworthiness and build confidence. When other people give more credence to ideas, we have social proof.

We might hear social proof in our conversations with friends and neighbors. It can sound like, "So we heard that our neighbors the Sullivans loved the new Italian restaurant in town." This is peer social proof.

It might be that we think we are long overdue for a raise at work. Then, at lunch one day, a co-worker happens to say, "Our friend Joe in finance just asked for a raise and got one!" Now we are certain that if Joe was able to get one, we likely can too. Someone like us has successfully done what we are thinking about doing – social proof.

Social proof is widely used on the Internet and mobile devices. My husband uses the smartphone app, Yelp. Yelp also has a website. It is designed to help people looking for restaurants and shopping places sort out both the good and the bad – as evaluated by others who leave reviews. Social proof by shared wisdom and experience.

We can find examples of social proof everywhere when we start to look and listen for it.

Robert Cialdini, best known for his 1984 book on persuasion and marketing, *Influence: The Psychology of Persuasion*, cites research findings that point to social proof as one of the six key principles of influence. By the way, do you notice how I have just used social proof?

One of Cialdini's experiments involved creating two types of signs for hotel guests in a particular hotel. One sign asked guests to help save the environment by recycling their towel. A second sign used social proof, telling guests that the majority of guests at this hotel recycled their towels. The findings were that the guests who discovered that other guests reused their towels were 26 percent more likely to recycle those.

Findings like this show how being mindful and making use of social proof can be rewarding in your attempts to influence others.

Can you think of a social proof example for you asking for something you want?

How do social skills fit?

> *"Your career success in the workplace of today - independent of technical expertise - depends on the quality of your people skills."*
>
> *–Max Messmer, author, Managing Your Career for Dummies*

There is a rule in selling that, "People buy from people who they know, like, and trust." The ability to get along with people to this degree in any work situation develops because of a learned set of social skills.

In *Chapter 7, Do You Have an Axe to Grind? Use a Positive Approach for Workplace Conflict*, I mentioned four skill areas that make up Emotional Intelligence:

> ➤ Two personal competencies are of the intrapersonal nature: self-awareness and self-management.

> ➤ Two social competencies or interpersonal skills: social awareness and relationship management.

Because intrapersonal skills are focused on our awareness of our interior life, introverts may be more predisposed to put them into action effectively. It is a focus on us as individuals rather than our interactions with others.

Extroverts may possess stronger interpersonal skills as their personality is, as the word suggests, focused on what is outside of themselves. The focus of these skills is on other people and their moods and behaviors.

If you are willing to help others to buy into an idea, act on a new process, buy a product, or act on some new procedure, all to help them, you can both use the social skills you already have as well as increase the effectiveness of ones you might hesitate to use.

Helping others is, in the context of selling and influencing, a focus on other people and their moods and behaviors.

When my speaking and training business began, it was imperative to have a video of a live presentation. My target audience at the time was companies with a sales team, and so my twenty-minute presentation for the promotional video focused on sales skills. After the final take with an audience of about forty people, there was time to talk with the director.

He told me something to encourage the uniqueness of my work at the time, saying "You are the only one talking about ideas like this." As we talked, he helped me uncover my message, rooted in my belief about what sales is all about, which at that time was a quiet message compared to the din of other programs about sales tactics, which used to work.

Tip
In sales, we help people to make decisions, to buy or at least do something different than what they are doing now, to solve a problem or fill a need.

Consider three social skill mistakes in selling and where they are with our ability and willingness to put into action in the regard of being helpful.

The three to consider now are listening, empathy, and understanding. When we understand the importance of them to others, and our inclination to put them into action both as introverts and human beings, we can assure ourselves we have a fit for sales and persuasion.

People want us to listen more

"Listening well is as powerful a means of communication and influence as to talk well."

–John Marshall, 30 years on the USA Supreme Court

The number one mistake that causes professional relationships to falter is not listening effectively. Listening includes small behaviors such as giving your full attention, responding to acknowledge understanding, reading non-verbal communication, maintaining eye contact, and asking clarifying questions, which, when put together, help to create a strong relationship.

A 1997 study by Ramsey and Sohi in *The Journal of Academy of Marketing Science* clearly established that a customer's perception of how well someone listens has a positive association with trust. That research was backed up in a later study in 2005 by Praveen Aggarwal, Stephen B. Castleberry, Rick Ridnour, and C. David Shepherd in the *Journal of Marketing Theory and Practice,* which supported the notion that listening and trust are closely related.

In 1999, Castleberry tested a scale to measure interpersonal listening specifically in the selling environment. While the main purpose was to further test the listening scale of fourteen listening behaviors, which did test reliable, one other result was confirmed. This was that there is a positive relationship between listening ability and sales performance.

Here is why these findings are important for us who consider ourselves to be more introverted.

With this positive correlation between listening, sales performance, and trust, we as introverts may have a decided advantage in that we listen more. This gives us ample opportunity to use our listening to mutual good.

We are comfortable with many of the behaviors that make up listening as an activity, such as giving our attention, asking clarifying and probing questions, and thinking things through before responding.

These behaviors can help us enhance those behaviors that extroverts might use more naturally, also associated with listening, like maintaining eye contact and reading non-verbal communication.

It is more about how the other person feels

"I've learned that people will forget what you said, people will forget what you did, but people will never forget how you made them feel."

–Maya Angelou

A second mistake is being presumptive instead of, and more than, being and acting curious. People unsuccessful in sales or who simply lack the skill to influence presume instead of asking questions. Behaving in this way is detrimental in two ways:

> By being presumptive or even jumping to a conclusion before hearing a customer through, we stand a chance of going off on a tangent only to find the rabbit trail leads nowhere.

> Also, presuming can leave the buyer or the customer feeling unimportant in the sales process when in fact, they control the buying.

Asking questions up front, listening, and taking the time to think through a response is essential to be an effective influencer.

Again, as introverts, we can parlay this already natural and comfortable trait to help us when we need to influence someone about almost anything.

Having the solutions before knowing all the angles of the problems is not effective in influencing. Instead, listen closely to the customer to clarify their needs. One thing we can do well as introverts is to allow the time and space for someone to hear themselves say something, and feel good about their own point of view. "Selling ain't telling, asking is." We clarify with asking a question, then give a little time for the other to talk things through with their point of view, and as that goes on, we listen more. Now, we have allowed the other person their needed space for personal expression.

When we give a solution before we even understand the full scope of a problem, this essential part of building a relationship with a customer is going to be left out.

By using our listening skills as effectively as possible, as a core part of creating a relationship, we can help the other person feel involved, engaged, and connected to what we finally propose.

People do remember how we make them feel.

When we ask questions and listen, we give the other person exactly what they might need to buy into our idea, our proposal, or our product: time to think things through, time to speak their own concerns and interests to someone willing to listen.

Being prepared

Just as any product a company makes will not sell itself, when we have a good idea, we have to sell it. We can originate a work process changing idea, even deliver a compelling presentation around it, but it takes being prepared for all the ensuing steps of selling.

My sales training was conducted in large corporations, mostly by extroverts and with many tactics that have since been abandoned.

There were many goals for us to meet: cold calls, follow-up calls, proposals, and of course, sales. I remember one of my first cold calls, those unsolicited calls salespeople make on potential customers.

In a hurry to meet the cold call goal I was totally ill-prepared as my manager and I walked into a business. After cordial small talk, I asked if the owner or the person who decided what office equipment to buy was available. When he approached us, with my manager again leading the way in the small talk department, his nod signaled to me to take over. "So Mr. Maurice, what do you all do here?"

It was a red-faced moment where my embarrassment could only be consoled by over apologizing for my blunder. It is the third biggest sales mistake: not being prepared.

While sales is a defined process, many salespeople either do not know it or follow it. Instead, their eye is on the end goal, causing them to miss opportunities.

Introverts can be successful in sales and influence because of our predisposition toward preparing. Acting in this way makes it more likely that the plan will be followed through.

There are key social skills in the sales process, regardless of who defines it. In my sales training, the steps I refer to are:

> **Get the person's attention**: This usually happens through marketing and promotion, but can also be achieved in the way you present yourself to the customer and articulate their need

> **Build rapport**: Communicate a caring and helpful attitude with the other person

> **Show genuine interest**: The person wants to know you are interested in their needs and what they want

> **Create desire**: Collaboratively uncover what the other wants and needs by questions, listening, and handling their concerns

> **Help the buyer to take action**: Get a commitment, whether it is yes or no

> **Be customer-focused**: Once you get a commitment, follow through in a way that gives the customer the sense of a beginning, rather than an end

Building rapport takes time, attention, and listening.

Showing interest during the sales and influence process means more listening, asking questions, and offering suggestions once you have the other person's information.

Handling concerns involves listening, asking questions, and clarifying.

Being customer focused means applying those sales and influencing skills to manage the relationship.

Tip

Selling and persuasion is less about us and more about the other person.

As you look at each of the six steps used in my training programs, you will see a process to include various social skills, and many which are quite comfortable for most introverts.

Trainique partnered with Nightingale Conant and surveyed 2,663 sales organizations (80 percent USA/20 percent UK) and found that 82 percent of them have either a poorly defined sales process or none at all.

Successful salespeople understand people and their business, because they are prepared along the sales process. While of course extroverts can be prepared and follow a successful plan, for most introverts, it is both preferred and second nature.

Enhancing the connection with key social skills

Listening, allowing time for personal expression, and being prepared for a mutually beneficial conversation can be pivotal to our sales and persuasion ability. The extrovert typically starts with the relationship yet may miss the key pieces that enhance the connection.

To get to know someone, we ask questions to find out about them. Then, we listen as they reply, often so we can grab onto something and go deeper into the conversation when either needed or useful.

We should then allow someone to find out something about us, if they haven't already. While early on in a relationship we might be slow to self-reveal, it often works to our advantage because we get more information about the other person.

When we comment on something or share more in the conversation, it takes the conversation either wider or deeper, and we are likely raising our "like" factor.

These two pieces, the getting to know you and sharing in the conversation, flow more naturally for us as we are able to find openings in the conversation to be helpful. What comes of a conversation in the flow of getting to know each other is often the building of trust: trust of us, trust of our expertise, and trust of us as a decent person.

With technology at our disposal to use regularly, we can use it to learn, practice, and even build some other social skills integral to building relationships that we might be uncomfortable with in person.

How to use social media to build our influencing skills

"Social media allows me to pick my times for social interaction."

–Guy Kawasaki, Silicon Valley, author, speaker, investor, business advisor

The assumption that introverts are not effective salespeople or master influencers is based on a misunderstanding of selling, influence, and introversion. If these assumptions were corrected, there might be more introverts working in sales roles and, indeed, maybe even more satisfied customers!

What is important in selling is flexibility. A good salesperson is someone who can comfortably move along the extrovert/introvert continuum and utilize the skills at different points along it. If selling had another label like buyer help or buying assistance, or simply the word influence, maybe it would attract more people.

But regardless, social media can be a tool to strengthen some of our social skills needed in the buying and selling process today. We can then take what we learn online and what we do with email and use those same strategies and actions in any influencing situation.

Consider using social media like a school for some social skills that you might believe you do not have, or you might not use enough when needed.

Millions of people use online social media every day. While it can be a distraction, when it is used properly, what we learn in the process can build our skills of social influence for any communication.

Such is the ubiquitous nature of the Internet; it provides a great platform for influence—it's unsurprising that a 'digital strategy' is so essential for businesses of all sizes. Another conclusion we can make is that just having an online presence can be influential.

But the more relevant point for us as introverts is that we can use online social media to build, assess, and then use our influence skills as needed.

This is because social media gives us an opportunity to rehearse social skills in a comfortable environment where we can think before we respond, and then put those same skills to use as comfortably outside the confines of social media.

Make a note

Engaging in online interactions will help build our self-confidence.

Rapport builds influence

Rapport is another area the introvert can use social media to deepen the strength of what we already do naturally.

Rapport is about creating a close relationship wherein both parties can thrive. Think of it like being in step with a dance partner when the level of rapport grows. It should be welcome in a professional relationship (although you may not want to be that intimate with a client!)

When face-to-face, extroverts can succeed at small talk while many introverts may find it difficult. One thing about using social media is that it provides an environment in which every instance of communication can be prepared. We are able to scan a profile, look at some of the topics someone else is talking about and what they are interested in.

A further benefit of online communication is that we do not have to talk about ourselves. When we say hello to introduce ourselves, we already have a clear topic at hand to discuss, whether this is something we noted in their profile or a conversation.

You must build trust in any sales or influence encounter, but bonding with the customer goes beyond the "Gee, nice office. Good-looking picture of your family", typical old type of sales opener. This is the kind of statement that even though it is a compliment, does little to build trust. It is superficial. Yes; it might show that you are observant and you may even be sincere, but it does little to create common ground. The customer has likely heard this from countless others. Comments like this today are relegated to the lowest level of small talk, something most introverts despise. Artificial communication like this is not liked by anyone these days and will not foster the relationship building anyone wants.

An observant introvert can turn this kind of rapport opener into something more effective. "Good-looking picture of your family. It looks like the background is a vacation or holiday you all took? Where is that exactly?" Now the conversation can move along and possibly get to something more meaningful.

Research of over 3,000 buyers by The Brooks Group, Bill Brooks: 74 percent found these well taught sales tactics to be a turn off, 21 percent who responded were neutral on this approach, and just 5 percent were accepting of it.

The benefit of being able to establish rapport is that as long as we can continue to be open and honest in communicating, the relationship will be maintained.

Make a note

We can use online social media with people who we already know to practice rapport building.

Persistence

Recently I was invited as a guest on a radio show interview with a highly extroverted radio show host. I learned that while she was concerned her about her online influence, fearing that one of her social media platforms was ineffective, she believed over time people would become more actively engaged with her and want to hear more of her message.

Social media success for anyone revolves around planning and persistence, something which most introverts know well. The introvert's inclination to prefer to plan things through is well documented. The attribute of conscientiousness is more often attributed to introverts. In this personality factor, we find the ability to persist and focus on the task at hand.

Ultimately, though, selling is a numbers game. You have to be talking to and influencing many people to be able to end up with the sales. In the context of social media influence, we can understand better what works for us to apply similar tactics face to face when necessary.

Whether you have fifty or fifteen hundred friends or connections online, people want to be heard. Our listening helps that happen. People want to be heard more than anything over the ever-increasing noise in the world. Since we already listen more, we can make than work to our advantage. We can use our conscientiousness to focus on what works for us as individuals in getting engagement and building influence. Then we have some powered up tools to take a similar approach off line.

For example, one thing that works to engage people online on almost any social media site is to offer valuable information. Sometimes they will comment, and sometimes they will share. What this means is that we are both building trust, and in that process, influence. As we keep focused on what we assess to be fruitful actions like this, it is helpful to think about making a similar approach work for us in the workplace. When we share valuable information on a regular basis with our workplace colleagues, it has the same effect.

Make a note

Use your preference for preparation and analyzing to carry you through to "inspect what you expect" to see in your influence through social media.

Being a giver

According to Joyce Shelleman, PhD, "The approach to building influence that works best for an introvert is the Law of Reciprocity." This term was coined by Allan Cohen and David Bradford, authors of *Influence Without Authority*, but is based on a long history of reciprocation in human influence.

We might think that influence is based on fast talk and being personable, traits typically exhibited by extroverts. But what I have found over time is that being a giver is influence. We as introverts undervalue what we can give. In life and business people are craving to be listened to for example. We can give our listening. As people express the need for information, it is highly likely we can refer them to a source for information. Think of any number of requests spoken directly or indirectly and then decide how you can fill that need. That is a giver.

Introverts can find it difficult to engage in networking, either online or in person.

It is built day by day in using what you have to offer – whether that is listening, information, or professional expertise.

We may be who we are and want to respect the authenticity of our natural tendencies. But when we want to do something better, or when we want to excel at something we have not yet, then what could serve us better than to use a tool like social media to take positive steps in the direction of change that could help us?

Make a note

The lesson for all introverts is that influence is not only found in extroverted ways of interacting with others. Instead, it is within the authenticity of who we are.

How do selling and influence challenge the introvert?

"The key to persuasion is not a clever phrase or a clever argument. The key to becoming a great persuader is understanding human nature and why we do what we do."

–*Kurt W. Mortensen, author of Maximum Influence*

Because of the apparently extroverted nature of sales and influence we might have to admit as someone more introverted, if we are not getting the results we want time after time, then we have to change something.

While it might challenge us, we can use the challenge to both leverage our innate nature and learn something new. It could be just the leap to sell any idea you have to improve something in the company you work. It might mean the difference to you having more customers in the next few months. Here are just a few introvert challenges and how to make them work for you.

How to balance an introvert and extrovert tendency

Jill Konrath, sales strategist and speaker, is an ambivert. While she has natural introvert tendencies, over time she has developed well-honed extrovert skills to the point that she even enjoys it. There is a caveat as she claims, "But after, I'm pooped."

For several years, she informally mentored a bright young introverted woman named Elizabeth. She was full of ideas on how to improve things in her company. But time after time, when she would share her suggestions, her colleagues would listen politely, then quickly turn their attention to other matters.

Elizabeth felt grossly unappreciated. Does that sound familiar? Often she would spend days and weeks researching the situation and thinking about how to make things better. When she finally felt she had figured out the best option, she would pull together a detailed plan outlining everything that needed to be done.

But her colleagues simply responded with a big yawn.

When she and Elizabeth discussed what was happening, it was clear that people were not listening, interest was low, and conversations moved nowhere. Yet she thought she was being smart doing it all herself.

The next time it happened, she coached her on a different approach. Her first step was to have one-on-one discussions with all her colleagues who would be involved in the ultimate decision. Indeed, you may have noticed that this is a recurring theme in this book: do pre-research in one-to-one conversations.

The topic? She needed to uncover the issue that needed resolution. She went around to each of them, shared her thoughts on what she was seeing, and then asked them for their opinions on it, how big of an issue it was, and what would happen if no action was taken.

After that, she would go back to her normal process until she came up with some ideas on how to address the challenge. But rather than finalizing her approach and mapping out the action plan, Elizabeth again had one-on-ones with her colleagues. She shared her thoughts, got their suggestions for improvement, and finally uncovered any potential hitches in her thinking.

She was finally ready to bring the idea to the meeting. But this time, when presenting it, Konrath told her to bring in her colleague's thoughts, comments, suggestions, and more.

The result? Everyone was engaged in the discussion. They debated several options she proposed and she got approval to go ahead with the project.

Elizabeth never let go of her approach to being prepared, and Konrath's coaching showed her a better way. When you feel challenged by moving something forward that you feel is important or that you may be passionate about, it is not always possible to do so on your own. Taking a solitary approach is not effective when change needs the support of others. It may sometimes be wiser to look outside yourself for answers to "how do I persuade them?"

Make a note

Have meetings with everyone in a more comfortable introvert way, one-to-one conversations. Persuasion results can escalate for the introvert with this approach.

Until we decide, nothing changes

Have you ever recognized you needed to change your approach, sought advice and yet, you did not act? Maybe you thought about fitting exercise into your daily work routine by instead of taking an hour for lunch, walk for fifteen minutes and reduce the eating time. Looking back over time, you find though you did not actually take that action.

We usually do not take action until we make a decision to do something. Up until that decision point, it can be a thought, a dream, a hope, and a wish.

I really believe the statement that "salespeople are not born." The skills and attitudes of people who sell can be learned only when there is a decision to do it. Considering how much attention gets put on the more extroverted behaviors – presenting, interpersonal skills we might think it does not serve the introvert well. Make a decision that selling and persuading is for non-salespeople, or those of us who prefer the introverted behaviors in the sales process – research, planning, and listening.

How profound is the effect of either our introversion or extroversion on work we do?

For one thing, introversion or extroversion is just one dimension of our personality. Introverts and selling – for some of us, it is kind of an oxymoron isn't it? They don't really go together.

In chapter one and three, we talked about some of the more common myths about introverts: introverts don't like to talk, have difficulty knowing what to say, are anti-social, and can fix their problems by becoming more like an extrovert.

Those certainly sound like some of the skills needed in selling!

Besides having us run for cover if we are in a situation that requires us to persuade someone to do something, believing erroneous statements like the myths we've mentioned might lead to the conclusion that introverts and selling do not go together.

We have to make a different decision about introverts and selling because a large proportion of everyday business situations are actually sales-oriented, even if you are not working in sales. Consider, for example:

> ➤ Presenting new ideas for acceptance and action
> ➤ Getting buy-in from your manager to try a new approach
> ➤ Competing for resources when the budget is tight
> ➤ Convincing one colleague or a department to support an idea

These are all everyday business tasks, but they all involve techniques or skills that are essential to selling.

Having conducted hundreds of workshops in my training career, I often ask participants at the opening of either a sales or networking topic, "Give me some words or phrases that come to your mind when you hear the word salesperson."

The words that start flowing are things like 'pushy', 'aggressive', 'talks too much', 'used car salesman', and similar words and phrases. The natural tendency is to think about a bad sales experience and all kinds of descriptors that match up with it.

However, when I change the question to "What are some words or phrases that come to mind about the person you worked with when you felt happy you bought something," the words and phrases are much different: he listened to me, she cared about me, my problem got solved, we collaborated, they were genuine.

Our perception of selling is skewed toward bad selling experiences, and that influences our dislike of it. But when you think about positive buying experiences, for most of us, selling seems to be a helpful situation. In this context, the words might even sound like skills introverts feel they possess.

Anne Miller, author of *The Tall Lady with the Iceberg*, and admittedly someone who prefers their time alone but more of an ambivert, has found she would get some clients not traditionally salespeople, like portfolio managers and information technology specialists. They love the research, talking about the findings but hate selling. "I don't like the pushiness of selling."

She talks about a book by Michael Devitt, *Language and Reality*, which makes the point that words do not simply describe reality, but can actually shape it and play a part in our experience of it. In simple terms, every word has a certain effect—an idea or a thought can be subtly changed by a different choice of word. She applies strategies that are similar to what I try to do with the openings of my workshops when dealing with her clients. Language therefore has the power to change the way we look at certain activities—or, indeed, even the way we feel about ourselves.

Make a note

Sales and influencing have many descriptive words that if we change them, will allow us to understand and clarify, that behaviors which are comfortable for the introvert are behaviors which make selling feeling more positive like helpfulness.

If we think closely, we should take the time to acknowledge that we do excel in small group collaboration, we do show up prepared, we do ask questions to understand more, and we are adept at offering different perspectives on a given idea or situation.

When we let go of acting in certain ingrained ways and modify our approach, when we change the way we look at activities by changing the words that describe it, introverts can become masterful in influence and sales.

Persuading quietly, subtly, and engagingly

If you want to be more successful at influencing others, we have to understand the other person. In being ourselves, and adding some scientific and psychological pieces to our communications, we will find we can easily begin to have more success in influence and selling.

Some actions are going to come more naturally and be more comfortable for introverts. Others might be new for us and will require a different understanding and a willingness to add something new.

Mirroring

As a certified Neuro Linguistic Practitioner, there are many pieces to this communication approach and personal development, which offered success to many of my coaching clients and participants in my workshops. Because I stumbled on this way of communicating years before my certification, even having no label for it, it was something I knew could work to influence people, used ethically and properly.

Introduced in the 1970s in the United States, Neuro Linguistic Programming (NLP) is reported work on the connection between neurological processes, language, and behavioral patterns.

In 1981, IBM released its IBM PC Jr. By this year, as an experienced sales manager, almost every salesperson went through either my sales training or some manufacturers'. Still, there was no way when these two events collided we could be prepared for the tremendous volume of sales.

The problem was that IBM could not deliver. Even my understanding of the national, even international scope of its success, did not deter me from communicating our disappointment with our IBM business development representative of having to let customers down.

When I telephoned him and we began to talk things through, I was angry and he was like the calm before the storm. We were solving nothing, and then, there was a shift. He subtly, and maybe even craftily, began to mirror my angry tone. He actually even changed his language to match my feelings, "I hear you are upset," to finally the right word, "I can hear you are angry."

Mirroring is a tactic that can help create strong rapport with someone else through observing and then modeling the other person, often with some micro-behavior like a body posture, hand gestures, language, and even vocal quality.

Granted, modeling anger is an advanced use of mirroring to employ, but this extreme example will easily explain the power of mirroring in influence. Within less than five minutes, the representative paced my vocal quality and was able to lead me to a calmer and more productive discussion of how to solve the problem. When I hung up the telephone, I felt amazed.

This example always goes against all logic and may even go against any type of customer service or communication training you have had. How often might you have heard, if the customer is angry, speak back calmly to them? Really, that does not work in my experience.

NLP rapport skills teach us how to communicate at an unconscious level. Mirroring, matching, pacing, and leading skills have the possibility to enable you to become "like" the other person. Indeed, we probably know this - we tend to like and trust people who are most like us.

Make a note

As introverts, we are keen to observe, and we listen more with both our ears and with our eyes. This trait can give us a decided advantage to improve influencing situations when we understand and use techniques like mirroring.

You first

As long as we focus on the introvert traits that are effective in the sphere of selling, we will always have the aptitude for it, and, moreover, to do it well. "You first," was the topic of a sermon of a pastor in a newly opened church in my community. When I heard it, I almost immediately thought about how introverts often put others first in their thoughts and actions.

Just what are some of those subtle thoughts and actions?

One action that comes naturally to us is to let others talk first. Think about our typical workplace behavior: we piggyback on to ideas in brainstorming, or we hold back before venturing into a networking group already in process.

In sales and influence, one of the best actions to take is to let the other person or the potential customer talk first. Letting the other person talk first allows them to get their ideas out and gives us the chance to decide when and how to respond to any concerns.

When the other person goes first, it gives us time to both hear what they are saying as well as for us to think about not just what to say, but how to say things to them in the way they will most understand.

One other key reason to let the other person talk first is to observe those silent communicators such as body language, facial expression and eye contact. Eye contact can actually be another natural trait advantage for those of us more introverted.

Many statistics bear out that if you want someone to know, feel or see that you are listening to them, you want to have more eye contact with them than not. While too much can be interpreted as staring, too little can mean lack of sincerity or caring.

A critical point about a positive amount of eye contact, besides communicating silently that we care about another, is that by looking at what is right in front of us can serve to preserve our energy. If we have to take in other activities around us, then it breaks our focus as well as taking our attention off of our listening.

Make a note

Allowing the other person the "You first," in communicating helps us focus our attention to learn more about them, their desires and their concerns, than if we were to take the lead.

Metaphors and stories sell

People are moved by emotions and interested in the facts. Consider that we buy on emotions and convince ourselves of having made the right decision based on facts.

Narratives and stories have always captured the human imagination – it is no surprise then that they can be effective tools when selling. Here are two ways to consider opening up a presentation about selling.

Which connects better for you, A:

Today we are going to spend some time learning sales skills. While many of us are anxious about selling, by the end of today's program, you will have the skills you need for more success. We will review the key elements and techniques that cover the gamut from prospecting to handling concerns, and all the way to asking for a decision. By the end of the day, you will know what parts of the sales process you need to learn or just tweak.

Or B:

Queasy about selling? Selling is like flying an airplane. If you've either piloted or flown in a plane, you know this. First you file a flight plan. Then you use your observation skills, handle turbulence when it comes up, stick to your plan, and land feeling good about the flight. With an all-inclusive flight plan, as we have prepared for you today to participate it, you will know where in the sales process you need to either learn or just tweak.

The first example, A, will certainly get nodding agreement that yes, these are the things that will help me sell better. Ultimately though, it is just a bit boring and ho-hum.

The second example, hopefully, pulls you in about your personal experiences with flying, all of which are hopefully good. It is more engaging with pulling you in with you having experienced the metaphor of flying. Knowing your metaphor has universal understanding is key. Hopefully, you understand flying or else, I may have missed the mark.

If you cannot find a metaphor then the next best source would be either your own stories, or stories from other people. What we look for is everyday things that most people will relate to.

Consider story telling in sales like a mini- presentation: it has a beginning, middle and an end. We hook people in at the beginning then make a connection with the story to the idea or product we are selling and in the end, ask for a call for action.

Make a note

Introverts can easily enjoy telling stories and once we learn the most comfortable way for us to do so, we will likely use them not just in sales and influence situation, but managing conflict, and negotiating.

The key is finding something for which you are both familiar with and then not over preparing it. Story telling can be a short as a simple metaphor that makes that connection of the unknown to something know by the listener.

Remember that we introverts enjoy the playground of ideas we find in our own mind. Story telling gives us respite there for the times we want might most want to be influential.

How being ourselves can give us an advantage

"To improve is to change; to be perfect is to change often."

–Winston Churchill

When we try to act like someone we are not, we sabotage ourselves. Introverts more than extroverts may do this simply because so much of what we engage in on a daily work day includes behaviors further along on the extrovert side of the introvert-extrovert continuum. Being in business meetings, giving presentations, taking telephone calls, any number of interaction activities can fool us into thinking that what we prefer to do is not useful. In fact, researching, preparing, thinking things through, communicating concisely in email, any number of solitary activities help strengthen us in the engagement.

By playing to our strengths and understanding what we do well, we can remain true to ourselves, which in turn will give us confidence in our professional lives.

Identify your preparation sweet spot

One of my introvert friends, Val Nelson, a life coach for introverts, told me about a marketing situation where she had to stop and assess why she was getting so drained so she would be able to identify what to do to get back on track.

She created a workshop called "Networking Secrets from an Ex-Wallflower." The first time she led it, the room was filled to capacity and she was pumped with energy to see the positive responses. But when she ran in again, she was more drained afterwards. She said, "I went over my own line of what feels energizing versus draining."

Whatever we do in sales and marketing efforts, we want to behave in a manner that energizes us. Or, we risk hurting our business successor even ourselves.

Too many people follow what is an old model of push selling, but today, in part due to the influence of social media, we can sell more with a pull model.

Val had to find her own sweet spot and in part what she did to do that, was tune in to her body. Was she feeling stress? Where was it? When?

One other key factor she shared with me for why her workshop works so well for her business is that she chose a topic that is very resonant and personal for her. That heartfelt passion gives her the energy to be in front of the room like that, and it makes it more effective for participants, and more likely to sign up for more.

Even with that passion, I can't forget to watch the energy. In general, the more planning we do the more it energizes, allowing us to explore more and think things deeply.

Make a note

The lesson for us more introverted: choose something that aligns with your heart and your body's energy. If you over plan, you may have missed your sweet spot of preparing.

Use the environment

One key to not having to act like an extrovert is to instead identify where both our extrovert and introvert tendencies appear at work. Once you know what makes up your role, you can find areas that bring out the best in you, and plan around the times when you might need to recharge.

All the roles we fulfil in both our professional and personal lives require both introvert and extrovert tasks. Regardless of our energy preference, we must all engage in a range of activities that fall in different places on the introvert-extrovert continuum. It has been suggested that workplaces are spaces that require and demand extroversion, but this, I think, is a little misleading.

In my view, the range of activities that comprise a typical day at work mean the situation is more complex and not as black and white as it might appear. For example, in the morning, we may be sending emails, researching and writing, planning presentations, while later on you may have to attend meetings, give presentations, and attend social events with clients or colleagues. Maybe you have suggested telecommuting, but were unable to sell that idea, at least before reading this book.

Or maybe you work in an open bull-pen like office and cannot find a way to create privacy.

Maybe you have exhausted all possibilities to improve the environment more to your liking.

It is not over for your success.

Look at your role or your job description, and as long you can plan to save your energy as you go through your day you will be able to manage the extrovert activities when you are called to act on them.

Make a note

What you can do to better manage your environment: prioritize your breaks to recharge, assert yourself in requests such as needing time to get back to another person, use email to communicate when you are able.

Summary

As stated earlier in this chapter, "Influence and persuasion each have a similar objective: to change either a person's thinking or behavior. Influence works silently and persuasion uses skills like presenting, conflict management, and negotiation."

Regardless of what situation comes to mind when we consider the twin notions of selling and persuasion, as an introvert, we already have solid and natural traits to lend to the skills needed to succeed. The success of either lies within our ability to influence. A key is to know who we are naturally, and understand that as an advantage to more success in this essential communications skill. Once acknowledged, we get to choose what to ramp up and improve:

> ➤ Expanding my understanding of selling and influence as isolated events to regard them as things that are essential in our everyday (professional) lives.

> ➤ Identifying the personal benefit of using social media to build influence skills.

> ➤ Willing to use logical persuasion, benefits statements, and social proof as just three influencing strategies.

> ➤ Acknowledging my introvert strengths of thinking things through, planning, and listening to allow a more successful influence position.

> ➤ Assessing when my introvert nature might be over used and I need to bring in more of an extrovert trait in selling or persuading.

➤ Being more observant so I can mirror others, taking my nature to not want to self-disclose to a "you first" approach and telling stories.

➤ Discovering my sweet spot of preparation.

➤ Improving the management of my environment to be more at ease in my everyday need to influence.

Thoughts to contemplate

➤ How do I personally feel about sales, persuasion, and influence? Do I see it as a regular occurring skill in everyday work situations or not? Why do I believe this?

➤ Think back to a recent idea you wanted to sell to your manager, another department, or even another employee. Was the outcome positive? Can I identify what I might have done too much of or what I did nothing with to my advantage?

➤ Select new ideas you may have discerned from this chapter. Select the top three that you believe could work effectively for you.

    ➢ In the next situation you identify as having potential for sales or persuasion, select one of the skills presented in this chapter to add to your conversation.

    ➢ Regardless of the outcome, evaluate your level of comfort with that one new skill.

    ➢ If it is uncomfortable for you, identify if you either need more practice or want to move on to new idea number two.

    ➢ Make it your goal in the next 90 days is to put a new skill into practice that helps you comfortably influence others with your ideas or sell your products or services.

As long as we need ideas to improve life, products and services to live, selling and persuasion will be in our lives. The interesting thing is that most introverts, not seeing themselves as salespeople, might dismiss their ability to persuade and sell. In fact, this is just incorrect.

Take time to examine your "authentic self". Then acknowledge what of our natural way of being supports effective persuasion and selling. Consider all the power tools of how we listen more, build deep relationships, plan and prepare, and even like others to speak first. All of these used in proper balance will help us to turn our communication skills into power persuasion and sales skills.

Bibliography

> Jill Konrath, *SNAP Selling* and *Selling to Big Companies*, http://www.jillkonrath.com

> Ramsey, Rosemary, and Ravipreet S. Sohi, *Listening to Your Customers: The Impact of Perceived Salesperson Listening Behavior on Relationship Outcomes, Journal of the Academy of Marketing Science*, 25 (Spring), 127-137, 1997

> Nicole B. Ellison, Charles Steinfield, Cliff Lampe, *The Benefits of Facebook "Friends":* Social Capital and College Students' Use of Online Social Network Sites, *Journal of Computer-Mediated Communication*, July 2007

> Joyce Shelleman, PhD, *The Introvert's Guide to Professional Success: How to Let Your Quiet Competence Be Your Career Advantage*, http://theintrovertsguide.blogspot.com/

> Val Nelson, Introvert Coach: Life/Career/Business, http://www.valnelson.com

> Anne Miller, presentation and sales specialist, http://www.annemiller.com, author, *The Tall Lady with the Iceberg*

>10

Quiet Communication can Triumph

"Quiet people have the loudest minds."

–Professor Stephen Hawking

We have now looked at a range of skills that can help you professionally (and maybe personally), and looked at ways that we can play to our strengths as introverts in the workplace. But where do we go now?

Hopefully, this book has helped you see that who you are naturally and how you prefer to act in this world can in fact be incredibly effective, even in environments and scenarios that you may have previously thought difficult, unfavorable for "who you are". With this increased awareness, I hope that you are inspired with a diverse range of techniques, ideas, and skills to give you more access to handle everyday work situations with ease and success.

As you grow in appreciation of who you are, it will be worthwhile to take time to go back in times of doubt to think about and reread any particular skill or skills that you initially wanted to improve. What you will find is a common thread.

At the beginning of this book, we solidified our understanding of ourselves. Now you have irrefutable evidence of our ability to be able to authentically communicate on every front to a mutual benefit.

Moving ahead with thread repair

There are certain tools that often need thread repair. Something gets worn out, something gets overused, or something just does not fit.

Let's consider that neither someone more introverted nor someone more extroverted has all the right tools at the right time. That would mean as introverts we have strengths that stand firm on their own:

➤ Listening

➤ Planning

➤ Preparation

➤ Thinking things through

➤ Think before we speak

➤ Deepening relationships

Of course, we might find we rely on our strengths to the degree we find them being stripped of their effectiveness.

For example, we referenced a few instances where our solo planning or preparation might leave us open for defeat because we did not fully consider the positions of others in conflict management or negotiations.

Or we might value one-to-one relationships and overlook how to use the keys to building them when we need them in a business meeting or a situation of influence.

Whether we overuse, underuse, or do not amplify what we already do well is when we need to consider thread repair.

Your next actions

Now the analysis, theory, and your evaluation of your own effectiveness is complete. What should you do next?

➤ We do have to take action, if not as we went along, then now that we have thought through the tips, strategies, ideas, and techniques.

➤ Move into action now with a written plan. Or go back to what you may have already put in an action plan to confirm you are taking the most effective steps to see positive change.

➤ Will you keep the ideas in mind as you go about your daily workplace interactions? What will be the benefit of this?

  ➤ Write out a prioritization of the top three essential skills that you want to improve the most.

  ➤ Identify specific personal benefits for each; one to three is helpful.

  ➤ Give it one night if you want to think about and make sure this will serve you best in your everyday business success.

  ➤ Now keep what you have written and confirmed to be important for you at the top of your mind or in clear view.

➤ Maybe it would be beneficial to revisit each essential skill assessment for a particular area you want to approve? And move from there to find chapter tips to take action on?

> ➢ If necessary, refer back to the chapter topic assessment for the top three skills you identified as your most important.

> ➢ For each of the selected skills, identify at least three new actions, strategies, and techniques that you will take for a skill area, using the results in your assessment to guide you.

Make a note

You can select either your strengths and act to make them stronger, or your weak points to strengthen them, or mix it up. The idea is to find what works best for you.

➤ Will you set some intentions or goals to put specific actions into place? And if you are going to do so, will you give yourself a timeline?

> ➢ For your number one priority of the three skill areas, with associated actions, assign a beginning and end date for a 30-day plan.

> ➢ Identify and ask a person who you know, like, and trust to keep you accountable to new actions and behaviors by checking in with you.

> ➢ Make the request for checking in on a mutually agreeable timeframe, for example once a week, and in a mutually agreeable format, for example, e-mail.

➤ Will you want to go back to some specific chapters to reread what you think you recall?

➤ Or will you want to engage in some further thinking about what to do next?

> ➢ As you progress in your first 30-day plan of action, you can always go back to a chapter to remind yourself what made you decide this change was important.

> ➢ Then think about whether you have actually been taking action, the greater effectiveness you are finding, or not.

> ➢ If you feel you are getting the results you want, then continue; remember, it is a 30-day plan. If you feel you are not getting the results you want, and you can honestly say you are acting on it, decide whether you are congruent with it.

> ➢ All change requires action, commitment, and time.

How you move forward is really up to you. Before you can see the view, you have to make it to the top of the mountain.

If you are an introvert, you have likely found that you already do some things that I have described in this book, but hopefully there are now some things you can do a lot more easily and confidently. Over and over again, I want you to know and understand that most of these essential skills require us to be true to who we are. When we pay attention to the congruency of our behaviors, we maintain our energy. The pure state of having more energy, on its own, can elevate our everyday business successes.

If you are an extrovert (and decided to read this book anyway!), you should by now have a greater awareness of what helps and what can sometimes hinder the introvert in everyday situations. Whatever your role in the workplace, you can now work to help create an environment that brings the best out of everyone, whether they are an extrovert or an introvert.

The world—and indeed workplaces—can benefit from a range of diverse perspectives. If we want to encourage creative thinking and innovative approaches to problems, diversity is absolutely essential. Introverts can play a big part in offering fresh approaches and new ideas – if we, as introverts, can push ourselves to develop our skills. We will be able to make a real impact, leading to influential change.

www.ingramcontent.com/pod-product-compliance
Lightning Source LLC
LaVergne TN
LVHW081339050326
832903LV00024B/1219